DID YOU KNOW

At what age your child can have a pet
of his own? What you should look for when
choosing a collar and leash?
Whether a dog should be allowed to sleep
in your bed or your child's bed?
How you can train your dog not to bark
excessively? How you can stop your
dog from chasing cars? How much exercise
your dog needs? What kinds of
dog food are the best? What you can do
about excessive shedding? How
you can rid your dog of fleas? What
are the main points to keep
in mind when selecting a puppy?

THE COMMON SENSE BOOK OF
PUPPY AND DOG CARE ANSWERS THESE
QUESTIONS AND HUNDREDS MORE.
IT IS THE INDISPENSABLE REFERENCE
BOOK FOR EVERYONE WHO
OWNS A DOG OR IS THINKING ABOUT
GETTING A DOG.

Books by Harry Miller

❧ **THE COMMON SENSE BOOK OF PUPPY AND DOG CARE**

❧ **THE COMMON SENSE BOOK OF KITTEN AND CAT CARE**

❧ Published by Bantam Books, Inc.

THE COMMON SENSE BOOK
OF PUPPY AND DOG CARE

HARRY MILLER
Director Emeritus, Gaines Dog Research Center

•

Foreword by Hadley C. Stephenson, B.S., D.V.M.

•

Second Edition · Revised

BANTAM BOOKS
TORONTO · NEW YORK · LONDON · SYDNEY

THE COMMON SENSE BOOK OF
PUPPY AND DOG CARE

A Bantam Book / September 1956
2nd printing . . . . . . June 1957   3rd printing . September 1957
4th printing . . . . . . October 1960
Bantam Reference Library revised edition / February 1963
6th printing . . . August 1963   15th printing . . February 1972
7th printing . . . . . April 1964   16th printing . . . August 1972
8th printing . . . . . April 1965   17th printing . . . August 1973
9th printing . November 1966   18th printing . . . October 1974
10th printing . September 1967   19th printing . . . January 1976
11th printing . . . October 1968   20th printing . . February 1977
12th printing . September 1969   21st printing . . . . . July 1978
13th printing . . . October 1970   22nd printing . December 1979
14th printing . . . . . June 1971   23rd printing . . February 1980
24th printing . . . . . October 1981

Library of Congress Catalog Card Number: 56-11111

Front cover photo by Walter Chandoha

ISBN 0-553-20775-X

Published simultaneously in the United States and Canada

Bantam Books are published by Bantam Books, Inc. Its trademark, consisting of the words "Bantam Books" and the por-
trayal of a rooster, is Registered in U.S. Patent and Trademark
Office and in other countries. Marca Registrada. Bantam
Books, Inc., 666 Fifth Avenue, New York, New York 10103.

PRINTED IN THE UNITED STATES OF AMERICA

31 30 29 28 27 26 25 24

☆ FOREWORD ☆

Why write a book? Every author has a purpose, be it to state a theory, support a cause, make available information which is difficult to find, or present new information for the first time. In this book, *The Common Sense Book of Puppy and Dog Care*, Harry Miller has drawn upon his extensive knowledge of dogs and his close association with many research projects devoted to their welfare: his cause—to help dogs live longer and better lives through lifetime care; the result—a book that can rightfully be called a classic in the field of dog care.

The puppy needs good care during his early formative months if he is to lead an active life when he is full grown and enjoy his final years. Consequently, this book discusses the growing puppy month by month and, in addition, devotes full chapters to the grown dog and the old dog. In the latter sections the latest findings of research in nutrition and veterinary medicine, general care and training are presented in a popular and practical manner.

Finally, *The Common Sense Book of Puppy and Dog Care* contains an index which makes all of its valuable information and sound advice readily available. If this advice is followed, more dogs will live to a ripe old age, more disease will be prevented, more dogs and more people will be happy.

HADLEY C. STEPHENSON, B.S., D.V.M.

☆ PREFACE ☆

Not less than 19 million American homes keep one or more dogs for sport, for protection, for companionship and fun around the house. The army of dog-owners would doubtless be larger still were it not for the fact that many people still believe the task of dog care to be more difficult than it really is.

In this book we have tried to approach the whole subject from a "common sense" standpoint. Let me illustrate:

Dogs come into homes at various stages in their lives, each stage presenting special problems that require particular attention. In this work we have tried to group these problems—and the answers to them—within the ages when they normally would occur. We understand that this has been done with baby books, but believe this is the first time anything of the kind has been attempted in a dog book.

We are strong believers in professional veterinary care for both the prevention and the cure of illness. However, all dog-owners do not live within easy reach of a veterinarian. Our recommendations, therefore, must take into consideration the practical necessities faced by many dog-owners.

We may have gone too far in recommending care for the young puppy like that given to a baby. In defense we can only plead that too much care is better than too little.

In the following pages we have tried to anticipate—and answer—every type of problem that the dog-owner may have to face in the lifetime care of his dog. Being human and fallible, we may have missed some. Therefore this final word to you: Our interest in your dog does not stop when you own a copy of this book. Any time you need an answer to any question on a dog topic, please feel free to write me at the office of the Gaines Dog Research Center, 250 Park Avenue, New York 17, N. Y. We will certainly do our best to help you—without charge.

This book would not have become a reality without the diligent efforts of a good friend, Josephine Rine, and my assistant, Evelyn Monté. To both, my heartfelt thanks and grateful appreciation.

HARRY MILLER

☆ CONTENTS ☆

CHAPTER 1

THE 2-3 MONTHS OLD PUPPY

Introduction to the Home

Let's suppose that you have just acquired your first puppy. You drive him home; you take him indoors and set him down. He is only eight to twelve weeks old, remember, and it's quite understandable if he is completely bewildered by all these new sights and faces. Perhaps you brought him home in your car. He had been bounced and jounced, or at least had butterflies in his stomach from the unaccustomed motion of riding in an automobile. All gone is that delightful playfulness he showed when you picked him out at the kennel or shop. Don't be surprised if he looks like a wilted bouquet.

However, puppies are not all alike. Even at this tender age they are individuals. While one puppy will seem utterly crushed by the strangeness of new surroundings another will trot about boldly as if anxious to investigate this charming place and all these lovely people. Whatever the pup's reaction to this new scene there are two important DON'TS: 1. Don't reach out quickly and make sudden grabs at him. 2. Don't permit the children to shriek over him in their delight. Sudden movements, unaccustomed loud noises frighten puppies. Your role is to gain his confidence. When you get that, it will serve you all of your dog's life, in obedience, in training, in whatever you want him to do or be. Talk to the new pup. He won't understand a word at this point but he will understand a friendly tone of voice and there is nothing more successful in creating confidence.

All of a sudden you are astonished at yourself for daring to bring home such a very young puppy. You feel so inadequate to cope with the problem. Hesitantly he comes toward you and looks up as if you were all in the whole world he could depend on. That does it! You pick him up in your arms and hold him close. He's yours and you are going to do the best you can.

You will, too. You are just as able to take on this job of puppy raising as anyone else. It's a wonderfully rewarding job and not at all hard to do. You can learn it, step by step, as the puppy grows. That you love him already and have anticipated his coming is proved by the fact that you have prepared for him.

The Puppy's Bed

Before the pup is brought home, consider the place where he is to stay while he's little. Young puppies need warmth and an even temperature. An unused bedroom is fine since its windows needn't be opened at night—or you can use a bathroom, pantry, or a discarded baby pen in a corner of the living room or kitchen. There are two good reasons for giving the young pup a special place. At this age puppies have very little control and when given the run of the house can't avoid soiling anywhere and everywhere. This makes for more difficult housebreaking later. Also, a puppy is not only safer but the feeling of security in having a place of his own helps him fit into his new life and its routine.

Arrange a box or bed of his own, not over-large but wide enough so he can stretch out and long enough to hold a thin pillow or blanket at one end and a few layers of spread newspapers at the other. The puppy may have been partially paper-broken when weaned. Whether he was or not, he soon gets the notion of what the paper is for because it is natural for him to leave his pillow when he is ready to eliminate. Always have a newspaper within easy reach.

His bedding, first of all, should be washable. You might use a small discarded cotton blanket, fold it down to pillow size to fit the puppy. Or you can use a piece of folded flannel, or blanket. It should be fairly thin; a thick cushion is too deep for the pup's short legs to negotiate. Whatever it is to be, have two or three on hand so that you can wash it, and air it in the sun periodically.

The bed or box itself may be as plain or as luxurious as you wish—the puppy will not care. For the small-sized dog, a high-sided carton will do, provided it is deep enough so that he cannot climb out in the night and get lost in the dark. And it should be underlaid with a carpet or blanket to keep its floor warm. For a cozy shelter for a toy breed pup, place two straight chairs back to back on either side of the carton and over them throw a blanket. Since the back of the chair will be higher than the top of the carton, he will get plenty of air without cross draft. Draft is a puppy's meanest enemy.

For puppies of the medium and larger-sized breeds, a wooden box is better because all puppies, regardless of age, are tempted to chew their way out if they can. A cage or crate with a door that can be closed is not necessary but can be very useful, especially for small dogs, and for house training. The man of the house can make an excellent puppy crate out of a packing case. Nail strips on the bottom to keep it an inch or two off the floor. For the front, make a door with four-sided frame, its center covered with wire. Don't use fine-mesh wire. It is too easily chewed and equally important, its close mesh can trap the puppy's toenails. Use quarter inch square mesh; nail or staple it on the outsides of the frame, and cover the edges with strips of molding. Fasten a good catch on the door, one the pup can't pop open by bouncing against it.

When a puppy is kept in an otherwise unused room do not shut the room door tightly at night; leave it open a crack so you can hear what goes on. Constant crying during the night can often be stopped by the simple command "Quiet!" so the puppy may know he's not entire alone.

You may prefer to keep the puppy's box in your own bedroom for a few nights until he learns to sleep by himself. Always place the crate so that its open side, or screen door, is safely turned away from any possible draft. If the room becomes cold, throw a blanket or shawl across the opening. Use your own judgment as to how much air to give the pup. Don't let him take cold, but don't smother him, either.

If you have a puppy of a sporting breed or one of the large breeds you may have planned to have him live in an outdoor kennel. In that case be sure to have a well-sealed, draft-proof dog house, one that has a snug box within filled with bedding material so that the puppy can make a warm nest. The building should be raised off the ground and so placed that the door faces away from the wind. It must be placed within an enclosure, such as a wire-fenced yard, or your pup may wander or be a prey to straying dogs or mischievous children.

So, after the comforting hug you've given your new puppy, you're going to place him in his box. He's had enough excitement for a while. Too many introductions, too much attention at first appearance will only be confusing. Probably he will just sit in his box and think things over, glad at least to be rid of the motion of the car. Since he has undoubtedly not been fed for several hours, he may whimper from hunger. If he remains quiet or sleeps, leave him alone.

If he whimpers, give him a snack, some warm milk or other accustomed food.

Crying At Night

You may be upset by the crying sessions of the first few nights. You feel very helpless and somehow to blame. This is a perfectly natural occurrence—nearly all puppies cry when they sleep alone in a new home for the first time. They miss the warmth and companionship of their litter mates.

Try to make up for this lack by providing something warm for the pup to snuggle up to. A rubber hot water bottle will serve wrapped with flannel for the puppy to cuddle up to. Fill it about two-thirds full of slightly hotter than lukewarm water. Electric heating pads have been used, but these are safe only when the connecting wire can be buried under the bedding so securely that it cannot be chewed. The loud tick of an alarm clock placed near the pup's bed may help to ease the lonely feeling.

Few Visitors

Next morning the puppy will be up bright and early literally screeching for something to eat. Open the crate door and let him scamper around the floor as you clean out his box and give him a change of blanket and newspapers. Keep the door of his room closed if there is any chance of his investigating the stairway and falling down.

Now your problems will begin—and they will not come from the puppy either. Everybody up and down the block is going to be interested in your pup; everybody is going to love him and itch to get their hands on him. And this can invite trouble. Perhaps they have a dog too, and out of the kindness of their hearts they will bring him to sniff noses with your puppy. Or possibly their puppy is home, sick, so cannot call in person; but he can send his germs on the hands, feet and clothing of his owners. This is one way contagion is spread, especially among young dogs. Your puppy may have been safeguarded by inoculation against the serious puppy diseases. If not, explain the situation to your visitors or make up some excuse. Then select a veterinarian, take your puppy there and have him inoculated so you won't have to fear contagion. (See page 16)

Aside from the possibility of disease, young puppies are easily excited, upset and over-tired by too many visitors. Until your pup has become used to his new home, try to avoid attention from strangers; also do what you can to guard him from loud noise and confusion.

How to Feed

Beginning on page 73 you will find a complete discussion of feeding. Read it as soon as you can. But right now you are faced with one hungry pup, and the suggestions below are made in line with the common sense approach to dog feeding there outlined.

The person from whom you got the puppy may have spoken to you about feeding, or given you a feeding chart. In either case, continue the same diet for a week or so while the pup is getting used to the daily routine as a new member of the family. But remember that feeding charts, in some cases, may have been designed only for the weanling pup. Many new owners follow the "baby" diet long after a husky, growing pup is ready for more substantial food.

Although some puppies are weaned to baby cereal and milk, the recommended method is to wean directly to a dry commercial meal or burger-type dog food, starting at three weeks of age, with the weaning process completed when the pups are 5-6 weeks old. (see page 122). In the latter case, you have no problem in changing the diet. If the pup has been on cereal and milk, he should be started on a regular dog food at about six weeks of age. However, since any sudden change of food is very apt to cause an upset, introduce new foods gradually. Add the commercial food a little at a time to the cereal and milk, increasing the amount until the cereal food is replaced. The puppy's food should be slightly warm, never too hot nor fed direct from the refrigerator.

If, by chance, your puppy arrives before you have prepared yourself with the regular food you are going to give him, it is safe to feed cooked or dry cereal, or toast mixed with slightly warm milk or meat broth or raw beef chopped in small bits. The growing pup requires even more food than a grown dog of the same breed but his stomach cannot hold that much in one feeding. So the puppy must be fed several times a day. At this age, four feedings are needed, morning, noon, early evening and shortly before bedtime. The period can fit the convenience of the household but they should always be about four hours apart. Changing feeding times prevents proper digestion and also upsets the routine that a pup likes and which makes raising him much easier for you.

In late evening offer milk and meal or, instead, a few biscuits.

Occasionally a pup will turn up his nose at one feeding. If your puppy refuses a fourth feeding, skip it but be sure to increase the amount of food in the other feedings.

The amount of food will differ according to the size of the breed. We have more than one hundred different breeds to consider, including a great many different sizes. Individuals, too, differ—even members of the same litter; some are pigs, others pickers. So no one cares to be too strict in recommending amounts of food.

Step on the bathroom scale with your puppy in your arms. By subtracting your own weight you can estimate the pup's weight. Then use the feeding chart as a guide, remembering that amounts are approximate.

As already stated, however, the individual puppy is the best measuring stick for the amount of food to be given in each feeding. As a rule, give as much as he will readily eat and use your own observation. You can soon tell if you are over-feeding just by looking at your pet.

The average young dog eats as if he were starving. Don't believe him for a minute; he gobbles by nature. Up to now he has been eating side by side with his brothers and sisters, so he eats fast. As time goes on he will acquire better manners. Occasionally, however, a puppy misses the competition of his litter mates and may not eat as readily without it. He may dawdle at first and need some coaxing, but in time will get used to eating alone.

Your pup may clean up his dish in a few minutes. Good! For the puppy who eats like an eager beaver and gains and grows is what you want. If he eats half his food and appears satisfied, take the dish away and give him a little less at the next feeding time. Allow enough time for him to complete his meal—20 minutes or so. Fix a fresh dishful for each feeding. Mixed food left standing is likely to become pasty or become sour in warm temperature. Furthermore, allowing the puppy to dawdle over eating will encourage "picky" eating habits.

If he skips one feeding do not worry or tempt him with tidbits. Remove the food and feed him again at the next scheduled time. But if he stops eating entirely and appears listless then make a quick visit to your veterinarian.

You will soon learn the right amount of food to give your puppy to keep him satisfied and well filled out without becoming over-fat. Watch the little fellow's stomach as he eats; if it is so enlarged that he sways and waddles when

```
┌─────────────────────────────────────────────┐
│              FEEDING CHART                   │
│         Age: Weaning - 3 Months              │
└─────────────────────────────────────────────┘
```

VERY SMALL BREEDS

(Averaging 5-15 lbs. weight as adults)

Wt. in lbs...................1-2½
Calories per day..................100-250
No. of feedings.....................4 or self-feeding
Meal (nugget)....................1-3 tablespoons per feeding
Meal (chunk).......................2-4 tablespoons per feeding
Burger-type (3 oz. patty)............⅛-¼ patty per feeding
Canned dog food (1 lb. can)........2-4 tablespoons per feeding

SMALL BREEDS

(Averaging 15-30 lbs. weight as adults)

Wt. in lbs...........................3-7
Calories per day....................300-700
No. of feedings.....................4 or self-feeding
Meal (nugget)......................¼-½ cup per feeding
Meal (chunk).......................¼-⅔ cup per feeding
Burger-type (3 oz. patty)............⅓-⅔ patty per feeding
Canned dog food (1 lb. can)........⅛-⅓ can per feeding

MEDIUM BREEDS

(Averaging 30-50 lbs. weight as adults)

Wt. in lbs..........................6-12
Calories per day....................500-1000
No. of feedings.....................4 or self-feeding
Meal (nugget).......................⅓-⅔ cup per feeding
Meal (chunk)........................½-¾ cup per feeding
Burger-type (3 oz. patty)............½-1 patty per feeding
Canned dog food (1 lb. can)........¼-½ can per feeding

LARGE BREEDS

(Averaging 50-80 lbs. weight as adults)

Wt. in lbs...........................10-15
Calories per day....................850-1050
No. of feedings.....................4 or self-feeding
Meal (nugget).......................½-¾ cup per feeding
Meal (chunk)........................¾-1 cup per feeding
Burger-type (3 oz. patty)............¾-1 patty per feeding
Canned dog food (1 lb. can)........⅓-½ can per feeding

VERY LARGE BREEDS

(Averaging 100-175 lbs. weight as adults)

Wt. in lbs..........................15-25
Calories per day....................1050-1600
No. of feedings.....................4 or self-feeding
Meal (nugget).......................¾-1 cup per feeding
Meal (chunk)........................1-1⅓ cups per feeding
Burger-type (3 oz. patty)............1-1½ patties per feeding
Canned dog food (1 lb. can)........½-¾ can per feeding

he gets through, then he may have had too much. Cut down on the next feeding.

After he has finished eating let him run around outdoors or on his "paper" for a few minutes to relieve himself. Puppies always have a bladder or bowel movement soon after eating. Then put him in his cage, room or yard to rest. Do not handle him much, and don't romp with him directly after eating. Increase the food amount gradually as the puppy grows.

Because the young puppy's food is very moist, water is not quite as neccessary now as it will be later. Sometimes puppies may actually overdrink water just before or after meals and upset their stomachs. Offer a drink regularly, then remove the dish. When kept in a very warm room, or during very hot weather, offer fresh water more often or keep it available. Unlike cats, dogs are fond of water; they delight to dabble in it and strew it around; water must be available for puppies that are on dry self-feeding. (see page 123).

Feeding Dishes

The feeding dish will depend on the length of the puppy's nose and the shape of his face. Flat-faced, short-nosed pups eat more easily from a shallow dish. Longer-nosed kinds can reach into a deeper dish, while the long-eared youngsters may need a slant-sided dish to help keep ear-flaps and fringes from dipping into the dinner.

However when the puppy is just learning to eat, he may be started on a fairly flat dish; then after a week or two given the type of pan best for his ears and muzzle. Do not use enamelware which may chip. Stainless steel make the best type of feeding dishes but oven-ware crockery or plastic are also serviceable.

Self-Feeding

If your puppy prefers his meal-type food dry—without the addition of any liquid—you might like to try something called self-feeding which is becoming very popular. The dog feeds himself from a container in which the dry food is always kept available. He can eat what he wants, when he wants it. When left alone in his "room," he has something to do; nibbling at his dry food will very likely take the place of nibbling at a chair leg or the corner of a linoleum rug. Also, if you are kept away from home past the puppy's regular feeding time, you know that he has food and can satisfy his hunger. An important advantage is that the blood nutrient level is maintained more evenly.

However, when starting self-feeding, do not begin at a regular meal-time—that is, when the dog is very hungry—or he may gorge himself beyond his needs. Feed him his regular meal, then put out the filled container.

Although some puppies may overeat and become fat on a self-feeding regime, most will eat the proper amount to keep in good weight and growing. Feeding dry food usually increases the need for water so the water dish must be kept filled for the pup on self-feeding.

You may not want to put the puppy entirely on self-feeding, in which case you may feed one or even two mixed feedings each day as well. However, keep the self-feeding container filled and available at all times.

Keeping Him Clean

After meals the puppy will need wiping off since his muzzle will be daubed up and his ears, if they are long, may have dragged through his dinner. Wipe off his mouth, his muzzle and his throat, with a slightly dampened cloth; otherwise the hair which is only puppy-fluff right now, will mat and annoy him until he scratches. No matter how dirty the puppy gets he should not be given a tub-bath until he is several months old! He can be wiped off with a dampened cloth or brushed clean and perhaps combed very gently to separate the hairs. Occasionally little clumps of hair mat together and irritate the skin. There is no harm in clipping these off, but use blunt-end scissors to avoid accidents. Puppies are unbelievably quick in turning, so do not risk injury to the eyes.

Don't worry too much about those tiny areas on the body where the hair seems glued to the skin and then finally falls out leaving a bald spot. Unless the skin appears angry-looking, such spots have resulted from nothing more than a few drops of milk. Rub them with a tiny bit of vaseline or castor oil on the end of your finger.

Trimming Toenails

Toenails grow rapidly and, in the case of the young puppy, they are not worn down to proper length because he usually walks on only soft or smooth flooring. The points are often sharp as needles. They'll prick holes in stockings or clothing but worse than that, as they grow they take on a curved shape which makes them difficult to disentangle once they are caught. When his nails do catch into things, the puppy may injure himself in trying to pull away. Long nails also make his footing less secure. Therefore, with blunt-end scissors or nail clippers, periodically nip off just the transparent tips of the nails. Remove only the point, without trying to shorten the nail, but merely blunting it. Do not cut into the "quick" which is quite sensitive and may bleed.

Dewclaws

On the inside of the legs, just above the feet, you may find a set of extra claws. At this age they are loosely attached by cartilage only. These are useless toes, something like thumbs, unsightly and often dangerous when they get caught in fabrics. Once in a while we come on certain breeds of dogs like the Great Pyrenees where dewclaws are left on; but for the most part they are just a nuisance and might as well be removed. The earlier they are removed the better since with growth they become attached to the leg bone. During early puppyhood the veterinarian can cut them off with scissors under local anesthesia. With older dogs, dewclaw removal is a more serious operation.

Soft Spot

Besides his joints, tendons and leg muscles which may be injured by a fall, the puppy has a very tender surface on top of his head known as the "soft spot." While the chance of incomplete or slow hardening of the skull differs in breeds or individuals, the top of the pup's head is always a highly vulnerable spot.

See to it that the pup is never dropped on his head. See that he doesn't strike himself against chairs, beds, and in fact any hard object as he may during those earliest play periods when he is just learning to use his legs. Perhaps the best answer to this problem is to give him a place to play where there is little or no furniture. Most important precaution of all is to instruct the children not to pick up the puppy until they have been taught how to hold him safely. (See page 20).

Play

The pup that plays quietly is usually playing safely, whereas the one that tears around boisterously may be exhausting himself nervously and physically. This does not mean that the normal puppy is not lively, for he certainly is. But just as he gets enough sleep by means of short naps, so does he get his best exercise in short sessions.

Don't egg him on to play when he tires or wants to rest. When he is ready to quit, leave him alone. It is a great mistake to excite the resting puppy, or to permit children to urge him on. He will play when he feels like it, and when he is tired he should stop.

Play is the young animal's instinctive method of exercise. He will find ways of playing by himself, too. The age-old game of chasing his tail is usually puppy play; but if he actually bites at his tail, look for matted hair, debris, or even a flea that might be annoying him. Since the normal puppy is chock-full of vim and vigor, he may exert himself beyond his strength. After a play period of twenty minutes or so, pick him up and put him in his box. Stopped in the midst of a boisterous game of chase and pull, he may rebel, but never mind! Shut him up and leave him alone. Before you know it, he'll be sound asleep.

The puppy that plays quietly in his own place or box cannot come to much harm no matter how long he keeps at it. His footing is secure because he is on his papers or his blanket. When taken out for play, however, he meets certain risks, not the least of which is slippery flooring. Many folks floor the puppy room with linoleum, or they let him scamper around the kitchen or bathroom, since these places suffer less from periodic mistakes. Nevertheless, the frisky pup is none too sure on his feet. He can easily slip and fall, injure a knee joint, or pull a tendon. Therefore, the puppy that plays on waxed linoleum or polished hardwood floors needs the protection of some kind of carpeting. Especially suitable is a discarded cotton rag rug that can be washed as often as needed.

Sleep

The puppy needs a lot of sleep. When he finishes eating he will usually feel sleepy so we put him on his paper or take him out to relieve himself and then put him in his crate for a nap. This helps his digestion, and avoids excitability.

He should not be allowed to romp directly after eating, anyway. Too much activity, handling or excitement may make him vomit his dinner. Keep him quiet and undisturbed for awhile, and before you know it he'll be napping. Or instead of going to sleep he may prefer to stretch out and quietly mouth his toys. This is all right, too.

Toys

The puppy needs toys to play with. Be sure they are the right kind of toys. Surprising indeed is the little rascal's ability to rip and tear things apart with his teeth. He is not being naughty but merely natural. Using his teeth is natural to a dog and the puppy learns this at a very early age.

In pet shops all manner of toys may be found, some more suitable than others. But whatever you buy, select it with this question in mind: can it be torn apart and can it be swallowed?

Don't give rubber toys which crumble easily, or those made of synthetic rubber. The latter, even if not swallowed, can irritate the stomach and intestines and do a great deal of harm. Toys with squeaking devices which might be chewed off and swallowed should also be avoided. Thin, soft, rubber balls will be destroyed in five minutes, the pieces perhaps swallowed and the puppy made seriously sick. Calico animals, sold as babies' playthings, will not last long under puppy punishment, and their cotton filling will be dug out and eaten. A pair of discarded stockings, knotted together, makes a good toy; also a bunched-up clean cloth, or a strip of heavy burlap stitched into a roll for the pup to haul about. The safest toys are those made of leather, "treated" natural bone or hard, natural rubber.

Stay away from painted toys like old broom handles. In chewing the pup may swallow paint flakes and lead paint poisoning can kill him. Non-poisonous paint must be used on children's toys, but the law does not apply to household articles, walls or woodwork.

Bones are sometimes given to puppies as playthings. Small bones like chop bones will be splintered and the sharp pieces may tear the throat and kill or injure the puppy. The larger, harder knuckle and shin bones cannot be splintered and are safe.

"Paper" Training and Housebreaking

The chances are that your puppy was started on paper breaking when he was weaned; even so, he is by no means perfectly broken as yet. He is too much of an infant to remember anything very long. So let's start again from the beginning.

Paper breaking has become standard practice for puppies too young to go out of doors, and not yet developed physically or mentally, to be trained. It means teaching the puppy to relieve himself on spread newspapers. It is convenient; but, to save the trouble and possible frustration in re-training to the outdoors later when the pup is older, it is better to start taking him outside from the beginning. However papers should be kept at one end of the puppy's sleeping place or pen (see page 2) for emergencies. Paper training is particularly suitable for small dogs and apartment living.

Following a nap, the puppy is usually ready to urinate. If you can be on hand just as he wakes, so much the better; if not, wake him gently after a reasonable period of sleep. Place him on the paper immediately. Do this several times each day and always the first thing in the morning if you can wake before he does. You will be surprised how soon he connects the feeling of paper beneath his feet with the duty expected of him. Always praise him so he will know that he has pleased you.

Burning all soiled papers is the most sanitary method of disposal; but while the puppy is learning save one soiled paper to remind him what the spread papers are for. Puppies, in fact all dogs, prefer to use a spot they have visited before, so we trade on this during the early stages of paper train-ing. However, remove all droppings promptly so the puppy doesn't play with them and, perhaps, get the habit of filth eating. (See page 31.)

When the puppy plays on the floor, we cover a large area with papers so he is more likely to hit the paper than not; then we gradually reduce the amount of paper until it covers only one small corner of the room. But, by all means, keep papers handy, and in sight everywhere the puppy may go. While he is little he cannot be expected to travel from one room to another for his needed toilet.

Watch him closely. When you see him sniffing the floor, hurrying round and round, he needs to relieve himself. Pick him up quickly and put him in the proper spot. Then be liberal with your praise. He may leave a trail—when he starts he can't stop—and though one spot may be easier to clean up, remember your object is to train your puppy and the proper place must be associated with the deed.

Now, if you prefer to train your puppy to go outdoors from the very first you can do so. For dogs that will eventually go outdoors for their "duties," it is the wiser course. It means that you must be ready to take the puppy out the first thing in the morning—usually early morning, too—in the begin-ning. Since a puppy needs to eliminate right after meals, that means another four trips, and still another walk just be-fore bedtime. That makes six trips at least, especially while he is young.

This may sound like more trouble than paper breaking but you will not have to retrain when breaking from paper to the outdoors. And, even at this early age, it is more practical with pups of the larger breeds. It has this one disadvantage—pups taken where other dogs have been may pick up disease from places where an infected dog has sniffed or urinated. However, when properly inoculated the puppy is protected. (See page 16.)

And this is how the crate comes in handy for outdoor breaking. The puppy won't soil his bed if he can possibly help it, but he will let you know very early in the morning his need to go out. Pull on some clothes in a hurry, then take the pup from the crate and carry him outdoors. Don't set him down until you get him outside, for he may squat immediately. Let him wander around until he finds a spot that he likes. If he doesn't do it right away, you must be patient. When he does, praise him extravagantly. Each time he does his duty give him a great show of approval. Try to avoid "mistakes" by watching the pup when he's indoors. When he starts to squat, hustle him outdoors. If you really work at it your pup will soon be on the way to being housetrained. You can't expect so young a pup to be completely broken. Mistakes are bound to happen with young pups since they can't control themselves when they get the urge.

Under certain conditions, both paper and outdoor training may be wise. Strangely, many dogs never forget their paper-breaking lessons, and this is often a very good thing. When the dog is ill or cannot go out of doors or when he is old and uncertain on slippery pavements, the paper toilet can be arranged indoors. The dog will remember what it is for.

The young puppy urinates frequently and in small amounts. At this age the bowels also move several times a day, the movements not quite formed but rather soft and of medium brown color. A change of food, particularly different milks, or even water, may loosen the bowels for a day or two, after which they return to normal. Overexcitement, more food than usual, or the strangeness of a new environment may also cause a temporary loose bowel condition. This need cause no alarm, unless the stools are definitely watery, black, or greatly increased in number. A highly-offensive odor suggests some type of infection, and the veterinarian should be consulted promptly.

Mucus in the stools, whether or not accompanied by pain and whimpering, may indicate simple indigestion, or a more serious problem such as worms (see pages 29-30). Rough food, such as dog biscuits, may be at fault, but consult your veterinarian.

Umbilical Hernia

Occasionally there is a soft, movable lump, beneath the skin of the puppy's stomach. When the puppy lies on his back, the lump disappears; when he stands up it descends again.

This is probably an umbilical hernia which occurred at the point of attachment with the placenta when the puppy was whelped. It is not painful, nor is it irritated; but may be subject to injury or unsightly. It may or may not correct itself in time. In any case, do not attempt any sort of home treatment. Your veterinarian will show you the way to bandage or otherwise remedy it, if necessary.

"Bargain" Puppies

We often say that there are no bargains in dogs; that you get what you pay for. That is true. At the same time, just as there are at times worthwhile sales in department stores, so there are bargains in dogs that can be purchased from kennels or pet shops at less than the usual prices. These can be as healthy, strong and friendly as any others; but they possess certain defects which bar them from competition in dog shows. That is why they are cheaper; they are excluded from the show ring, but certainly not from the home.

Among such things are unmatched eyes, the one being blue, the other brown. The blue eye we call a china, fish, or pearl eye. Only in breeds like Old English Sheepdogs, blue merle Collies, Dalmatians, etc., are unmatched eyes considered acceptable in the show ring; in other breeds they are deemed "faults."

Another defect of about equal importance (or unimportance to the pet owner) is "pink nose." Except in certain breeds the young puppy's nose is ordinarily black. It is usually pink at birth and begins to darken immediately. Once in a while the melanin, or darkening agent in the skin, stops at the spotting stage, and then we have a pink and black or what is termed a butterfly nose. Though not considered desirable for show dogs, you can be sure that the defect will in no manner affect the puppy as a pet in the home. In any litter some pups will be more promising as show dogs than others, so command premium prices. When the breeder asks less for their littermates, it does not necessarily mean there is anything wrong with the less expensive pup.

Inoculation

Science has removed many of the hazards of dog-keeping. Nowhere is this more true than in the case of those killers, distemper and infectious canine hepatitis.

Usually the dam is immune to these diseases either because she has had them and recovered, or because she has been inoculated against them. The colostrum in her milk which the puppies get in the first few hours of nursing gives them protection while nursing and for about two weeks after weaning. Beyond this period the pup is on his own and will require the protection of inoculation.

Injections of serum for temporary immunity can be given the young puppy every two weeks. Usually, puppy shots are given between the eighth and twelfth weeks. Your puppy may have been inoculated already—ask the kennel or shop where you purchased him. But by all means get in touch with your veterinarian for the follow-up injections.

The Veterinarian

Early inspection of every young puppy by the veterinarian is a matter of good common sense. Most breeders and pet shops are experienced and reliable enough to offer for sale only puppies which are in good health. Some, unfortunately, are not as careful as they might be. Many a pup is purchased on impulse before the buyer is sure about the standing of the kennel or pet shop. Then too, in the twinkle of an eye things can happen which change a sound and healthy youngster into an ailing or injured one requiring immediate skillful aid.

And so, even before any faint shadow of trouble, get acquainted with a veterinarian of your choice. You cannot, of course, sit down with him and have a cup of tea. He's a busy man. But you can ask your dog-owning neighbors about the nearby veterinarians. Find out who's who and why, and be guided accordingly.

Find out where he lives and what his office hours are; all about him. Then, when you need him, you will know exactly where to go. Today, veterinarians do not often go to one's home. Their more complicated equipment for examination and treatment is office-bound, so usually you must go to them. This is not too hard a task, however. You will find conscientious and well-trained veterinarians conveniently located almost everywhere.

There is a common belief that going to a veterinarian involves great expense. This is not so. In the main, fees are moderate; approximately five dollars. One visit may be all that is necessary. The important point is to seek the veterinarian's assistance before the ailment is advanced and the treatment expensive or unnecessarily difficult. Some large cities have pet clinics for those unable to pay normal fees. Telephone directories usually list these, in addition to locations for veterinary practitioners.

CHAPTER 2

THE 3-5 MONTHS OLD PUPPY

The Developing Puppy

Your puppy is growing rapidly now, not only in size but in other ways also. He is much more certain on his feet than he was a short time ago: his leg muscles are stronger, his coordination better. Most striking, perhaps, is the development of his intelligence. He seems more aware of his surroundings, more eager to reach out and make friends with the people around him. He wants to play, play, play, and he expects everyone to join in with him. He especially recognizes children. They too are always on the go, and that pleases him. They are little and, since his line of vision is close to the ground, he appeals to them even more than to the grown-ups for his ever-ready frolicking.

Message to Parents

Because so many puppies are purchased as children's pets, we are going to take time out to talk to parents. Some of them hesitate to add a dog to the household for fear it will injure the child.

You need have no cause for fear. Without exception puppies are friendly creatures. Born with complete confidence in people, they cannot be anything but friendly unless their trust is destroyed by ignorance or neglect. Of course, in playing with a small child, a pup may topple the child over—that is not the dog's fault and the bumbling puppy is sorry immediately. It is the fault of parents who, without thinking about it, gave the dog to too young a child. Actually, the dog risks the greater harm. Quietly, he takes an unbelievable amount of pummeling, and he'd give his very life for the child if he could.

In addition to the physical protection he gives the child,

the dog provides constant companionship. Rainy days present fewer problems for the only child in the house when the dog is around. Letting the youngster think the dog is his and his alone develops his sense of responsibility. In caring for the dog he learns how to treat an inferior with justice and humanity. Such wholesome friendship can teach him the proper attitude toward any member of society who suffers physical or other misfortune. Failure to grasp this lesson causes some of the greatest evils of society. The child must learn that the world is not his, to do with as he likes; only when he treats others with kindness and understanding can he really grow as a human being. Without a shadow of a doubt the dog plays a big part in the social education of youth.

The dog will not teach the child kindness unassisted—you will have to help. By his patience the dog may even give the child an exaggerated idea of his own powers and privileges for the dog is unbelievably long-suffering. The slightest growl is a real exception. Ordinarily the dog merely gets up and walks away.

Sometimes children, and even grown-ups, tease a puppy because he is so "cute" when he gets angry and tries to bite with his baby teeth. This is a serious mistake. Besides the cruelty of tormenting a pup, it is very likely to make him mean-tempered and snappish as he grows older.

What about the dog's service to grown-ups? It is as great as that given the child. Let us disregard for the moment the war dogs, herding dogs, farm and factory guard dogs and leaders of the blind. Thousands of these have paid, and are paying, many times over for any favors man has extended the dog. Let us salute instead the millions of dogs in private homes where as pets and companions, by their response and love, they make life happier and less lonely.

The Child and the Dog

At what age can a child have a pup of his own as companion? This question cannot be answered exactly because it depends on the amount of help given by the parents. Regard for others is one of the things a child must learn as he grows. He cannot be expected to treat a puppy with kindness without help. He will learn however, if he sees his parents handle the puppy carefully, and if they insist at every step of the way that he be gentle and considerate.

No child is old enough to play with a puppy by himself until he has learned to be kind. He must be taught not to chase the pup to make him run. He must be taught not to stick his fingers in the puppy's eyes and ears; not to pull his hair or tail, not to lift him by the legs, not to drop him on his head or to step on him or frighten him with screams and cries. A child must learn never to "corner" a dog (or any animal for that matter). It is natural for animals to protect themselves when cornered and a pup that has the most gentle nature may snap or bite to protect himself under certain conditions. All such things have been done to dogs by many children who knew no better because their parents did not realize the need for teaching them.

And so the age at which the child may be given a puppy of his own will depend upon the child and the amount of time given by the parents for teaching and example, as well as for watching over the play-times of both little ones.

How to Pick Up the Puppy

Always use both hands to pick up the puppy. Place one hand between the forelegs to support the chest, the other hand under the belly to support the hind parts. As you lift, take care not to spread the youngster's elbows. Held with both hands in this manner, the pup cannot use his feet to wriggle free, nor is he strained as when lifted at one end only. Never grab him by the scruff of the neck—it hurts him and frightens him by throwing him off balance. Never use his tail as a handle, since the tail is easily injured.

Put him down as carefully as you lift him up. Suppose you are holding him on your lap. Keep one hand ready to stop him in case he should suddenly try to leap off or squirm to the floor. When you put him down, lift him in both hands and put him on the floor carefully so that all four feet touch at about the same instant.

Very young children should not pick up the puppy at all. They go through the phase of dropping things on the floor and you cannot do anything about it *except* by your own watchfulness. Try to prevent puppy-dropping by seeing that the child does not lift the pup; if he should, get to his side as quickly as possible. Naturally, puppies of the smaller breeds suffer greatest damage since they are most easily lifted. Older children can be taught the proper method of picking up and putting down an animal, but even they should be told to sit on the floor when they handle a tiny pup.

Naming

The puppy is now ready to start his education. His first lessons will be simple enough to fit his youthful understanding. His name of course can be whatever you choose, for this is merely a call name to use at home. If he is a pedigreed dog and to be registered later (see page 113), he can then be given a more formal name. The every day name, however, should be short and crisp sounding.

Every time you approach the puppy, speak his name clearly, distinctly, and in a moderate tone of voice. Shouting is not needed; he hears much better than you do. Loud noises may frighten and confuse him. In a short time he will connect his name with himself. Maybe he'll reply with a tiny yip, perhaps he will run toward you. This is excellent. Play up to it by kneeling or stooping down as he approaches. A full-grown person, standing, can be a fearsome thing to a little dog way down there on the floor, so get down to his level and your voice will have far more appeal.

Collar and Leash

You are going to need more than one collar before the puppy grows up so don't spend too much on this first one. Select a lightweight, narrow collar, the round sort rather than the flat as it is less wearing on the tender skin of the neck. It should fit exactly right, that is, loose enough to be comfortable but not so loose that it can slip over the head when the pup balks at the leash. To make sure that it fits, buckle it in the center hole. See if you can slip one finger between collar and neck—that spells comfort—and then with both hands see if you can pull it off without unfastening it. If you can, then it is not safe, for the puppy may put a paw through and hobble himself.

Attach the collar for a short time each day, especially during play times. He may be one of those devil-may-care youngsters that doesn't mind a bit, or he may resent it by pawing and rubbing himself along the rug. Don't worry. He'll get used to it, but right now try it on him for short periods only, perhaps just before meal time.

Next comes the small lesson of the leash. When the puppy has learned to accept the collar, tie to it a piece of string, or light-weight leash, depending on the size of the puppy. Let him trail it over the floor, wherever he wishes to go. He'll be a bit bewildered, especially if it catches on a chair leg and gives him a yank. Stand by and see that the pup doesn't tangle himself up and become frightened or injured.

After a few sessions of trailing, pick up the end and guide the pup around the room or your yard. This is the first time he has been made to do something he may not choose to do. If he balks, drop the leash, play with him a moment, then pick it up and try again. As you guide him along, talk to him continually, praise him, tell him what a very good dog he is. Soon he will disregard the tug at his neck. For outdoor walking, use a lightweight leash, as even a tiny toy pup may break a string, get away and run into street traffic.

These earliest and simplest lessons have been dealt with at length to stress the need for patience and understanding. Avoid frightening the puppy now and you will also be paving the way for all later teaching.

"Bed!" "Place!"

When a dog does something especially smart or surprising, we like to fall back on the instinct theory. "Oh, he does that instinctively," we exclaim. Maybe he does, then again maybe his mother taught him.

Plenty of supposedly instinctive animal knowledge is taught the young by the mother. Even under domestication today, puppies learn much from their dam, if they are free to trail her, and she is free to show them the sights and the dangers. When we get a young puppy, we are literally taking him out of school; so let's get him right back in again and teach him what a little dog on his own ought to know.

Simplest of all the puppy's obedience lessons is "Go to Bed!" or merely "Bed!" or "Place!" or whatever expression you may want to use. Its advantages are too many to name; you will find that out as you go along.

Remove his toys from his bed, and use one of them to start a little game. Take his toy away, give it back, then take it away again. Naturally, he'll want it. Hold it up so he can see it and, as you walk toward his box say "Go to Bed!" He will scamper after you, and as he sees you drop the toy in the box he will jump to get it. You are telling him to do what he is already doing, but the point is that you are impressing upon his mind the sound of the order "Go to Bed" at the very moment he is hopping in. Repeating the order will soon associate the words with the act. When he understands what is wanted, you can skip the toy. Merely issue the command and give a signal with your hand in the direction of the box.

Don't overtire the pupil by continuing the lesson longer than five minutes at a time. Four or five lessons daily are enough. Be regular in your teaching, be patient, and above all be encouraging. "Go to Bed!" is an order, not a punishment, so be cheerful, sociable about it. All the lessons will not go well. Sometimes the pup will be confused; he'll look up at you, worried, as if to say "What am I to do?" Stop everything. Pet him, talk to him. Wait a while and then start all over again. Once he gets the idea, his eyes will shine as he scampers to obey. Then, be liberal with your praise.

A young puppy's memory is short, so little and often is a good teaching rule. Several short training periods per day are best, without one day skipped if it can be avoided. Even after the lesson has been learned, use it often or the puppy will forget. Gradually increase the distance until the youngster can be sent to bed from another room.

The Carrying Case

Conditioning the puppy to the carrying case is best done while he is young. Grown dogs have shown resentment and fear of being shut up in a bag. Of course, if yours is one of the larger breeds, you will not be carrying him in a satchel. He will ride free in the car, or he will be crated when he may have to travel by plane or railroad. Nevertheless, at some time during puppyhood the large dog, too, may have to be taken somewhere in a bag; so it is common sense to teach them all that the modern carrying case is nothing to fear.

Place the puppy's own blanket or pillow in the case so he will feel at home, and open both ends so he can see out. Put the bag down on the floor. Maybe he will hop in; if not, lift him in, lower the top and latch it. Don't attempt to move the bag, but just sit down beside him so he will know you are there; if he cries reassure him by talking. Open up the top and let him hop out if he likes, or if he cares to take a nap in the bag, so much the better. Leave the bag around for a while so it will be familiar to him. Next time you put him in, carry the bag around a little to accustom him to the motion. Carry him further and further, down the street a ways, just so he will learn to accept it as a matter of course.

Feeding

The puppy's basic diet continues without change (refer to "Basic Nutrition and Feeding," page 73). However, as the puppy grows he needs more food so we increase the amount in each separate feeding. We also mix his food so that it is drier, more crumbly and less moist than for the younger puppy.

The amount fed at any age can usually best be determined by watching your pup. He will show weight changes almost from day to day. If he is getting too much on the plump side, reduce the quantity. If he appears thin and seems anxious for more to eat, increase the amount. The quantity also depends on the puppy's breed and activity. The feeding chart for the different-sized pups can serve as a guide. (See page 25.)

When the puppy reaches four months of age you can reduce the number of feedings to three a day—morning, noon and evening. But, of course, to make up for the dropped feeding and also because the puppy is growing all the time, you will increase the quantity.

If you prefer to vary your pup's menu, the morning feeding can be commercial dog meal moistened with slightly warm water or milk, the noon feeding biscuits, and the evening feeding either meal moistened with meat broth, burger patty or canned dog food.

In buying commercial dog food be sure to get the best kind you can buy, since whatever else you add, this is the foundation of your dog's diet.

Under certain circumstances, you may want to feed dry dog meal alone. This can be done on a self-feeding regime which is described on pages 8-9.

And do not forget to offer a drink of fresh water several times during the day, but not directly before feeding or after hard play or exercise. If it is not convenient to offer water to your pup, keep a filled water bowl available.

During the teething stage, usually occurring at the age of four months, a large shank bone is a good thing for the puppy to chew on; it helps the teething process, gives him exercise and a lot of innocent pleasure. Other than that the best use for bones is to boil them and use the broth in the dog's regular feed. Never give the puppy fowl or chop bones that are sharp or may splinter and be swallowed.

Mischievousness

Every healthy puppy is going to be mischievous. You might as well make up your mind to it and not worry about it. Worry more when your puppy is so good he never tears up anything; this one needs a bracer, for he's below par!

When we say that puppy mischievousness is not a fault but a virtue, we can hear objections popping up on all sides. But his teeth, you know, are his fingers, and he must use them if he has the normal vitality and curiosity of the healthy young animal. Books and magazines within reach will be gnawed; that hanging corner of the table cover will be yanked unmercifully. The world is his, and everything he can grab is a toy to play with.

FEEDING CHART

Age: 3 - 5 Months

VERY SMALL BREEDS
(Averaging 5-15 lbs. weight as adults)

Wt. in lbs.................................3-10
Calories per day.....................300-850
No. of feedings.....................3 or self-feeding
Meal (nugget).......................¼-¾ cup per feeding
Meal (chunk)........................⅓-1 cup per feeding
Burger-type (3 oz. patty)............⅓-1 patty per feeding
Canned dog food (1 lb. can).......¼-½ can per feeding

SMALL BREEDS
(Averaging 15-30 lbs. weight as adults)

Wt. in lbs.................................5-14
Calories per day.....................500-1000
No. of feedings.....................3 or self feeding
Meal (nugget).......................½-1 cup per feeding
Meal (chunk)........................⅔-1¼ cup per feeding
Burger-type (3 oz. patty)............⅔-1⅓ patties per feeding
Canned dog food (1 lb. can).......⅓-⅔ can per feeding

MEDIUM BREEDS
(Averaging 30-50 lbs. weight as adults)

Wt. in lbs.................................15-25
Calories per day.....................1050-1600
No. of feedings.....................3 or self feeding
Meal (nugget).......................1-1½ cups per feeding
Meal (chunk)........................1-1¾ cups per feeding
Burger-type (3 oz. patty)............1⅓-2 patties per feeding
Canned dog food (1 lb. can).......¾-1 can per feeding

LARGE BREEDS
(Averaging 50-80 lbs. weight as adults)

Wt. in lbs.................................20-35
Calories per day.....................1400-2250
No. of feedings.....................3 or self-feeding
Meal (nugget).......................1¼-2 cups per feeding
Meal (chunk)........................1½-2½ cups per feeding
Burger-type (3 oz. patty)............2-3 patties per feeding
Canned dog food (1 lb. can).......1-1½ cans per feeding

VERY LARGE BREEDS
(Averaging 100-175 lbs. weight as adults)

Wt. in lbs.................................35-50
Calories per day.....................2250-3100
No. of feedings.....................3 or self-feeding
Meal (nugget).......................2-2¾ cups per feeding
Meal (chunk)........................2½-3½ cups per feeding
Burger-type (3 oz. patty)............3-4 patties per feeding
Canned dog food (1 lb. can).......1½-2 cans per feeding

25

There is just one way to prevent all this. Keep things out of his reach. You cannot teach him yet to leave certain objects alone. So be sure to provide interesting toys to push and pull and tear and wreak his small vengeance on; and then remove all else from his inquiring teeth.

A special warning about base plugs: Electric outlets with their wires attached are fair game for any pup. He'll chew them and possibly cause a fire or shock himself. If a puppy does get a shock from chewing through an electric cord and stiffens out unconscious, *always unplug the cord from the wall* before touching the pup. Then use artificial respiration on your dog (see pages 147-48) and put aromatic spirits of ammonia to his nose. Meanwhile notify your veterinarian. One thing more—do not drop rubber bands, paper clips, and such on the floor, because everything goes into the curious puppy's mouth and may be swallowed.

The Play Pen

To get enough exercise the puppy must have more space to play in now. He may be very mischievous, too, so he cannot be given the freedom of the house. Put a gate in the doorway of the room you want him to stay in. At this age, dogs of the larger or heavier coated breeds, can, of course, spend much of their time in an outdoor enclosure. A baby-pen can be used for a tiny dog. You can make it or buy it.

Four wired frames can be screwed together and bolted to a wooden platform with castors or wheels. If the height of the pen is an inch or two less than the width of the house doors, it can be carried from one room to another, or outdoors.

When covering the frames, nail the wire on the outside. It is less costly to tear your clothing than to have the puppy injure his eyes when he attempts to chew the wire. You can protect your clothing, too, of course, by edging the frames with staples.

Since you may wish to use the play pen to confine the pup when you leave him alone, it is wise to add a bed in which he can curl up for a nap. For most puppies, a wooden box will serve. Cut out a square or, if preferred, a U-shaped piece from the side to serve as an entrance. Hinge the top for a cover that can be raised for cleaning, or left open if the weather is very warm. Place a blanket or other bedding inside, and there you have a snug little harbor free from draft and chill. The puppy left in a wire enclosure outdoors must have a really sturdy type of dog house. Occasionally a pup will refuse bedding of any kind and claw it all out of his box, basket or kennel. Don't worry about it. If he prefers a bare bed, there is nothing you can do about it.

Can He Go Outdoors?

Can the puppy of this age be taken out of doors? Of course. But use common sense. If it rains or snows the pup belongs inside the house. If it is definitely cold, or very hot, keep him indoors. Wind, draft and too much direct sunlight can prove harmful. So avoid them. This is most important with small and medium sized breeds. The larger breeds at this age will be well accustomed to outdoor living.

Bear in mind that most puppy coats are not thick and weather resistant enough to keep him warm, or screen his body from the sun's rays. He is more sensitive to cold, too, since he has more body surface for his weight than the grown dog.

In fairly warm weather a certain amount of exercise on natural grass is good; but it is not safe for any length of time. Especially when left to himself, the puppy will dig up dirt and stones and may swallow them. He'll delight to sprawl out on the grass, but if he lies there very long he may get chilled from the dampness even though the ground seems warm. If the owner plays with him for ten or fifteen minutes, two or three times daily in good weather, that is fine, and that will be enough. Keep the youngster moving and he will benefit from the outing.

The safest type of outing for the pup of this age is in the play pen (see page 26) or a fenced yard. Place the pen in the sun when it is cool, and in the shade when it is hot. Face one long side and one short side with canvas as a wind shield. The outdoor yard for the larger breeds should have some shade as well as sun, and a place protected from drafts or wind, such as a box or doghouse.

Keeping the Dog in the Cellar

How about keeping the pup in the cellar? It depends entirely upon the cellar! A dark, damp, poorly ventilated cellar is no fit place for a dog of any age—it is just as unpleasant and unhealthful for him as it would be for you. The average cellar, however, is not what it used to be, particularly in today's modern home. If it is light, dry and clean, it can serve for at least part of the time. It can be his bedroom for sleeping at night, for instance, if care is taken to guard against dampness. Construct a wooden platform, raised off the floor for under ventilation, shield the sides against draft, and furnish a good, comfortable box or basket for the pup to stretch out in. (Watch those wicker baskets, though; dogs sometimes chew them and swallow the pieces to their, and your, sorrow!)

Due to the lack of sunlight in even the best cellar, however, the dog should not be made to spend too much of his time down there during the day. To make a long story short, the cellar that is fit for you is equally fit for the dog, as part time shelter.

Sleeping with People

Should the puppy he allowed to sleep in your or your child's bed? By all means, if you want it that way. So long as he is sweet and clean, no harm will be done grown-ups or children except in the rare case of human allergy to dog hair. Taking the puppy with them is one of the best means of persuading children to go quietly to bed. It is also a great comforter for lonely folk, young, old or middle-aged.

So far as the puppy himself is concerned, he sleeps warm and draft-free, with no danger of chilling when the house heat goes down. If you are afraid of coddling your puppy, remember that some need coddling—if such a term may be used to mean sleeping warmly. A puppy's energy is limited; it can be used for keeping warm, or for growing. So, let him grow.

There are drawbacks to letting the pup sleep with people. Once you start it, you may have to keep it up. The puppy himself will be quite definite telling you that. Furthermore, sleeping covered will "soften" him to a certain degree. He should not sleep in bed one night and in a cold room alone the next.

The short-coated, thin-skinned little puppy accustomed to sleeping covered should be given a blanket to curl up in for day-time naps. Make a flannel cover for the blanket or pillow, and leave the ends open so he can get inside. The older puppy knows enough to do this; when warm enough he sleeps outside, when chilly he crawls in, snug as a bug in a rug. If you have occasion to board out a dog that has always slept in bed, tell the kennel so that they can provide the additional night warmth required. If they cannot, then take the dog elsewhere.

Change of Teeth

Toward the end of the 3-5 months period, the puppy will begin to change his teeth. In the course of his life, he has two sets, temporary and permanent. The temporary set, sometimes called milk teeth, are shed around the fifth month (earlier in some cases), after which they are gradually replaced by the permanent teeth.

The milk teeth consist of six quite tiny teeth, upper and lower, directly in the front part of the jaws. On each side, upper and lower, is a fang-like or shearing tooth (the canines), and behind them the molars.

The puppy starts to cut his baby teeth at three or four weeks of age, and by six or seven weeks he has his full set of thirty-two temporary teeth. For the time being, the milk teeth are strong enough for chewing rather soft foods; but since his jaw strength has not yet developed, they cannot crack or crush really hard substances. Nor are they strong enough to support the puppy's weight without injury. A common method of play is to let the puppy grab a rag and hang on as you lift him high. Owners often do this as a matter of pride, to prove what a good grip the youngster has. Needless to say, lifting by the teeth is bad practice, and ought never to be permitted.

During the fourth or fifth month, you may notice that the gums are swollen and angry-looking. The little teeth gradually loosen and fall out. The puppy rarely if ever cries from toothache, yet his mouth is sore; he champs his teeth together, may vomit occasionally, lose his appetite and act as if he had lost his last friend. However, change of teeth does not always disturb puppies. Some puppies go through it without batting an eye. But practically all puppies chew on things at this stage. You can help the puppy by providing a hard knuckle bone which he will chew on in an attempt to pull his own teeth. (See page 35.)

When a baby tooth refuses to give way to the permanent tooth coming up beneath it, it will be pushed aside rather than out. Then the veterinarian will have to extract the baby tooth. But give the puppy time; don't be too eager to get those baby teeth out. Ordinarily, they will shed themselves and you won't even notice the process. However, if you see two teeth, one large and one small, trying to occupy the same place in the jaw, then do something about it.

Worming

Contrary to what people may say, not all puppies have worms. So do not dose your puppy with strong and dangerous medicines merely because you think he needs it. Be very sure before you go ahead, and then proceed with caution and exactness.

Since most dog breeders worm their puppies before delivering them to new owners, your puppy may not need worming again for several months, if at all. However, since worms are fairly common in young dogs, it is wise to be constantly on the watch for them.

Signs of worms are many, for they upset the puppy in various ways. His abdomen may appear bloated or overfat especially after eating—and more than the amount of food he ate would seem to warrant. He may spit up, or vomit often in small amounts. He may act dumpish and be disinterested in play. His appetite possibly is irregular—one day he may eat hungrily, and another day refuse food entirely. The bowels, too, may be unusually loose or watery. Round worms, which resemble one to three inch pieces of string, are often expelled in the stools. They may also be vomited. This is the most common kind of worm with which young puppies are infested.

If worms are suspected or actually seen in the stools, it is wiser for the new dog-owner to let his veterinarian prescribe the dosage instead of trying to do it himself. Take the pup, or a specimen of his stool, to the veterinarian, who will, by microscopic examination, determine the type of worm present, if any, and prescribe medication. The fee for the examination will be modest. The average dose recommended on the package of worm remedy cannot take into consideration the condition of every individual puppy; meaning that your puppy may be less rugged than normal. He may be weakened by the worms or some other ailment and his resistance lowered for the time being. If such is the case, even the normal dose for his size and weight might be dangerous. That is why the veterinarian's prescription is preferable to patent remedies.

With present-day remedies, it is not difficult to rid a puppy of round worms. Directions for dosing will be found on worm medicines sold in drug and pet stores. If you buy one of these, be sure you get it in the *puppy* size, since it comes packed in both puppy and grown dog dosages.

The amount of worm medicine varies with the puppy's age and weight. This is where the danger lies, when the inexperienced dog owner attempts home worming. Worm remedies are irritating to tender intestinal membranes. They are hard on the digestion, too. With some worm medicines it is important to give them only after a period of fasting. The dose is usually directed to be given the first thing in the morning, on an empty stomach, that is, before any food or even milk is allowed. And then, no food for at least two hours or the specified time. You will find detailed directions on the package. *Be sure you follow them to the letter.*

Stool Eating

Once in a while a puppy will eat his own droppings. This disgusts and disturbs the owner but it is not serious and need not become a habit. The cause is difficult to determine. He may be merely hungry—puppies are always hungry and always ready to pick up whatever offers. Therefore, it may be a good idea to keep some dry prepared dog meal or biscuits in his play area for him to nibble on when he suddenly feels like eating.

Filth eating may result from teething and from mineral deficiency, especially a lack of salt, so sprinkle a little iodized salt on his food once daily. Boredom, inactivity and too much confinement are believed to be the main reasons and point to the need for more attention, more exercise and a good assortment of toys so he'll have something to drag about. Puppies often start by playing with stools. Since the uncollected stools may actually be responsible for the practice, clean up all stools promptly. Scolding is not effective, although a sharp "Ah-ah" or "No" in a disgusted tone of voice will stop a puppy when you catch him at it. Then, of course, remove the stools. Sprinkling one or two stools with cayenne pepper or Worcestershire sauce is sometimes successful in breaking the habit. Watchfulness is the best way to correct filth eating.

Things to Watch Out For

There are certain infectious diseases which will prove far less serious if treated without delay. Symptoms include listlessness, loss of appetite, coughing, running eyes and nose, and quick, high fever. If you notice any of these signs, get the pup immediately to the veterinarian.

As you brush the puppy's coat every day, watch out for fleas and lice (see page 83)—they infest the young as well as the older puppy. Look sharply along the back and at the root of the tail, under the vent and the forelegs, the creases of the ears. If you see the slightest trace of the pests, or their black, granular leavings, get to work with the fine comb, and use flea powder on the puppy and his bed.

☆ CHAPTER 3 ☆

THE 5-7 MONTHS OLD PUPPY

Adolescence

This is the age of gangling youth, a trying period for any young dog. Ordinarily, it is his most unattractive age. He has lost his puppy plumpness and may appear to be all legs and neck. He is leaving behind some of his sweet, trusting puppy ways, but has not yet acquired any grown dog dignity and good sense. He is rambunctious, barks more and generally asserts himself. His coat is undergoing changes, too. Gone is the soft, fine hair and in its place are the beginnings of his two-ply adult coat.

Dog Licenses

He is still very much a puppy and, if normally healthy and intelligent, something of a little wild Indian. But, according to the record books of his municipality's town hall, he rates as a grown dog at six months and so must be licensed.

If you are new to dog-keeping and unfamiliar with your town's dog ordinance, ask the town clerk exactly what the laws are. Towns differ widely in this respect, some being more strict than others. However, you must get a license from your town clerk or whatever agency issues them when the puppy reaches six months of age; and it must be renewed yearly.

In return for the license fee you will receive a properly filled out printed form containing the dog's license number. Be sure that on this form, a copy of which is retained at headquarters, you have written in the dog's call name, breed. markings, and sex. This is important. If the dog strays and some good soul picks him up, his license number will tally with his description, hence he can be identified as yours and returned to you. This is why the metal license tag which you will be given with the receipt, should be stapled to the dog's collar or clamped to its attached ring.

The collar should be worn at all times, since its license tag serves as a form of identification. The puppy may slip out the door, chase after someone and get lost. If he is found without his license tag, he may be picked up by the local dog-catcher and popped into the pound, after which you may or may not see him again. If he wears his license tag, he will be held for a few days during which you can claim him.

Another means of identification is the collar plate engraved with the name and address of the owner. Neither the license tag nor the collar plate, however, can always be depended on to furnish positive proof of ownership. If the dog strays and gets in a fight with another dog, the collar is sometimes chewed off and if the dog is stolen the collar is usually destroyed.

There are three foolproof methods of identifying a dog and proving ownership, namely tattooing, and nose or paw printing, but they are not as yet in general use. The dog can be tattooed on the inner flank of the ear-flap with a number, initial or symbol. This is not painful and the marking cannot be removed. Nose and paw printing are dependable identification, since each dog has a whorl pattern on his nose and footpads as distinctly individual as that of a man's fingerprints.

Feeding

Most 5-7 months old puppies will not need the same number of daily feedings as they did when they were younger. So we will now skip the bedtime feeding and give only three meals a day, morning, noon and evening. Some puppies at 6 or 7 months may even show a preference for two instead of three feedings. But in either case, the amount of food must be increased to make up for the skipped meals and also because his rapid growth puts an extra demand on the puppy at this stage.

The amount of food required depends on the individual puppy, the extent of his activity, exercise, size and weight. You will find a complete discussion in the chapter on "Basic Nutrition and Feeding," page 73.

The main thing to keep in mind is that at least three-fourths of the puppy's diet should be a balanced, prepared dog food which will give him all the necessary food elements. You will probably be able to judge the amount of food needed to keep your puppy satisfied and in good weight, neither too fat nor too thin, by observing him. The feeding chart, based on the puppy's weight and caloric need, can serve as a guide:

FEEDING CHART
Age: 5 - 7 Months

VERY SMALL BREEDS
(Averaging 5-15 lbs. weight as adults)
Wt. in lbs.................................4-12
Calories per day....................400-1000
No. of feedings......................2 or self-feeding
Meal (nugget)......................½-1½ cups per feeding
Meal (chunk)......................⅔-1⅔ cups per feeding
Burger-type (3 oz. patty)............¾-2 patties per feeding
Canned dog food (1 lb. can)........½-1 can per feeding

SMALL BREEDS
(Averaging 15-30 lbs. weight as adults)
Wt. in lbs............................12-24
Calories per day....................1000-1550
No. of feedings......................2 or self-feeding
Meal (nugget)......................1⅓-2 cups per feeding
Meal (chunk)......................1⅔-2⅔ cups per feeding
Burger-type (3 oz. patty)............2-3 patties per feeding
Canned dog food (1 lb. can)........1-1½ cans per feeding

MEDIUM BREEDS
(Averaging 30-50 lbs. weight as adults)
Wt. in lbs............................20-35
Calories per day....................1400-2250
No. of feedings......................2 or self-feeding
Meal (nugget)......................2-3 cups per feeding
Meal (chunk)......................2⅓-3¾ cups per feeding
Burger-type (3 oz. patty)............2¾-4½ patties per feeding
Canned dog food (1 lb. can)........1½-2¼ cans per feeding

LARGE BREEDS
(Averaging 50-80 lbs. weight as adults)
Wt. in lbs............................40-50
Calories per day....................2550-3100
No. of feedings......................2 or self-feeding
Meal (nugget)......................3½-4¼ cups per feeding
Meal (chunk)......................4⅓-5¼ cups per feeding
Burger-type (3 oz. patty)............5-6 patties per feeding
Canned dog food (1 lb. can)........2½-3 cans per feeding

VERY LARGE BREEDS
(Averaging 100-175 lbs. weight as adults)
Wt. in lbs............................55-90
Calories per day....................3400-5600
No. of feedings......................2 or self-feeding
Meal (nugget)......................4⅔-7⅔ cups per feeding
Meal (chunk)......................5¾-9½ cups per feeding
Burger-type (3 oz. patty)............6¾-11 patties per feeding
Canned dog food (1 lb. can)........3½-5⅔ cans per feeding

There is a method called self-feeding, in which dry dog meal is kept out for the dog to eat at will. Although its use is more likely to appeal to the person who keeps his dog, or dogs, in an outdoor kennel, it can also be adapted to the house pet. The self-feeding method is described on pages 8-9.

Bones—should they or should they not be given to your dog? Let us look at the factors against bones—they provide little nourishment, can cause constipation, irritate and even tear the digestive tract when swallowed. Continuous gnawing of bones wears down the teeth. On the other hand, bones provide chewing exercise and most dogs enjoy them tremendously. At one time bones were considered quite valuable; but today they are looked upon as more risk than nutrition. If you feed bones to your dog, limit the number to about one a week. Never give him one near his regular feeding time—and do not give him any kind except a large bone, such as a beef shank bone. Poultry, chop and other small bones are too sharp, may splinter or be swallowed and do great harm.

Do not forget that your dog needs water as well as food. In fact, a dog can live without food a great deal longer than he can without water to drink. Keep fresh water in a bowl where he can drink at will unless you make it a practice to offer him a drink several times a day. In hot weather, water easily becomes warm or fouled by insects so it should be renewed frequently.

Drooling

Folks worry sometimes when they see saliva stringing down from the corners of the dog's mouth. It is very common and usually occurs while he is waiting for his food. The sight or the smell of the filled dish is enough to start the mouth watering until it spills over. Drooling is common, too, when the dog feels sick at the stomach as when riding in the car. Teething also causes it, as does a piece of bone or a splinter of wood caught between two teeth, so look for the cause. If the drooling continues, have your veterinarian examine the mouth—a sore tooth or torn gum may be the cause.

Draft

Let us say it once again: draft is the puppy's meanest enemy! It is the enemy of all dogs, in fact, since even the strong and healthy adult cannot hold his own against it.

At an age when the pup is too young to be left alone in his yard, he is sometimes tied out on the porch for his airing.

Here many a youngster comes to grief. The weather is warm and pleasant, but the open porch may be drafty. Seemingly mild breezes often sweep around a house to chill the puppy on the porch.

He may get bronchitis, and cough and cough. He may catch cold. His eyes run, his nose runs, and he feels miserable even as you and I. Don't let this happen. The only porch safe for the small puppy's airing is the one closed on three sides. Put the puppy pen out there, and in it place a covered box with its entrance turned away from the porch's open side. Even then, watch the puppy, and if he acts shivery and uncomfortable, bring him inside.

Sunshine and Panting

Direct sunlight out of doors is very good for the puppy, but in summer or in warm climates too much is harmful. The first sign of over-heating will be increased panting. The dog's body cannot rid itself of extra heat as rapidly as can the human being. The dog perspires mostly through his tongue rather than through pores in the skin. As he pants, his tongue drips, and if he continues to pant he loses a lot of body fluid. Give him water to drink, and leave him in a semi-dark, cooler place until the panting ceases. For the young dog ten or fifteen minutes of direct sunlight will be enough, unless he has shelter into which he can crawl when he gets too hot.

Spaying

If your dog is a female, you will want to decide whether or not she should be spayed. This operation is often performed to prevent the female from being bred and having puppies. It does away with the female's three weeks "season" which attracts male dogs to her. During her "season" which occurs every six months, you would have to put her in a boarding kennel or keep her confined indoors for safekeeping.

What are the disadvantages of spaying? The spayed female is ineligible to compete in the show ring, and naturally she can never have puppies. For those who desire a puppy merely as a pet, companion, watchdog or guard, these things are not disadvantages. On the other hand, if you should want to enter your dog in dog shows, or to breed her at some later time, then certainly she should not be spayed.

As far as the pet in the home is concerned, the spayed female is ideal. When the operation is performed before she comes in season for the first time, there is every chance that, if correctly fed and exercised, she will not become over-fat. Contrary to report, her disposition is not changed, nor is her later activity or alertness impaired. The younger the operation is performed, the simpler it is since a much smaller incision is necessary and therefore recovery is more rapid. At this age, healing takes about one week, and in from two to three weeks, the patient is back to normal. At first, however, physical exertion, particularly jumping and running up and down stairs, should be avoided.

The fifth or sixth month is a good time for spaying, for ordinarily this is well before the initial seasonal period. The operation can, of course, be done later, if desired.

Sweaters and Raincoats

When the pup goes out walking he is going to need pro-tection against wintertime cold. The general rule is this: When you put on a topcoat yourself, put a sweater on the dog if he is accustomed to living in a heated house. Of course, when let out for a few minutes to scamper around the yard, or taken on a brisk walk he need not be bundled up; but when he is left out for any length of time or walked in cold or wind, he should wear his sweater.

Should all dogs wear sweaters? The larger, long-coated kinds do not wear clothing of any sort, especially when full-grown. By that time their dense undercoat, overlaid with a coarser outer coat, shields the body quite well from the cold. However, as we have noted before, the thin puppy coat is not weather-resisting. So if your pet is still carrying his puppy coat during his first winter, keep him moving out-doors, dry him well if his coat gets wet. As for the thin-skinned, fine-haired small breeds kept as house pets, these will need sweaters on cold days.

Pet shops can furnish attractive coats and sweaters, some just for looks, others for use. When choosing first make sure that the coat covers the chest since this needs protection most. Fancy coats which cover only the back and shoulders may be pretty to look at, but they are not much good against the cold. Raincoats, of course, serve a different purpose, and protect the back rather than the chest. These save the owner a lot of time, too, since the dog that is walked in the rain uncovered has to be thoroughly dried when he comes in.

Get the puppy used to clothing of some sort while he is little for you never know when he may need it. In illness, the housebroken dog often insists upon going outdoors to relieve himself, and at such times he will need special protection. Be careful when you put on the sweater the first few times. Don't frighten the animal into resistance by dragging it over his head and ears. Instead, take the sweater in your left hand, run your right hand through the collar, and spread it enough to slip it on gently. Better do without those little sleeves for the forelegs; they add to the difficulty of putting the sweater on.

"No" for Destructiveness

This is the age of greatest destructiveness if you permit it to be. The normal puppy is playful as a kitten; his jaw strength is rapidly increasing; his gums and his teeth are losing their sensitivity, and he is eager to try them out on everything. Add to this the fact that he does not know right from wrong, and you have on your hands an animal capable of doing considerable damage.

We are not going to punish the puppy for stealing, chewing, breaking; instead, we will teach him what he may and may not do. We'll teach him the important lesson *"No!"* We must be firm but kindly; firm because the puppy feels greater security when controlled; kindly because we don't want to destroy his confidence in us. He thrives on praise, and he stops, surprised, when scolded.

Approval and disapproval can be shown by tone of voice. The higher-pitched, encouraging *"Good dog!"* means approval, while the lower-pitched, definite *"No!"* signifies correction. It takes time for this tone difference to register with the puppy, but the understanding will come if we keep at it. Repeated lessons will do it if the pup is normally intelligent, and most puppies are.

Suppose we find him blissfully gnawing on the table leg. Quickly get one of his toys, maybe his knuckle-bone. We pull him from the table leg as we scold, *"No!"* He stops in surprise, and then we offer him his bone. As he takes it, we praise him. Then we watch him. If he returns to the table, we order *"No!"* again, and immediately shut him in his crate or another room and leave him alone. Sooner or later, he gets the idea that he may chew certain things but not others.

This lesson is difficult to teach. Much of the trouble, however, is caused by temptations that we leave in his path. We make it too hard for him by not using our own common sense. Take the case of the table leg again. When we are at home we scold him for chewing it, then we go out and leave him alone to chew it to his heart's content. There is no one around to follow up the lesson, consequently that lesson is lost.

Once you insist that the puppy leave something alone, see that he obeys, or remove the tempting object from his reach. If you give him an old stocking-doll to play with, don't blame him when he noses into the closet and drags out a perfectly good pair. That is your fault, not his. As a rule, the puppy is less destructive when given something to do. Suppose we teach him how to walk properly on leash.

Heeling

Since leash control is required by law in some communities, begin correct leash-walking at a fairly early age. Also, the puppy will need more exercise than he can get in his play pen, and he will have to get used to the sights and sounds of the street. The first leash lessons were discussed in the preceding chapter. By this time the puppy is probably used to being led with the leash fastened to his collar.

Heeling is just a fancy name for walking correctly under leash control; it means walking with the dog's right shoulder about on a line with the owner's left knee. When this lesson has been learned, the leash will be held in the left hand, the right being free for other duties. However, throughout the training period the leash will be shortened by coiling and is held in the right hand. The left hand grasps that part of the leash closer to the dog's collar. Just how near the collar the hand can be placed will depend upon the size of the dog.

Keep the dog on your left side. Walk at a fairly brisk pace. Find a quiet path or sidewalk so the pupil's attention will not be attracted by passing people. The idea is to make him walk willingly, easily. He may charge ahead like a little bull or balk and pull back. If he pulls ahead, tug sharply on the leash as you command *"Heel!"* to keep him in line. Here the stiffly-held left arm will help especially if he tries to jump up against you or pull to the side. Every time he goes off the straight and narrow, be ready with the order *"Heel!"* Keep saying *"Heel!"* from time to time.

Remember the difference between command and correction. All commands are issued in a calm, clear tone. The sharp word, and the jerk upon the leash are corrections to be used, for instance, when the dog stops to sniff the ground. And when he understands and obeys, be liberal with your praise. Several lessons daily, of about ten minutes each, will be about right. The puppy tires easily and then becomes confused, so little and often is the rule.

Conditioning to Noise

The longer the puppy is protected from noise and confusion, the greater will be the shock when he encounters them. You walk along the street—pop goes the exhaust as a car goes whizzing by. The puppy shies. He is not only frightened; his ear drums actually hurt. Stoop down, reassure him, and if the noise continues, put your hands over his ears to deaden the sound.

He will undoubtedly have already learned that the world is not an altogether quiet place. We cannot stop noises but we can see that the pup gets used to them gradually.

Make some sort of racket at home; for instance, just before you feed him rattle the pan unnecessarily. He enjoys his food so he will be less disturbed by the noise that goes with something pleasant. When he has learned to walk fairly well on leash, take him along the highway where traffic is heavy. Have a biscuit or two in your pocket, and if fire engines roar past, offer him the tidbit then and there. All this noise, he begins to think, is not so bad after all!

Hot Weather Tips

It is easier to keep a puppy warm than to keep him cool. When he becomes overheated he perspires mostly through his tongue, so he needs plenty of drinking water to replace the fluids lost. A pan of water placed for him in the morning is not enough. Provide it fresh and cool several times daily. He is not particular about his drinking water—he will lap it as he finds it. Be sure that both the water dish and the water are clean.

Exercise in morning and evening hours during hot weather, and stay out of the noonday sun. See to it also that his yard has a section of shade. Puppies may get snappy and grown dogs cranky if bothered too much in hot weather.

Do not worry if he goes a little off his feed during a long hot spell—he seems quite sensible about eating less at such a time. Give him the same kind of food but not quite so much of it. And do not take him for long rides in the car; he is better off at home. Do not shave off his coat since it helps to screen the skin against sunburn and insect bites. Daily brushing will remove much of the undercoat and dead hair which add to overheating and discomfort. Heavy coats can be thinned out but not given a crew cut.

Never use poison weed killers or plant sprays where your puppy plays. They are poisonous and can kill your dog or make him very sick. Fresh paint and varnish must also be kept out of reach.

CHAPTER 4

THE 7-10 MONTHS OLD PUPPY

Nearing Adulthood

Changes are now taking place very quickly. You can almost see your pup grow. He is still a bit awkward, and still enthusiastic about everything, especially play. But he has lost something of that baby look—he watches you as if he knew what you are saying. As a matter of fact, he probably does, for the more you talk to him, the sooner he will begin to understand. Talk to him simply and clearly—and often. Dogs love conversation.

At seven months he is shooting up on his legs; as he nears ten months he will begin to broaden out. Unless, of course, he happens to be one of those ultra-low breeds whose framework develops somewhat differently from the average.

Because of his growth and his increased activity, he needs more food, but not as many feedings a day since he can digest larger amounts of food at a time.

How to Feed

Until the puppy reaches eleven or twelve months of age we will feed him morning and evening with, possibly, a snack at noon.

The feeding chart can be used as a guide to the amount of food your pup needs, in line with his size and age. (See page 44.)

The amounts given in the chart can, of course, be changed to fit the individual pup. An active, well-exercised dog will burn up more food than one of more quiet habits. An amount that is right for one puppy will make another overweight. You can arrive at the amounts to feed by watching your pup's weight. If he is well filled out and seems satisfied with less food, feed less. If he seems forever hungry and is shooting up fast, feed more.

Dogs of the small breeds are reaching maturity at this age so their food needs drop off. With maturity they will eat less of their own accord. But dogs of the large breeds do not mature until well over a year of age so their food requirements are still those for growth. In fact, many pups of the large breeds may seem almost to have bottomless pits for stomachs at this age.

Tidbits and Supplements

Although your dog's diet will be mostly commercial dog food, there are usually good table leftovers in every household that can be included in his feeding. Economy can be combined with taste variety and you may be sure that your dog is getting proper nourishment when the scraps are only additions to a good prepared dog food. Leftover meat, fat trimmings and vegetables can be mixed in the food along with leftover soups and gravies. Remember that such additions should never be more than one-fourth of the total amount of the food in order to prevent nutritional or digestive upsets. A teaspoonful of a vegetable oil or fresh fat, such as bacon drippings, can be mixed in the pup's food occasionally.

Some dogs get bed-time tidbits all their lives; it is very much of a household ceremony as the various members of the family go to the refrigerator for the same purpose. This is just a snack, however: a dog biscuit fed from the hand. Feeding tidbits and adding table scraps has this disadvantage —it can form poor eating habits.

Although the majority of dogs of this age are hungry and wolf their food, some may be slow, even picky at times. Do not try to find something the dog likes when he refuses the food offered. If he is normal and active, remove his dish and offer nothing else until next meal time. If you let him grow choosy instead of eating what you give him, he may lead you a merry chase for many a day. Some dogs, too, show great good sense by skipping a meal now and then for no apparent reason. A feeding or two refused occasionally need cause no alarm. By always refusing one of two feedings, a dog shows that he is ready to have the number reduced to one.

The multi-flavor dog biscuits now on the market are ideal for "reward" or snack feeding. They are nourishing and offer plenty of taste variety.

If you prefer, there is a method known as self-feeding

VERY SMALL BREEDS
(Averaging 5-15 lbs. weight as adults)

Wt. in lbs.............................5-15
Calories per day.....................500-1050
No. of feedings......................2 or self-feeding
Meal (nugget)........................⅔-1½ cups per feeding
Meal (chunk).........................1-1¾ cups per feeding
Burger-type (3 oz. patty)............1-2 patties per feeding
Canned dog food (1 lb. can).........½-1 can per feeding

SMALL BREEDS
(Averaging 15-30 lbs. weight as adults)

Wt. in lbs...........................15-30
Calories per day.....................1050-1900
No. of feedings......................2 or self-feeding
Meal (nugget)........................1½-2½ cups per feeding
Meal (chunk).........................1¾-3¼ cups per feeding
Burger-type (3 oz. patty)............2-3¾ patties per feeding
Canned dog food (1 lb. can).........1-2 cans per feeding

MEDIUM BREEDS
(Averaging 30-50 lbs. weight as adults)

Wt. in lbs...........................30-45
Calories per day.....................1900-2800
No. of feedings......................2 or self-feeding
Meal (nugget)........................2½-3¾ cups per feeding
Meal (chunk).........................3¼-4¾ cups per feeding
Burger-type (3 oz. patty)............3¾-5½ patties per feeding
Canned dog food (1 lb. can).........2-2½ cans per feeding

LARGE BREEDS
(Averaging 50-80 lbs. weight as adults)

Wt. in lbs...........................50-70
Calories per day.....................3100-4350
No. of feedings......................2 or self-feeding
Meal (nugget)........................4¼-6 cups per feeding
Meal (chunk).........................5¼-7⅓ cups per feeding
Burger-type (3 oz. patty)............6-8½ patties per feeding
Canned dog food (1 lb. can).........3-4⅓ cans per feeding

VERY LARGE BREEDS
(Averaging 100-175 lbs. weight as adults)

Wt. in lbs...........................80-100
Calories per day.....................4950-6200
No. of feedings......................2 or self-feeding
Meal (nugget)........................6¾-8½ cups per feeding
Meal (chunk).........................8⅓-10½ cups per feeding
Burger-type (3 oz. patty)............9¾-12¼ patties per feeding
Canned dag food (1 lb can)..........5-6¼ cans per feeding

which has worked out satisfactorily. This is explained on pages 8-9.

Give your pup water to drink. Keep it fresh. Dogs dislike "stale" water as much as we do and often will not drink enough unless it is kept fresh.

The Female's First Seasonal Period

If your dog is a female, your most important concern at this age will be safety during her first seasonal period. The average female comes in season at eight months of age although some begin at six or seven months, others not until ten or twelve months. She will have another period every six months. A few females come in season only once each year while some may go to the other extreme and come in three times. The female whose periods are oftener than once every six months should be examined by the veterinarian.

Early signs include extra friskiness and affection, more than usual urination and swelling of the vulva. Occasional mucus discharge for a few days is followed by a bloody discharge which continues usually for two weeks. During the third week the vulva swelling goes down and the discharge lessens as the parts return to normal.

During her season the female will be attractive to male dogs and can be bred by them; in fact, that is the *only time she can be bred*. Heroic measures are needed for her protection. She cannot be allowed out alone for one minute. Either board her out for the entire three weeks or confine her securely. The instant she sets foot out of doors, the males from far and wide will congregate, to your annoyance and her danger.

Every time a female in season squats to urinate or sets foot on the ground she leaves an odor for male dogs. The next-door male carries the telltale odor on his feet, and so on, dog by dog. This is why males you've never seen before will hang around your yard. If the female is habitually kept in an outdoor kennel run, shut her in her yard for the entire three weeks. The fencing must, of course, be escapeproof. It must also keep out visiting dogs who will try to climb over or dig under it. There is a monetary consideration here also. Some municipalities levy a substantial fine against the owner who allows the female in season to run at large. Don't blame male dogs if they congregate on your doorstep. It is your fault for allowing your female the opportunity to attract them.

For lack of a fence or protected yard, the female will have

to be hand-exercised—on leash, of course. Little dogs can be carried under one's arm some distance from the premises and then set down for relief, picked up and carried home again. This helps to break the trail so that wandering males, although attracted by the scent, will be unable to follow it to its source. To exercise your larger female when in season, carry her from your door to your car, to a corner lot or country area and, upon your return, carry her into your house.

If your female has an accidental mating, get her to the veterinarian immediately. He may be able to prevent conception by hormone injection or other treatment. However, one mischance need not ruin your female for future breeding or having purebred puppies. Each litter is complete in itself, with no bearing on any later litter.

Care of the House Pet in Season

The care of the house pet in season presents certain problems. Some females, especially those of the smaller sizes, flow so little that it is hardly noticeable, others flow enough to spot furniture, floors and coverings.

Of course, furniture can be protected with covers, which is not too great a task when the female is kept in a single room. Where she has the run of the house, however, she can be dressed in commercially available sanitary panties. There is also a contraption for harnessing on the female to avert mating. At least that is the idea. But the vigor of male dogs make such contraptions not altogether safe. They cannot be completely relied upon. Neither can ointments, liquids, or pills taken internally, advertised as protective for females in season; though they are helpful in disguising the scent.

The sensible procedure is to imitate the practice of the professional kennelman who shuts the female in season securely in a compartment or separate room. In the home, enclosures of the sort should be locked or otherwise safeguarded against accidental opening. Likewise, screen doors opening onto the street should be carefully locked or latched lest the female push them open and slip out.

Remember, wherever the female sits down and whatever the amount of her flow, the scent will advertise her condition until a rousing good rain wipes it out. And when the female has returned to normal, that is, after three full weeks, give her a good soap-and-water bath to remove all possible scent.

Caring for the female in season is not too difficult a task, but if you now decide you would like to have her spayed (see page 36) you can still have it done. The operation is not performed during any seasonal period. Wait until about midway between seasons.

Fences and Fencing

Whether yours is a male or female, he or she is going to be safer and healthier if provided with a fenced yard in which to play and exercise. But, you will say, your dog loves his home and will not wander away. Nevertheless, all dogs at some time in their lives may roam if they get the chance. And this urge may be strongest at the approach to maturity. Your dog may find his way home again, but his disheveled state will tell a tale of travels with other escapees. It is no reflection on the comforts of home when your dog takes off for parts unknown. He's a sociable creature, and he loves to travel in packs. In fact, the pack instinct is something which man, with all the frills of domestication, has not succeeded in eliminating.

There will come a time when the scent of a wandering female will blind the male to all other joys and prompt him to follow her to the ends of the earth. The female may also get the wanderlust, especially when near or actually in season.

To confine a dog properly, the fence must be high enough so that he cannot jump over—the exact height of course depends upon his size. You want to keep your dog in, and other dogs out, so choose a heavy wire fence such as fox fencing, or soldered mesh like chain-link, rather than a loosely woven, light mesh that can be spread apart. The wire should be sunk at least six inches in the ground, and the posts driven well below the frost line. Dogs can dig under a fence; the only way to discourage them is to sink the wire into the earth or pour a concrete wall a few inches thick into the ground. A diagonal mesh that pinches their feet helps prevent dogs from climbing, as does an overhang of about a foot, braced inward, all around the top. The most effective fence for the female in season is doubled wired; that is, a fence within a fence, about a foot apart.

The gate must be strong and rigid so it cannot be pried open at the bottom. Use a good latch, one that will not be accidentally opened by delivery men or by curious children. And remember that many dogs can use their paws like hands to turn a knob or lift a latch.

Trolley-line Leash

Without a fence the puppy may occasionally have to take

his airing tied out in the back yard. String a stout wire across the yard and fasten it securely to two posts, after first attaching a swiveled ring so that it will slide easily along the length of wire. One end of the leash is then latched into the ring, the other end to the dog's collar. A swivel at both ends of the leash will allow turning as the dog runs up and down.

The danger of such a trolley-line exerciser is that the leash may tangle hobbling the dog and in extreme cases even choking him. The space all along the wire must be kept free of objects on which the leash might catch.

The dog on a trolley-line cannot stray. But he is at the mercy of other dogs who are free to enter his yard and plague him. He cannot fight back or protect himself, so he should not be left unless someone can keep an eye on him. He should also have walks or other exercise as the small space in which he is free to run, always up and down, never across and around, can make him restless and excitable.

The Outdoor Shelter

The dog left in the yard even temporarily will require a shelter—a snug barrel-kennel for example, where he can go when it rains or snows. In a small house of this sort, the animal's own body heat is thrown back to him to warm him in winter. The bottom should be raised off the ground, the entrance protected by a flap of burlap to serve as a windshield, and the whole, of course, must be leak-proof. Such a shelter can be kept in the open in mild weather, and hauled into the barn or garage if the weather becomes unusually severe.

For summer, a platform sunshade will be enjoyed. Build a wooden platform long enough for the dog to stretch out on: put it on four legs just high enough for him to crawl under. When he wants to sun himself, he will lie on top; when he wants to cool off he'll dig in below. Now, damp ground, we have always been told, is not a safe bed for a dog to lie on; even so, in extremely hot weather a dog finds a deep and shaded wallow of good brown earth the coolest place to be.

The dog living outside in all weather will need a really sturdy house. Remember, though, that only the heavily coated or more rugged dogs can stand full-time outdoor living in winter.

The permanent shelter has a double floor, with tar paper or insulation between the layers. Roof and side walls are insulated, and the roof pitched to prevent the puddling of rain water. Hinge one-half of the roof so it may be laid back from time to time for airing and cleaning. Face its entrance east or south, at least away from prevailing winds; and for extremely cold weather attach a portable vestibule or right-angled storm door to keep the wind out—this can be merely two sides of a box.

The all-year dog-house needs floor space fully twice as long as the adult dog, with a bed placed at the back, well away from the door and protected by a partition. Bedding, which may be held in place by a slotted slide, may be of cedar shavings or cured hay or straw—not new hay or grass which is damp. If there are no shade trees, make a lattice across the front and over part of the entrance. Convert it in warm weather with a length or two of deck canvas.

Shade trees are more satisfactory than any awning. They give off moisture, helping to equalize the temperature in summer; they are windbreaks in winter and keep the snow from drifting quite so much into the yard. However, trees should not be too close to the siding—leave several feet beyond their widest spread to allow for the circulation of air. If trees are already grown, this can be provided for when the dog shelter is built; if the house comes first, then allowance must be made for the growth of the trees. Avoid fruit trees for the dog's yard if they are going to be sprayed with material which can poison the dog when dropped on the grass or licked off the feet.

Whether the yard is designed for part-time or full-time use, outfit it with a container for water—if possible of fountain type to keep the water cool and clean.

Excessive Barking

From now on for many months to come life is going to be one lesson after another, but the dog will thrive on it. Learning things keeps him out of mischief by giving him something to do, something to think about. Training matures him mentally; and he almost wiggles out of his skin with pride when you praise him for work well done.

Your puppy has learned to love you very much; you are his whole world and, if he has anything to say about it, you are not going to leave him alone, no sir. To make a long story short, he barks when you go out—the neighbors have complained. This will never do.

The first step is to teach him not to bark unnecessarily. To do this correctly we must decide what barking is right and what is wrong. To discourage all barking is to limit his value as a watchdog. So we correct only when the dog barks continually and for no apparent reason.

Go *to* the barker. Never ask him to come to you for correction. With one hand hold the muzzle tightly shut even if it hurts. Use the other hand to fingerpoint as you command *"Quiet!"* Occasionally a few such sessions will be enough, but if the bad habit is of long standing, or the dog unusually stubborn, then something more spectacular than the muzzle grip has to be used. You can surprise the yappy one into silence by means of a harsh sound—drop a frying pan or tin. Empty tin cans tied together also can be thrown at the dog as you command *"Quiet!"* This lesson can also be taught quite successfully by dousing him with a shot from a water pistol or by dashing a glass of cold water in the dog's face.

Once you teach the *"Quiet!"* lesson, the dog will remain quiet while you are with him, but the minute you are out of sight he may get right to work again with that bark. Those living in settled communities, or in apartments, have to be quite sure their dogs behave when left alone. So, put on your hat and coat; let the dog know you are going out. Order him to *"Bed!"* or *"Place!"* with an old sweater of yours to lie on or one of your old shoes to snuggle up to, then say plainly and slowly, *"Quiet!"* Go right on out, but stay fairly close to the door so you can listen in.

Don't let him fool you by stealing to the door and sniffing out the fact that you are waiting just outside. That is why you ordered him to *"Place!"*—to keep him away from the door. When he starts to whine and bark dash back in again and say *"Quiet!"*, *"Place!"* With a folded newspaper or stick, rap the floor on the side of his box as you issue the command. You will have to repeat this performance many times, and you may find yourself spending what seems like hours just outside the door waiting for the barks to begin. But keep at it until you are sure that the dog has learned the lesson. Leaving him for short periods at first will also let him understand that you are eventually going to return. If he feels assured of your return he will learn to be quite contented alone. Young puppies that have learned this in the cradle, so to speak, rarely have to be trained to stay alone quietly.

Jumping Up on People

Jumping up on people on the street or in the home can be annoying, embarrassing and frightening to strangers. It is a bad habit easily broken if caught in the start. It is unfair to allow our dogs to jump on us when we are in old work clothes but resent it when we are all dressed up to go out. The dog can't tell the difference. As the animal leaps toward you in greeting, bring your knee up, or if it is a visitor who is being jumped on, tell him to do the same. The bent knee catches the jumper in the chest. If this does not work try reaching out with one foot and stepping on his hind toes and he will soon understand that his greeting must be given on all fours.

However, do not discourage the greeting entirely, else you snub the dog for his expression of joy. As you correct him for an unnecessarily boisterous greeting, you substitute another form. The moment he is on all fours, you pet him or shake hands with him, if he has learned that enjoyable little trick (see page 106).

The Sit Exercise

Another method of greeting concerns the *Sit*. When the dog rushes to meet you or someone else, you command *"Sit!"*, whereupon he sits down instead of pawing or jumping and acting generally objectionable. Bright puppies are often taught to *Sit* before they are taught to *Heel*. The two lessons do go together because they are used so often when the puppy is walking on leash. One lesson at a time, though, in teaching.

The puppy is trotting along at your left side. The leash is held in your right hand, your left hand just now being reserved for something else. Coil up the leash into a fairly short length. You stop, and as you command *"Sit!"*, you lift gently on the leash to hold the puppy's head up, while with your left hand you press his haunches into a sitting position. Press gently, slowly, and do not remove your hand too quickly. You want the dog to sit but not to lie down, so you may have to continue the upward pull on the leash. And as you issue the order *keep your feet still*. If you move your feet the puppy will move.

The first few times the puppy may be surprised at the pressure and perhaps even try to break away. If he resists, order *"Heel!"* immediately and gaily and start walking to calm him down. (Learning to *Heel* is explained on pages 39-40). Then try the *Sit* again. Keep at it, and in about ten days or so your pupil will be performing perfectly.

If he lies down instead of sitting as he should, the chances are that your hold on the leash was incorrect. A slow, firm up-pull on the leash as you issue the order *"Sit!"* should produce the right pressure. When your grip on the leash is not strong enough, and the dog lies down, do not try to correct by jerking. The mistake was yours, not the dog's. Reach down, and with your right hand between the forelegs, raise him to the sitting position, then pet him to show approval.

If he gets up the instant you take your hand away, that, too, is your fault. Keep your hand pressed to the rump long enough for him to understand what you want, even if it takes several seconds. Gradually less pressure and time will be needed and finally none at all; likewise the up-pull on the leash can soon be skipped. Should the dog sit diagonally instead of squarely, nudge his quarters to the right or left so that he heads directly forward.

Turns

The pupil must now learn that you will not always walk straight ahead, that you may turn to right or left and that he must turn with you without tangling you up or making you fall over him.

You are walking forward now, the dog on your left side, the leash-end coiled in your right hand, and your left hand fingering the leash loosely but ready to stiffen your hold at the proper moment. Command *"Heel!"* if only to alert the pupil's attention as you turn sharply, squarely to the left, at the same instant tightening up on the leash with your left hand to prevent the dog from walking across your path. You turn on the left foot and bring your right foot around into the new direction. If the dog bumps against you instead of turning, jerk the leash and say *"Heel!"* rather sharply. He will probably bump your right leg as it swings on the turn, and this combined with the leash-jerk will teach him what to do.

The right turn is done the same way, although the dog in this case has further to go. You turn on your right foot, swing your left around and, as you order *"Heel!"*, bring the dog around with you and on a taut leash.

Car Chasing

Car chasing is a problem in most communities. This bad habit should be broken before the dog comes to harm or causes an accident. Cars on the road are not the only danger, either; many pets have been laid low right in their own driveways while the family car was being backed out. Therefore the dog should be taught to give wide berth to any moving vehicle.

Training can be begun in the home driveway if it is long enough, or on the street at a time when there is little or no traffic. Let one member of the family take the dog into the yard, or on the sidewalk, on a fairly long leash. As the car is run slowly down the road, have someone sitting with the driver, ready to shoot a water pistol into the dog's face as he approaches the car and you order sharply and immediately *"No!"* This has a frightening effect upon most dogs and will discourage them. The use of your own car is best because, being familiar with it, the dog runs up to it expecting a ride. Controlled by the leash, he gets near enough to be "shot," but not near enough to risk injury. Sometimes this is all that is needed to teach him to stay away from moving wheels.

If, however, the dog is a confirmed auto chaser, stronger measures may be needed. Have an assistant drive a car up and down a quiet street. He will know what you are doing and will therefore be on guard to prevent injuring the dog. Snap on a long leash or rope and walk the dog along the side of the road, letting the leash out to full length as he lunges. As he nears the wheels, jerk him off his feet so sharply that he tumbles over and command *"No!"* This may have to be repeated many times but though it may seem rather severe punishment, a few dogs need it for their own safety.

Objectionable Habits in Males

The urge of approaching maturity sometimes causes the male dog to begin the quite objectionable habit of riding one's arm or ankle when over-excited in play. About the only way to deal with it is to grasp the dog by the collar or back of the neck, give him a quick shake and say sharply *"No, No!"* If while on leash, he tries the trick on someone else, yank him off balance as you give the command. Lack of exercise has been suggested as a cause. Give more leash exercise and other activities to find out whether this might help.

Probably because children and dogs roughhouse together, the dog unfortunately misbehaves in this manner more often with children than with grown-ups. Parents should instruct the child accordingly. When they actually see it happening, they can simply say, "Don't let Rover do that!" There is no need, however, for parents to be embarrassed at such a time. Animals are animals; they're made that way. And on the brighter side, once the dog is fully grown he will probably have outgrown the habit. If he doesn't outgrow it see your veterinarian, since a tiny cyst on the penis might be causing the trouble.

The male's testicles should be descended and visible. If they are not descended by this time, or if only one can be seen, take the dog to the veterinarian.

Objectionable Habits in Females

The female, prompted by a desire to mate, occasionally mounts a male or another female. When this happens during the seasonal period it is a natural occurrence. It is obvious, though, that the female should be isolated at such times. (see pages 46-47.)

Should this continue when she is not in season, she had best be examined by the veterinarian since ovarian cysts or tiny growths in the vagina may be the cause. Furthermore, the odor given off by cysts and infections may attract the attention of a male dog who will probably attempt to breed her.

Infections of this kind may cause the female to undergo seasonal periods more often than normally. She is not actually "in season," although she appears to be for a period of a few days at a time when she discharges a very small amount of mucus. If the female comes in season, or seems to be, at other than her regular six month intervals, she should be examined by the veterinarian. Two periods per year are enough; more than two would suggest spaying (see pages 36-37) to avoid any chance of malignancy.

CHAPTER 5

THE GROWN DOG

Maturity

The dog of small or medium-sized breed will probably have reached his full height by the time he is ten months of age, although his shape will continue to change for a few months longer. Larger breeds mature more slowly so these keep on increasing in size. Except for the slow developing kinds, growth beyond the ten-months stage is mostly rib-spread or rounding out, and settling down into the body shape of the breed. In most cases, then, we may consider the ten-months-old dog as an adult.

While the basic food requirements are the same as those of the earlier, or 7-10 months stage, the amount of food eaten daily will be slightly but not a great deal more. However, since more food will be taken at one time, the number of meals can now be cut to two, or even a single meal each day. We will not make this change all at once because the dog may have learned to expect a morning or noon feeding, so he has a feeling of hunger at this former feeding period. For perhaps two weeks, offer a biscuit and thereafter nothing at all at noon. When cutting down the number of meals, though, supply more food at the remaining meal time. And serve it at room temperature or warmed, but never too cold or too hot.

How to Feed

The feeding of the grown dog can be as complicated or as simple as you choose to make it. Simplicity seems to make the most sense.

By this time you have probably found a good commercial dog food which the dog enjoys. Perhaps it is the dry type moistened with water or milk, broth or soup, or the "wet" type served right out of the can. Perhaps you use both types, feeding mixed or separately. High quality dog foods contain more than enough proteins, carbohydrates, minerals and vitamins for a complete and balanced diet.

One pound of canned food averages 500 calories; one pound of the high quality dry meal about 1600 calories; burger-type about 250 calories per patty. For adult dogs it has been estimated that the daily food needs vary from 30 to 60 calories for each pound of body weight per day, depending upon the dog's activity. The hard working or very active dog as well as the growing puppy naturally needs more food than the grown dog which spends most of his time lying around the house. The amount of food is reckoned not entirely on the dog's body weight but also on the amount of body surface area. Strange as it may seem, the larger dog often needs less food in proportion to his weight than the slightly smaller dog. For further information turn to the chapter "Basic Nutrition and Feeding."

In general the amount of food will vary with breed and size of the dog. For an easy and complete diet a feeding chart is provided. Due to varied activity as well as to individual differences, this may not hold true for all dogs; but it is accurate enough to serve as a starter. The owner, after trial, will arrive at the right daily quantity.

Once he is used to one feeding a day, the dog usually prefers it that way. Two feedings may be continued, if you like. If you care to continue with two feedings a day you may divide the above amounts or vary the menu by a breakfast of dry dog food and milk. For dinner, which is the main feeding, mix the meal with broth or soup or with water, together with canned food or whatever leftover meat or vegetables you happen to have at the time. Vegetables may be fed; they are not necessary but they do have a laxative effect which will help the under-exercised dog. Cooked carrots, onions, spinach, beet tops and string beans are especially suitable.

Practically all kinds of meat leftovers may be given the grown dog. Because it often contains dangerous parasites, rabbit or pork should always be thoroughly cooked. Fish should also be cooked and, of course, carefully boned.

Although bones can be given occasionally (see page 35), they are not food unless considerable meat clings to them. Provide only large, hard bones such as knuckle, shank or shin; no poultry or chop bones which may splinter and pierce throat or gullet. When we read that the dog is a carnivorous animal we may get the notion that he requires nothing but meat. As a matter of fact, today's dog is not carnivorous.

```
┌─────────────────────────────────────┐
│            FEEDING CHART            │
│             Adult Dogs              │
└─────────────────────────────────────┘
```

VERY SMALL BREEDS
(Averaging 5-15 lbs. weight as adults)

Wt. in lbs.	5-15
Calories per day	250-550
No. of feedings	1 or self-feeding
Meal (nugget)	1-2¼ patties per feeding
Meal (chunk)	1-2 cups per feeding
Burger-type (3 oz. patty)	1½-2½ cups per feeding
Canned dog food (1 lb. can)	½-1 can per feeding

SMALL BREEDS
(Averaging 15-30 lbs. weight as adults)

Wt. in lbs.	15-30
Calories per day	550-950
No. of feedings	1 or self-feeding
Meal (nugget)	1 ½-2 ½ cups per feeding
Meal (chunk)	2-3¼ cups per feeding
Burger-type (3 oz. patty)	2¼-3¾ patties per feeding
Canned dog food (1 lb. can)	1-2 cans per feeding

MEDIUM BREEDS
(Averaging 30-50 lbs. weight as adults)

Wt. in lbs.	30-50
Calories per day	950-1550
No. of feedings	1 or self-feeding
Meal (nugget)	2½-4¼ cups per feeding
Meal (chunk)	3¼-5¼ cups per feeding
Burger-type (3 oz. patty)	3¾-6 patties per feeding
Canned dog food (1 lb. can)	2-3 cans per feeding

LARGE BREEDS
(Averaging 50-80 lbs. weight as adults)

Wt. in lbs.	50-80
Calories per day	1550-2500
No. of feedings	1 or self-feeding
Meal (nugget)	4¼-6¾ cups per feeding
Meal (chunk)	5¼-8½ cups per feeding
Burger-type (3 oz. patty)	6-10 patties per feeding
Canned dog food (1 lb. can)	3-5 cans per feeding

VERY LARGE BREEDS
(Averaging 100-175 lbs. weight as adults)

Wt. in lbs.	100-175
Calories per day	3100-5450
No. of feedings	1 or self-feeding
Meal (nugget)	8½-15 cups per feeding
Meal (chunk)	10½-18½ cups per feeding
Burger-type (3 oz. patty)	12¼-21½ patties per feeding
Canned dog food (1 lb. can)	6¼-11 cans per feeding

True enough, in his wild state he ate nothing but meat but he ate the entire animal, glandular organs, bones and even intestinal contents as well as muscle flesh, which, all told, made a fairly complete diet. Meat as furnished nowadays is not a complete diet. Moreover, the dog's instinct has been killed by modern civilization and if he were given a choice, he probably would not choose as good a diet as you can provide.

Certain dogs show a liking for "odd" foods such as fruits, raw vegetables, nuts or candy sweets. Such things are not harmful if given only occasionally. Do not let them interfere with the regular feedings.

Self-feeding, which is keeping dry dog food available to the dog to eat at will, has become an accepted method of feeding in recent years, especially for kenneled dogs. It can be started with puppies and continued throughout their life, or the grown dog may be put on self-feeding. For details on this method of feeding turn to pages 8-9.

Remember that your dog requires water to drink. It may be offered at various intervals or kept available in a drinking bowl. Keep it full and fresh, especially during hot weather.

Weight and Weighing

Whether or not the amount of food given is correct will be indicated to some extent by his weight. Once grown, the properly-tended animal maintains his weight fairly well. Do not, however, try to judge the dog's weight by looking at him. Ounces and pounds can accumulate unnoticed; likewise a heavy or fluffy coat can hide a thin body.

So, from time to time put the dog on the scales. The wriggling puppy can be rolled in a bath towel for weighing. If the older dog is small enough to be picked up, step on the scale with him in your arms. Then weigh yourself alone. The difference is the dog's weight.

When weight increases out of proportion to overall size, you can be fairly sure your dog is eating too much. When weight decreases, feed more, and at the same time have the dog examined for worms, particularly tapeworm. Worms weaken the dog, which is reflected by paleness of the mouth and eyes. Look carefully at the gums; pull down the underside of the eye rims. These should be a normal red, neither faded nor fiery.

Even though the dog seems to be in the best of health, veterinary examinations from time-to-time are worth while— every 2 or 3 months for the puppy, every 6 months or year for the grown dog.

Behavior on the Street

When a dog walks with you on the street, he will meet people and other dogs. You want to keep him from taking too much interest in them, but friend and stranger alike will have other ideas. They'll call him "nice doggy," they'll pat him, smile and whistle.

Your dog has already learned not to jump up on people (see pages 50-51); even so he may greet the stranger by pawing, licking or just acting silly. If he is the reserved, offish type, he may frighten the stranger by growling or bristling. This is not ugliness; your dog is only trying to say *"Won't you please leave me alone?"* You know that your dog is kindness itself, certainly not a biter. But what you may not have learned is that a dog can be goaded beyond endurance into anger, even as you or I.

In a case like this we cannot very well correct the dog; he's doing all right.

What a pity people do not treat dogs with the same dignity shown each other. Strangers do not rush up to one another and act as if they had been friends all their lives! Yet this they do to the dog, and the dog has every right to resent it. Pat a strange dog on the head and what happens? He may snap because he cannot keep your hand in sight. Hold your hand down perfectly still, giving him time to get your scent. When he makes up his mind he may show friendliness or he will ignore you. Do not try to make friends with a strange dog. Wait for him to make friends with you.

When passing a dog on the street, your dog will react according to his previous association with other dogs. If he is used to their company, he'll probably give them a welcoming wiggle and continue on. But if he has never met other dogs he may be shy or fearful, or he may kick up quite a fuss, snarling and tugging on the leash, or he may be awfully anxious to make friends.

The fearful and the over-friendly dog is not corrected at a time like this. He needs a carefully chosen doggy friend to play with occasionally. The snarling one, however, is yanked sharply by the leash as you order *"No!"* Then make him *Sit* until the other dog has gone by. Next time, when you see another dog approaching, make your dog *Sit* immediately. If the dogs are friendly you and the other owner may let them play together a while.

The Stay

The *Stay* is an elaboration of *Sit*, and a most useful exercise, too. Your dog will be ready to learn it as soon as he has learned to *Sit*. The new exercise will take longer to teach because it demands more of the pupil.

Tell your dog to sit, holding the leash in your left hand, with you at his right. Bring your right hand up to his face, palm flat, and say in a firm tone of voice, *"Stay!"*. If he moves, give a short jerk back on the leash, and make him sit, repeating the command. Do it for only a few seconds at a time at first, then for longer, and move away from him, letting the leash go slack. If he gets up to follow you, go back to the same spot, and make him sit and stay again. This training should also be followed when the dog is lying down, or standing, so that you can walk around him or away while he stays.

Coming When Called

You may have decided not to bother with this lesson. Your dog almost always comes when called, so why waste time?

If he is not taught, the dog comes when called because he wants to. Sooner or later he will refuse. You'll call him one day but he'll keep on going and risk his life in a fight or under a truck. So let's teach him to come whether he wants to or not.

Attach the long check cord to the collar, order *"Sit-Stay!"* then walk away from the dog the length of the cord. Now face the pupil and command *"Come!"* If he does not start toward you, stoop down and slap your knee with your hand as an added invitation. If he still refuses, give a light tug on the cord to get him going. Practice day after day, until the dog returns promptly no matter how far you let him out on the cord.

Later, try him off leash in a fenced yard or some place where he can't run out with traffic. If he keeps on going instead of obeying your call, turn around and walk away from him. Perhaps he wants to romp; perhaps he's teasing you, and will be so disappointed when you do not chase him, that he'll change his mind and come back. When he comes, do not forget the praise. And never, never call your dog to you for a scolding or disciplining. Always go to him in such cases.

Dogs, Gardens and Lawns

Coming when called is a very useful command in teaching your dog to observe your own property line and to keep him from bothering your own or your neighbor's garden and shrubbery. If your property is large, walk around the edge once or twice a day, first with your dog on a long leash, later without a leash. When he starts to go toward the street or the next-door yard, say *"No!"* sternly, then call him to you and pat if he comes. Do this repeatedly. If your command doesn't work when he's off leash, go back to using the leash again.

If this doesn't work, get an assistant. He will stand outside your hedge or somewhere in the forbidden territory, armed with some empty tin cans. When your dog ignores your call and bounces beyond the "line" the assistant will shout *"Go back!"*, clatter the tins and even throw some toward your dog. You will, of course, welcome your dog warmly when he comes back to you for "protection." Such measures, however, are usually unnecessary if you take regular "boundary" walks and keep watch when you turn your dog out alone. Call him to you for a pat or a tidbit every once in a while. Of course, you must remember that a passing dog or cat or a female in season on the next block may cause even the best-intentioned dog to stray from his own yard.

Dogs get spring fever and nothing is better to roll in or dig up than the soft earth of a freshly-sown lawn or a flower garden. If dogs are constantly warned *"No!"* and called back when they go for your flower garden or special shrubbery they will probably soon give it a wide berth. A few dousings with a garden hose or water pistol will also discourage, not only your own dog, but any visitors as well.

The commercial dog repellents, or hot cayenne pepper scattered around plants and shrubbery will help discourage a dog's attention. The repellents have an odor that a dog dislikes, the pepper will irritate his nose and make him sneeze. All such material has to be renewed frequently, especially after rain. And, of course, the least trouble is to put up a low wire fence around a garden to protect it from dogs.

Wandering

In many areas it's against the law to let dogs roam loose. Even where there is no law, it's best to have a wire enclosure for your dog or a "trolley line" outdoors except when you can be with or near him. (See pages 47-48.) Although many persons think that a dog must be free to be happy, a dog gets much more enjoyment out of life in being with his family and knowing he is wanted. Dogs who get much attention at home rarely become wanderers. If your dog is called once in a while, and spoken to, he won't be so inclined to stray away. There should also be regular play periods, walks, and, of course, times when you bring him indoors. Just feeding a dog well won't keep him at home. If he doesn't get the attention and friendship he needs at home, he'll search for it elsewhere.

Occasionally there is a dog who is a happy-go-lucky tramp by nature but that is the exception rather than the rule. If your dog does wander away one time and you have to find him to bring him home, don't waste time scolding him. It won't mean anything to him. Take him home, tie him up and treat him coolly for a while. In other words, you let him know you are displeased but that you want him with you. And see that he gets more attention at home.

Digging

There are many reasons why dogs dig holes in the ground. Certain breeds, such as the terriers, follow their natural instinct to hunt underground. They may actually be looking for a mole or field mouse or, in fantasy, digging out foxes or lions. With a determined digger there's not much you can do except to give him a place where he can dig when he feels the urge. Of course, dogs dig to bury a bone or some other morsel. And in the summer, dogs mostly dig to find the cool spot the deep earth provides for them to lie in. That's another reason for giving the dog a cool shady place outdoors.

Digging also comes about when a dog is bored. Here again, play periods, a few toys or a shank bone, more time in the house and regular walks and exercise, will help prevent the habit.

Exercise

How much exercise and what kind of exercise does a dog need? Few dogs get enough. In settled communities the dog must be exercised on leash, and this takes time. It is time well spent, for exercise is the great conditioner. The steady pace of controlled leash walking is more valuable than the occasional dashing hither and yon of the yard-confined dog. Furthermore, even in a sizeable yard, a dog can be as lazy as he likes.

If possible walk the dog on leash twice daily as far as he can go without seeming tired. Three trips around the block every day are far better than three miles on Sundays only, for the dog becomes used to exercise just as we do. For the dog, the walk should be as long as his legs, in other words one city block for the short-legged dog equals several for the long-legged one. When you are uncertain about the distance your dog can walk, start with a few blocks, then gradually increase the distance each day. In addition to leash-walking, your dog should be exercised and played with regularly in his yard, or he can be taken for a free run in woods and fields.

Do not feed immediately before or after exercise. When it is very hot, walk him only in the cool of the evening or early morning. Do not expect him to hold his own on icy pavements, for he slips easily. If you get caught in a shower, dry him off when he comes in, and when returning home from a tramp, check his feet for thorns, mudballs or blisters, and his coat for burrs and ticks.

Swimming

Swimming is very enjoyable exercise. Not all dogs, however, swim by nature, but some can be taught. Get the pet into shallow water by floating his ball. If you, too, are in the water, he will wade in to get it, and may swim when he reaches out beyond his depth. The dog's swimming stroke is much like walking—that's why we call it a dog paddle. He does not have to learn either stroke or timing, but he does have to keep his body fairly upright and his chin above the waterline. If he does not start swimming, don't push him; let him play around in shallow water to get the feeling of it. Later you can guide him beyond his depth while holding your hand under his chest.

Next, take him out into deeper water, always turning him toward shore before he begins to swim. He will continue swimming with paddling strokes until he reaches the bank and clambers up.

Wherever you encourage your dog to swim, be sure there is a graded exit, that is, a slight rise or bank up which he can scramble. The dog cannot pull himself up out of a straight-sided pool. Unwatched and unaided, he can easily drown this way. Even if he tries and fails by his own efforts he may be so frightened or exhausted that he will refuse to enter the water again. Once a dog learns to enjoy the water, he will jump in by himself, especially when chasing a stick or ball.

When he has finished his swim, dry him thoroughly with towels or electric hair dryer. Be particular about the ears dry them out. If the water is salt, rinse his coat with fresh water. Salt water dries the coat, often irritates the skin and causes itching and scratching.

CHAPTER 6

THE OLD DOG

Helping the Dog to Live Longer

Albert Payson Terhune once said: "The pity of it is that the dog lives for so short a time." Isn't it so!

Things look brighter, however, because modern management and medicines are helping the dog to live longer. While seventeen years is somewhat unusual, it is no longer news when a dog reaches that age; the dog believed to be the oldest known in America lived for twenty-six years.

The development of a six-months-old puppy may be compared with that of a child of six years, the year-old dog with the youth of fifteen. After two years the dog's aging slows, with each single year equalling about four years in man. In age, the ten-year-old dog compares to the fifty-six-year-old man, the sixteen-year-old dog to the man of eighty years.

We are never ready to give up our good companion, so how do we go about helping him to live longer? The pup with long-lived parents has a better chance of reaching a good old age, if he is correctly fed, housed and cared for. A good tight fence is very important to the life of today's dog. If you have a back yard, enclose it so that you can open your door and let the dog out by himself. Latch the exit gate to the front on the inside only. This sort of fence, which keeps your dog in and the neighbors' dogs out, will prolong your life too perhaps, since you won't be forever worrying about where your dog is. He'll be safe.

Aging is so gradual we hardly notice the changes taking place. There is a slowing-up in every way—repair following injury, recovery after illness. The body's reaction to drugs is not as strong or as fast as the younger animals. It cannot fight infections as well, and so disease may be less acute and less noticeable. The digestion is not as good because the gastric juices, too, are slowing down. Sight and hearing may weaken. The female dog, however, has no menopause; and the male can scent and trail a female almost as long as he can put one foot before the other.

Much as we regret the effects of age, we have to accept them. It is best to know what to expect so that we will be ready to deal with them.

Less Exercise, More Rest

The first thing to watch for is tiring after exercise. The old dog cannot walk as fast or as far. Do not take long walks at a stretch; rather, walk him little and often. Use a more leisurely pace, stopping several times for rest along the way. Do not make him run up and down the stairs, for his heart is not as strong as it used to be. Do not play with him if he does not want to. Those games of catch and run and fetch which he used to enjoy, may still interest him, so don't let him think he is being put on the shelf by stopping them entirely; do cut down on the time and see that he doesn't get overtired.

Doubtless he will want to sleep more now. Let him, and be sure his bed is a little softer, as well as warmer in winter, cooler in summer. He feels the cold and the heat as he never did before. Remember this when you bathe him and have the room and the water warm. Don't wash unless absolutely necessary; instead wipe him off with a damp cloth or use a dry shampoo to keep him sweet and clean. Brush him—he'll like it, and it helps to stimulate the skin.

Impaired Hearing

Deafness, which is quite usual, need not stop the animal's activity but it may risk his safety. The first sign may be inattention or disregard of your commands. Your dog is not being disobedient, he cannot hear your call. Now, a dog can hear with his feet, as it were, so as his hearing weakens you can use ground tapping to attract his attention. Of, if his sight is still good and he is looking your way, you can wave him in by motion of hand and arm. Often when one sense fails, another sense tries to make up for it, therefore it is not unusual to find the deaf dog looking instead of listening for commands. He will watch you more closely than ever before.

Failing Sight

Blindness is more serious, although much can be done to protect the animal from injury. Though not entirely blind, the old dog sometimes becomes fearful because he cannot see objects clearly. The condition may go unnoticed around the house where everything is familiar, but if you change the furniture about, you may notice that he stumbles and perhaps hesitates to move. "Blue eye" or filmed eyeballs in an old dog may mean cataracts which, of course, will need veterinary attention. Do not permit too much sun bathing if the pupils are enlarged.

The totally blind dog can get along fairly well and still enjoy life if a little extra care is taken for his safety and comfort. As long as he can smell and feel and hear his loved ones, he doesn't seem to mind at all. Keep his things in the usual places. He will remember where they are and can find his water dish, his bed, his favorite toy or bone and if need be, his paper. He will still enjoy riding in the car for his chief pleasure in going places is to sniff the scents along the way.

When picked up and set down he may not know where he is, and so may bump into objects until he gets his bearings. Therefore, when you pick him up, set him down again in his own bed or chair whose familiar scent will tell him exactly where he is. He can then make his way from one room to another without getting lost.

Broken or Worn Teeth

The teeth should be watched carefully, and diseased or broken ones removed by the veterinarian while the dog is still strong enough to withstand the shock. The loss of a few teeth need not mean liquid feeding. Canned dog food and broth or milk-soaked dog meal are handled very well. Don't give hard biscuit even though broken into bits. Although the teeth may be in fairly good condition, the gums may grow soft and spongy and bleed; in this case wipe the mouth with mild salt water night and morning.

Constipation

Constipation is caused by too little exercise and possibly the lack of coarse foods. Strong laxatives should not be given to the old animal.

Watch the bowels daily. If the stools are hard and expelled only with unusual effort, give milk of magnesia in small doses —about 2 or 3 teaspoonsful for a 20-pound dog. Some dogs will need the dose two or three times weekly—you can judge the amount and the best timing by watching the results. However, do not expect any laxative to work as quickly as when the dog was young. Don't give mineral oil since it may interfere with normal digestion. The B complex vitamins are in wide use today to improve intestinal health. If your old dog has a health problem, there are special foods available through your veterinarian for different disease conditions.

Feeding

The old dog sometimes does not get the full benefit from his food. He may become thin, and his coat harsh and dry. Have your veterinarian look him over to find the cause and correct it. A commercial vitamin preparation made especially for dogs may be suggested. Or try feeding oftener. Give two feedings instead of one per day; or three instead of two, the smaller amounts at each feeding are easier on the digestive system. And you might add a few treats now and then, such as custard.

The old dog is especially sensitive to changes. These may cause either meal-skipping or overeating. A new feeding dish, or a different person preparing the food, may affect the dog.

The Temperature

Watch carefully for any changes in appearance. Even though slight, these are more important now. When he was young a quick, high fever resulted when the forces of the body were fighting against an infection. The old dog cannot fight infection as effectively—he takes it lying down, as it were.

If anything seems wrong, take the temperature (see page 127). Even a one degree rise, which may mean nothing in a younger dog, is a danger sign in the old fellow. Though infection spreads slowly, nevertheless it does spread. Successful treatment must begin before damaging headway is made.

Growths

Growths are a common part of the aging process. Frequently no larger than a finger nail at first, they may remain small for a time and then suddenly begin to grow. At first they are quite loose, being attached only to the skin, then as they get larger they grow down into the flesh.

Growths are especially common on the breasts of unspayed females, though they may be found on almost any part of the head or body of any dog. The flaps of the ears, the eyelids, and the flesh between the toes are likely places also. If they are mistaken for boils and treated by the amateur, results may be unfortunate. Whether they are simple cysts or more serious tumors, they should receive immediate treatment by your veterinarian.

Warts on old dogs are usually hard, round and smooth. Young dogs sometimes have warts that are soft, flat and rough-textured. Warts are believed to be caused by a virus. They usually are found in the mouth or on the genital organs. Often they disappear without treatment. In any case, they do little harm unless there are so many in the mouth that they interfere with eating. There are several treatments for removing warts. A bit of dry ice, salicylic acid ointment, or a drop of castor oil on the wart daily are helpful. They should not be cut as they may bleed. There is a vaccine for warts which can be obtained through your veterinarian.

Whatever the age of the dog, no growth should be disregarded. Handled by the competent surgeon in its earliest stages, the average growth can be permanently removed; if neglected for any length of time, it may become deeply imbedded and malignant.

Obesity

The old dog may take on weight because he exercises less. When normal in every other respect, the gain is not serious. But sooner or later the dog gets tired very quickly, becoming short-breathed and actually lazy as the fat accumulates around the heart and squeezes the blood vessels. This is where real trouble begins. Dropsy may set in or the heart begin to fail.

A case of this kind can often be avoided by watching the weight. A dog can take on fat unnoticed until it becomes harmful. Make it a practice, then, to put the old dog on the scales at least once each month.

However, the over-fat dog, perhaps weakened by age, should not be put on a drastic dieting. First, increase the number of daily meals, but reduce the total amount of food served. Cut down on tidbits and "extras," if you have gotten into a habit of giving these. This should cause a gradual loss of weight without weakening the patient.

Do not be too strict and take away everything the old dog enjoys. There are lots of non-fattening foods he can have. He has not long to live perhaps, so he is entitled to all the pleasure you can provide.

Watch the Toenails

Long toenails strain the feet and make walking difficult.

The old dog's nails rarely wear down to comfortable length, so shorten with clippers or a coarse file purchased at your pet store for the purpose. The pastern or wrist joints often weaken with age and then the arch flattens and the foot lets down. The nails can no longer grip the ground and so they grow rapidly.

Whatever the state of the nails, however, the old dog is practically sure to become uncertain on his feet. He may not even try to jump any more or, if he does, he falls back. If he is used to snoozing on your bed, don't deny him this privilege; he'll miss it. Instead, place a low chair beside the bed so he can hop up in easy stages. The same goes for those windows he enjoys looking out of to watch the world go by. Arrange a low chair or an ottoman close to the window so he can sit there and watch for you to come home.

Uncertain gait or stiffness in the hindquarters is often caused by age, but may be due to nothing more than constipation. Watch the bowels, then, and treat accordingly. Should this fail to limber him up, see your veterinarian about the possible presence of rheumatism.

Jealousy

All of a sudden one day you are going to imagine how still the house will be when the old fellow is gone. You decide to get a puppy, before the old one leaves. When the new member of the family arrives, the old dog's nose is going to be out of joint. He has been for so long the center of attraction, beloved and well-tended, and now everybody ohs and ahs over the cute newcomer. Pet the old boy first before you handle the little one! When both dogs clamor for attention at once, pet both at the same time or neither.

Without fear the pup plagues the old dog to play, bites his ears, jumps at him in great glee. Perhaps already out of sorts at having to share attention around the home, the old one may resent the young one's onslaughts and perhaps nips him to put him in his place. Jealousy is powerful in doggy relationships.

Be very careful when introducing a new puppy to the old dog. First, keep the pup in his cage where the oldster can sniff around him and say hello without being rushed, and meantime pet the old fellow lavishly. Feed the two separately, and watch them when they run together for the first few days. Always pay particular attention to the old dog to keep him from feeling neglected and ignored. Do not permit the two to sleep together or be alone together until definite signs of friendliness are shown by the old dog. Before you know it, they'll be the best of friends.

Cat and Dog

Dogs and cats need not be enemies although they are often made so by thoughtless owners who shout "sic 'em" to the dog every time he sees a cat. Don't ever be guilty of doing this!

When introduced carefully, as when puppy and kitten are brought up together, they become firm friends. True enough, some dogs run after cats at the slightest opportunity. The cat flees, the dog legs it after him. That is precisely why he does it, because movement excites the age-old desire to pursue. The cat in the home, however, will affect the dog differently; here is an animal to be sniffed, investigated, and finally accepted with affection.

When bringing a cat into a home where there is a dog, it's a good idea to keep them in separate rooms for a few days. In that way the dog can smell that a cat has joined the household, and the cat smells the presence of a dog. Then when they are brought together they are more prepared for the introduction.

A kitten and a puppy of fairly equal age apparently do not recognize each other as cat and dog but merely as playfellows. The kitten brought into an old dog's family circle, or the puppy added to the old cat's household, immediately become competitors for notice and affection. If you get a cat when the dog is already grown, or old, choose a kitten, and then go ahead in the same manner as when introducing a puppy to the old dog.

Boarding the Dog Out

It may be necessary occasionally to board your dog out. Perhaps you are traveling to a place where dogs are not welcome, perhaps your female is in season and you cannot guard her properly at home. Now, placing in the hands of strangers a pet that has grown fixed in his ways as dogs do when they grow old is a drastic change. Select a boarding kennel of good reputation, and pay without quibble the price asked. Such accommodations are not cheap; if they are, they may not be good.

Have your dog as healthy, clean and flea-free when you take him as you expect him to be when you get him back again. Explain to the kennelman any conditions or habits that might make your pet difficult to handle. This is only fair to the person who cares for him in your absence; it is likewise only fair to your dog. Ask permission to leave your shoe or old sweater whose scent will comfort him. And, of course, provide a good collar and leash. Deliver the dog a few days early, then telephone to make sure he is getting along before you leave.

If you can possibly avoid it, do not board the old dog out at all unless he already is used to it. He grieves more than the young one since, as we have already said, he cannot as easily adjust himself to changes.

Putting Him to Sleep

Journey's end. It comes no matter how much we would like the journey to continue. The life of our pet seems to have been short, all the more because it has been so happy.

Let the veterinarian decide whether the time has come to say good-bye—he can decide better than you for he will be scientific rather than emotional. Veterinarians no longer say "Put him out of the way" because they do not know what else to do. Better trained now, they are lengthening life and easing pain more certainly and humanely than ever before.

Even so, there comes a time when the penalties of age pile up and nothing remains but to put the sufferer to sleep. Euthanasia as practiced today does exactly that. The dog literally goes to sleep before the lethal dose takes effect. When the needle is administered by the competent veterinarian, there is no pain, no struggle, no knowledge of what is happening. It is all so calm and quiet that you can hold the dog right in your arms.

CHAPTER 7

BASIC NUTRITION AND FEEDING

The Balanced Diet

Like all living things, the dog has certain nutritional requirements. And, to keep healthy, dogs must be properly fed.

Fortunately, the dog's nutritional needs have received a great deal of study during the past 25 years. Dogs have been used in feeding experiments which have taught us many things about the human diet. As a result there is more scientific knowledge about the food needs of the dog than of most other animals.

Most important in the feeding of any animal is a balanced diet which contains all of the many nutrients which he needs. The adult dog can live on a wide variety of diets, but many of these will not keep him in the best of health. A poor diet may even shorten his life by several years. The growing puppy is even less able to stand a poor diet.

Also remember that most of the important food substances, or nutrients, are not stored within the dog's body for any length of time. The principal exceptions are fat, which is stored in nearly all parts of the body, and vitamins A and D, which are stored for a time in the liver. Therefore, if these nutrients are to be fully used, they must not only be made available at each meal; they must also be present in the food in the correctly balanced amounts. Too much of one food substance can upset the contributions of some of the others.

The accompanying table lists the dog's known needs for proteins, fats, carbohydrates, minerals and vitamins.

The Essential Nutrients

Protein is the most important nutrient in a dog's diet. However, if it is to be fully used, certain amounts of vita-

Ingredients	Known Requirements	Typical Dog Food (Dry Type)
Protein	18 - 20%	25%
Fat	3 - 5%	7%
Carbohydrate	30 - 70%	48%

Vitamins

	Known Requirements		Typical Dog Food (Dry Type)	
A	900.0	USP Units/lb.	3000.0	USP Units/lb.
D	200.0	" " "	1000.0	" " "
E	20.0	" " "	55.0	" " "
Thiamine	.16	Mgms./lb.	1.5	Mgms./lb.
Riboflavin	.4	" "	2.5	" "
Niacin	.5	" "	20.0	" "
Pyridoxin	.2	" "	1.5	" "
Pantothenic Acid	.5	" "	6.0	" "
Folic Acid	Not established		0.5	" "
Choline	300.0	Mgms./lb.	500.0	" "
Biotin	Not established		.06	" "
Inositol	Not established		350.0	" "

Minerals

	Known Requirements		Typical Dog Food (Dry Type)	
Calcium	2.4	Gms./lb.	8.15	Gms./lb.
Phosphorus	3.4	" "	5.89	" "
Sodium Chloride	2.0	" "	3.85	" "
Magnesium	.40	" "	.82	" "
Potassium	2.0	" "	2.99	" "
Iron	.012	" "	.12	" "
Copper	.15	Mgms./lb.	.6	Mgms./lb.
Cobalt	.0005	" "	.0005	" "
Iodine	.25	" "	.36	" "
Manganese	1.0	" "	10.57	" "
Zinc	1.0	" "	21.1	" "
Fluorine	Not established		Trace	
Aluminum	Not established		Trace	
Silicon	Not established		Trace	
Sulphur	Not established		Trace	

mins and minerals must also be present, as well as enough carbohydrates and fats. Protein is needed for body growth and repair and must be of good quality.

Fat gives energy or calories. However, fat does contain three essential fatty acids which act like vitamins. These fatty acids are needed for a good skin and coat.

Carbohydrates produce energy and are also important to health. Much of the fibre needed for bulk is a form of carbohydrate.

There are at least fifteen known minerals that are needed for good health. There are probably others which are present in such small amounts that we aren't sure exactly what they are. Calcium and phosphorus are needed for teeth and bones as well as for a healthy heart and blood system. Iron, copper and cobalt are needed for good red blood cells. Iodine prevents goiter.

Without the vitamins there can be no life. Not enough of certain vitamins can cause rickets, poor bone and body growth, poor coat, poor appetite and nervous disorders.

The Ready-to-Eat Foods

The proteins, fats, carbohydrates, minerals and vitamins your dog needs can be given to him one of two ways. You can shop for separate foods, prepare, mix and cook them, or you can use the high-quality ready-to-serve dog foods found on store shelves.

Most dog-owners find that a dry dog food is the common sense course. It is the easiest and most economical way to feed a dog. Mixing many foods into a well-balanced diet requires knowledge which few of us have. The chances of the average dog owner coming up with a diet as nourishing as those put out by manufacturers who employ nutrition specialists and maintain research kennels, is indeed slim.

In making a quality dog food the reputable manufacturer usually builds in a "safety factor" over and above the known requirements. In this way he is able to allow for the unbalancing of his food by those dog owners who like to mix in "extras" or table scraps. Even so, manufacturers caution, such table scraps and "extras" should never be more than one quarter of the total diet.

The great advantage of feeding prepared foods is that it involves very little time or work; the dog enjoys his food because of the variety (meal, biscuits, canned etc.); and you can be sure that he is getting proper nourishment. Also, it does away with digestive upsets which are common in dogs that are switched from one kind of food to another, as when table leftovers only are fed. Another danger in feeding only table scraps is that the dog will get mostly carbohydrates and fat trimmings that have few vitamins, little protein and not enough minerals.

Types of Dog Food

There are several kinds of commercial or prepared dog foods widely used today:

Expanded Dog Meal—Sold in two basic forms—large chunk and small nugget—the main difference is size. Some form a gravy when warm water is added. These "homogenized" types are produced by blending all of the ingredients necessary for a complete and total diet for the dog, adding water, cooking, dehydrating and packaging. They contain about 10 per cent moisture, 90 per cent food solids, the caloric value is about 1600 calories per pound. These products can be fed as they come from the package or with added water. They are ideal for the self-feeding method (see pages 8-9).

Burger-patty—The newest type of dog food, termed an intermediate moisture product since it contains about 25 per cent moisture and 75 per cent food solids, and can be likened to a canned dog food without the can. It is produced by a method which allows the product to be stored without refrigeration. Two three-ounce patties are nutritionally equal to one sixteen-ounce can of a complete high grade canned dog food. There are about 250 calories per patty.

Dog Biscuits and Bits—Blends of wheat flour and other ingredients including dehydrated meat by-products, vitamins, minerals and fats, prepared by mixing with water and baking. They contain about 10 per cent moisture and 90 per cent food solids; the caloric value about 1500 calories per pound. These products are considered complete diets and are found in forms which vary in color and sometimes shape to differentiate flavors.

Canned Dog Food (Complete)—A blend of meat or meat by-products, vitamins, minerals and fats, prepared by blending the ingredients, cooking, canning and sterilizing. They contain about 75 per cent moisture and 25 per cent food solids. The better grades run about 500 calories per pound. They are generally fed as they come from the can or can be mixed with other dog foods. There are some canned foods which are primarily meat or meat by-products. They are not considered complete diets but are intended for mixing with complete dry dog foods.

The highest quality brands, which you will find are usually priced a few cents a pound over cheaper brands, are complete and balanced. You don't have to add anything for growth and general maintenance. In special cases, such as hard working hunting dogs, sled dogs or racing dogs, when a female is in whelp, or when puppies are in their early rapid-growth period, extra fat, minerals or vitamins may be added. But remember that too many extras can be harmful. It is actually possible to cause nutritional deficiencies by giving overdoses of vitamins and mineral supplements.

Occasionally a dog can't use all elements of his food, although he may be getting a balanced diet. Or, like certain people, a dog may need unusual amounts of some particular nutrients. In such cases it is better to add the special foods to the regular diet rather than to change the entire diet. Your veterinarian should be consulted in such cases. The prepared foods are, of course, made for the average, normal animal.

It is always a good idea to try to follow the manufacturer's feeding suggestions. However, the directions on the label are also for the "average" dog. Many a small, very active dog may actually eat almost as much as a very large one who spends his time lying on the porch. It will therefore take trial and error to find the amount of food your dog should have every day. This will depend upon his activity, size, breed, age and physical make-up. Reduce or increase the amount of his food when you see how much he will eat readily and whether he is gaining or losing weight. Some dogs get fat because they continue to get as much food as they received as rapid-growing and hard-playing puppies. Pups actually need about twice as much food for their weight as do mature dogs.

Serving the Food

If your dog is fed on meal-type food and seems to prefer it rather dry, you might try the self-feeding method described on pages 8-9.

An adult dog can eat a full day's food at one meal. Kennel owners usually feed their dogs only once a day, and that is not a bad rule for the family dog. However, if you wish, you can give him a part of the day's ration in the morning.

Try to feed your dog at the same hour or hours every day. He likes this regularity, which will also keep his appetite steady and his bowel movements regular.

It is important that the dog's food be mixed fresh each time. Don't keep it standing until it becomes unappetizing. The food should never be served hot or chilled. Prepared dog food of the dry type should be kept in a cool, dry place protected from mice or insects. Canned dog food, after it has been opened, should be kept under refrigeration. Burger-type food doesn't require refrigeration but should be kept wrapped until used.

There will be days when your dog will sniff at his dinner and walk away, or leave it after a nibble or two. This is nothing to be alarmed about in a grown and healthy dog—even if he refuses his food for a day or so. In his wild state the dog led a feast-or-famine existence and this may be the dog's natural way of giving his stomach a rest. Tempting him with tidbits will only encourage "picky" eating habits. Simply take the food away and prepare a fresh dish for the next regular meal time.

Water

Don't forget to offer fresh, cool water to your dog several times a day, but not within an hour before or an hour after feeding or immediately after strenuous exercise. (If he has water available at all times he will not be tempted to drink too much at meal times.)

Feeding Fallacies

Although they have been proved false there are several common superstitions about feeding dogs that continue to be handed down in families or handed out by self-appointed authorities.

While you are raising your puppy, someone will probably tell you not to give him milk because "milk makes worms." This could not possibly be true unless the milk contained worm eggs, which is not likely. Puppies which are given only milk after weaning might well become run down from the combination of worms they already have, and an inadequate diet; but milk does not manufacture worms.

Another old wives' tale is that raw meat will make a dog vicious. The basis for this belief is difficult to imagine. It is true that a dog fed *nothing* but raw meat would be getting an insufficient diet and so, perhaps, might not be in the best of spirits. However, if a dog is irritable look for other reasons than the addition of raw meat to his regular food.

Raw meat is sometimes also blamed as a cause of worms. This, too, is a "saying" that can be discounted. A dog may get tapeworm from eating a rabbit he has caught or, possibly from uncooked pork; but there is no other connection.

Another popular superstition is that feeding garlic or raw onions will "cure" worms in a dog. Worms are eliminated only by medicines that are made of much stronger stuff than any amount of garlic. Because worm medicines are so strong, you should turn a deaf ear to those who say "he just needs worming" whenever your puppy seems to be ailing. The pup may need worming but on the other hand, he may be suffering from any of a dozen serious illnesses. Don't weaken him further by dosing with worm medicine. See your veterinarian.

When anyone tells you to feed your dog raw eggs to make his coat shiny, remember that uncooked white of egg destroys an important vitamin, biotin, in the intestines. Whole eggs should be cooked. The yolks of eggs can be fed raw.

Many people worry when their dogs "wolf" their food. A dog's digestion doesn't start in his mouth as it does in humans. Eating fast and swallowing food whole is natural for a dog, and probably a hangover from the time when dogs ran with a pack and had to grab to get their share.

A block of sulphur placed in a dog's water bowl is credited with everything from "preventing" worms to curing skin diseases. Sulphur has no medicinal or nutritional value, and is just an ornament in the water dish.

A very common belief is that dogs should not be given the smallest speck of leftover potatoes because "starch CAN'T be digested by dogs." This was disproved many years ago by scientific tests. Dogs can digest cooked starch just as people can. The carbohydrates, so essential in the dog's properly balanced diet, come partly from starches. This does not mean, however, that a diet of only potatoes, macaroni or bread is recommended.

CHAPTER 8

GENERAL CARE AND GROOMING

Given proper attention, the dog's teeth, coat, eyes, ears, nose and feet can be kept in good condition. Daily grooming may seem bothersome, but it will save you time and effort in the long run. Many minor disorders of skin, teeth or feet may be avoided completely; others will be caught in their earliest stages when cure will be fairly simple.

Tooth Troubles

Early adulthood is a good time to have the teeth examined to make sure that the permanent ones are straight, not crowded too closely together, free from disease, and not worn by stone-carrying and gnawing. The amount of actual tooth decay among dogs is negligible. However, the dog's teeth cannot repair themselves; once the enamel is worn off, they remain damaged and may need treatment or extraction.

Guard against tartar, that yellowish, hard deposit on one or more teeth. The least of its harm is its unsightly color, but the real danger is that it menaces the life of the tooth to which it clings. It is most serious as it pushes into the gum, breaking the membrane which is the tooth's main brace. With this support gone, the tooth may loosen and fall out. The condition may not be painful. On the other hand, if food particles work down into gum cavities and decompose to cause abscesses there will be considerable suffering. When tartar is noticed, take the dog to the veterinarian who can scrape the teeth expertly before any damage has been done. It is also helpful to feed some dry meal or biscuits which require chewing.

Bones and hard substances are, in a manner of speaking, the dog's toothbrush. Not that they actually clean the teeth; they perform an even better service than that. They stimulate the blood supply as they rub over the gums. Therefore, the gnawing of bones and the chewing of coarse, hard food helps keep the entire mouth healthy. That is why as the puppy grows we gradually discontinue very moist foods and instead, feed drier, more crumbly mixtures. And then, when the second teeth are in, we give hard-baked biscuits occasionally.

All through the dog's life you may keep his teeth clean by wiping them regularly with a damp cloth dipped in salt or baking soda. A gentle rotating motion will stimulate the gums as well as actually clean the teeth. The dog accustomed to this attention from puppyhood does not object. He rather enjoys being fussed over.

Do not expect the dog to announce a toothache by crying. He suffers in silence, while rubbing his jaw on the affected side along the floor or perhaps pawing it. He eats gingerly, mouthing his food with his lips rather than with his teeth. He may drool, too (see page 35). All of which may indicate a decayed, broken or otherwise sensitive tooth, or possibly a piece of bone wedged between two teeth. At any rate, it means an uncomfortable mouth requiring professional aid.

Care of the Coat

By this time the puppy coat has been replaced by a stronger, tougher kind of hair which, according to breed, may be long, short or medium. Most coats are two-ply. The long-haired and the medium-haired kinds, especially, have an outer coat varying in coarseness, and an under coat, thick and dense.

The short, smooth-haired dogs have a double coat also. However, it is less noticeable because the under coat is neither downy nor flat-lying. Thus, it is almost impossible to tell the top coat from the under coat. When the under coat sheds out in warm weather, the chief change observed is the thinner covering of the whole.

The coat is the dog's complexion. A rich, full, glossy coat usually means that all is well within; whereas a dry, lifeless coat with hair constantly shedding means that something is wrong. Normally, the coat sheds out twice each year, spring and fall, although some shedding goes on all the time. Heavy shedding between seasons may be caused by a lack of strength, as, following illness, while dryness may result from too much washing or an overheated apartment. A temporary faded look may merely mean that the old coat is on the wane, since the hair loses its vigor and color just before it is cast.

Brushing

Regular brushing helps to keep the hair in good condition by stimulating the skin and by preventing tangles and mats. Also, it keeps the dog comfortable by removing loosened, dead hair before it can tickle the dog into scratching (or drops on your rugs or upholstery!). When you see your dog rolling vigorously in the grass, or pulling himself back and forth under the sofa edge, you may be fairly sure he is shedding his coat, and is trying to get rid of it himself.

Mats and Tangles

Get a long or a short-bristled brush, or even a smooth mitt, whichever is suitable for your dog's type of coat. There are many kinds to choose from at your pet supply store. Select a comb, too, a blunt-toothed one that will not scratch the skin. When combing out the tangles, just ease them out gently, holding the tuft close to the skin with the thumb and forefingers. Don't hurt the dog by pulling.

Mats of tar or chewing gum can be removed by rubbing with a piece of ice. Acetone, applied with a piece of cotton, will also remove such nuisances. With the fingers, work mineral oil into tangles of burr and beggar lice which can be taken off without harming the coat. However, use the comb only when necessary. Your best tool is the brush.

Brush the hair every day. Brush as if you meant it, going over every single part of the head and body, legs and tail. Brush always in the way you wish the hair to lie. In other words, if yours is a short, smooth-haired dog, brush in the direction of hair growth to keep it trained down tight to the skin. If your pet's is a stand-off type of coat, then brush against the grain to bring the hair up and away from the body. Take it slowly, do not neglect one inch. Brush out the ear fringes, the mane on the neck, the frill or apron on the chest, the skirts on the hindparts. Either sit on the floor beside him, or place him on a table so you both will be comfortable. So long as the dog enjoys it, keep at it as long as you wish, but if he grows tired or restless, stop for a while.

Removing the coat as it is shed by faithful brushing every day will go a long way toward keeping the upholstery free of hairs. However, a few hairs on the furniture are not the worst of evils—gentle rubbing with dampened sandpaper or with Scotch tape will pick them up, while a dry sponge will serve to scrape them off the clothing.

Excessive Shedding

It may seem as though some dogs are continually shedding. Those quartered out of doors shed more definitely in the spring and fall; whereas those kept in the house may cast their coats more or less constantly. It may be that the natural light cycle has something to do with it. At any rate, to stop continual shedding, try mixing into the food a spoonful or two of fresh fat such as bacon drippings, melted lard, or finely chopped suet. Make sure the fat is fresh, never rancid.

You might also try sponging the coat with a mixture of three or four tablespoonsful of bay rum or vinegar in a small basin of water, then dry thoroughly. Brush the dog daily as usual and massage the skin with the fingers. Do not bathe unless absolutely necessary since baths tend to dry the skin, causing itchiness. Worms, too, may cause brittleness and shedding of the hair. So have the dog checked for worms. (See pages 137-38.)

External Parasites

Fleas—All dogs have fleas at one time or another, so it is no disgrace. At certain seasons of the year, mostly in late summer, fleas nest in the ground and jump on the dog as he goes by. Their eggs can hatch indoors as well, especially in the dog's bedding. Since they multiply at an amazing rate, lose no time in dealing with them.

What harm do fleas do? We used to call them the dog's best exerciser, and let it go at that. We have learned better! Fleas can be the cause of so-called summer eczema and "hot spots"; even one flea on a dog hypersensitive to flea bites. They irritate the dog by constant jumping; they keep him awake nights with their biting. They spread tapeworm and open the way to skin diseases. Dogs that are kept free of fleas seldom have skin troubles. And last but not least, fleas can ruin a good coat by inflaming and irritating the skin.

Get out a fine comb, and powder him thoroughly with a commercial flea powder. Then go over him, inch by inch. The powder will numb the fleas so they are more easily removed, but the paper he stands on must be burned to get rid of them and the eggs that are also combed out. The pests will be found mostly around the root of the tail, the ears and neck, and under the legs. These are favorite hiding places, but they move like lightning so may be found anywhere at all. The black, grainy deposits around flea nests are excrement that can be dissolved by washing.

The fleas may jump off as you comb and hide in baseboard or floor cracks where they breed. Sweep or vacuum thoroughly; use flea powder on the dog's bed and other places where he lies. *Read the label* on your flea powder container carefully, however, before you begin, and be very sure that the remedy you purchase was *manufactured to use on dogs*. Not all insect powders are safe to dust on animals that lick themselves. The dog is one of these, hence he must have a dusting powder that will not poison him. There are also available vermin dips which are time-savers for de-fleaing large dogs and there are special flea soaps. However they are very strong and if used too often may irritate sensitive skins. The effect is quite lasting—in between bathing can be done with castile or some other mild soap. Be sure to remove and destroy old bedding and disinfect the dog's house or bed.

Lice—Lice are equally annoying. They do not move about like fleas but hook into the skin, hold fast and suck the blood. In fact they suck so closely beneath the hair as to defy detection. Lice nits can be found, attached to the hairs; these hatch on the dog. Unless you look carefully or use a magnifying glass, you'll miss them. Although bluish in color, they are no larger than the head of a pin. The adult lice are small and white and may be missed at a casual glance, but if your dog is scratching, and you find signs of dirt but no fleas, look thoroughly. The skin will usually be reddened in spots by the lice sucking. It is best to use a powder or dip sold for just this purpose, and to use it repeatedly until the dog is completely cleared.

Ticks—The tick is another pest which seems to become more common with the years, especially among dogs that roam woods and fields in certain sections of the country. The insect's barbed proboscis pierces the skin and, as it sucks the blood, it grows to about one third of an inch and becomes bluish in color. Then it drops off and hides in furniture, baseboards and floor cracks. This means that beds and bedding of infested animals must be thoroughly cleaned and disinfected.

Ticks cannot be removed by combing but must be pulled off by tweezers, or if you don't mind, your hand. Pull slowly, trying to get the head as well as the body. Otherwise, the claws left behind may set up an infection. Wipe spots that look sore with alcohol or iodine. Dips should be used regularly in tick-ridden areas, and flea powder will also help. Treating your lawn or the dog's yard with insecticide (but keeping the dog out of it until it is thoroughly washed in) will help if ticks are bad in your neighborhood.

An effective wash to kill ticks on a dog may be made of four ounces of derris or cube root powder containing three to five percent of rotenone and one ounce of flaked soap in a gallon of tepid water. Protect the dog's eyes by applying vaseline or oil around them. The same wash with half the amount of derris can be used for fleas. Powders with 5-10 percent DDT are safe for use on grown dogs to remove fleas, lice or ticks; but they are too toxic to be used on puppies or bitches that are nursing puppies.

Bathing and Dry Cleaning

Those who believed in bathing their dogs and those who did not used to be quite determined in their opposition to the theories of the other. However, time and modern research have taught us the advantage of moderation in this as in most phases of dog care. Now we bathe the dog occasionally.

We do not put puppies in a tub of water until they are at least five or six months of age, and we do not wash any dog directly after eating. But for the average dog, a good soap-and-water bath every eight weeks or so keeps him really clean, stimulates his skin without drying his coat and makes him feel "top of the morning."

In cold weather be sure the room is warm so the wet dog won't be chilled. Use your own bath-tub if you like. It won't harm it. You can lay a little ball of steel wool in the drain to hold back and collect the hairs. Have the water comfortably warm, not burning hot; the soap mild. The dog's skin is tender and since some soaps irritate, it is best to purchase a mild type put out especially for dogs, or plain castile soap.

To prepare the dog for his bath, first plug his ears loosely with cotton, and put a drop of castor oil, cod liver oil or mineral oil in each eye. When the dog has learned to enjoy his bath and cooperates with you these steps can be skipped; but if he resists or is in any way hard to handle, his eyes and ears must be protected from soapy water or he will fight harder the next time.

Stand him in water up to the middle of his legs, leaving enough free space to hand-scrub him well underneath. Wet him all over thoroughly, but gently to avoid fright. With the washcloth go over his face with clear water, then soap well from the top of the head down over the neck, the back, and around the tail, the underbody, legs and feet, giving particular attention to the undersides of legs, the base of the tail and between the toes.

Massage the soap in thoroughly with the fingers so that it reaches the skin. Rinse quickly, then soap again. The first soaping loosens the dirt, the second removes it. Rinsing is important, for even a light amount of soap left to dry in the hair causes dandruff and scratching. A few drops of vinegar added to the final rinse water helps to remove the soap. A mild bluing rinse makes white dogs whiter, and a teaspoonful of glycerine in the rinse water makes smooth coats glossier.

Now lift the dog out of the tub and dry him with turkish towels, chamois, or hot-air electric dryer. It takes a lot of time to dry a heavy coat well, so go slowly with towel or chamois. Do not brush or comb the coat when it is wet; rub it with a towel or cloth or fluff it with the electric dryer. In winter or in unseasonable cold weather shut the dog up in a warm, draft-free room for two hours or more. The coat may seem dry, yet remains damp underneath. Be sure the dog is absolutely dry before letting him go outdoors.

The way you give the dog his first few over-all washes will do much toward making him like a bath, and once he does, he will save you time and trouble by lending himself willingly to the job. There are occasional dogs that battle their way through every bath, with two or more members of the family required to assist. For the most part, however, fear of the bath is unnecessary and can be avoided if the handling is gentle but firm and the water temperature moderate.

A dog can be dry-cleaned too—that is, washed without water. Although not as effective, this type of cleansing can serve in winter weather. Commercial dry shampoo, cornmeal or fine cedar for light-colored coats, or orris root for dark ones may be sifted into the skin and then brushed vigorously out again. Much of the dirt and extra oils will be removed and the coat will be made soft and fluffy. Dry powders such as chalk can be used for white dogs, or a good non-oily hair tonic may be sprinkled over the coat, massaged in with the fingertips, rubbed dry with the towel, then brushed.

Clipping

When the temperature goes up, we pity the dog with the heavy coat. He's so hot, we think, perhaps we should have him clipped. Don't do it! Nature knew what she was about when she provided the dog's sensitive skin with a good covering of hair to shield it from the sun and to screen it from the bites of gnats, mosquitoes and flies. In preparation for the summer's heat, the under coat sheds out—this underlayer is what holds in the body's heat—leaving most of the outer coat intact to prevent sunburn. If we clip the dog in summer we may make him more uncomfortable than he was before.

Special Hair Styles

The wire-coated terriers will require periodic trimming and plucking, probably twice each year, to keep the coat free from tangles and hard in texture. Left untrimmed, the hair grows long and thick making the dog quite uncomfortable. Also, he looks rather like a stray, instead of a stylish, well-tended pet.

With a dull penknife held between thumb and forefinger, you can pluck out loosening hairs as the terrier coat is cast. You might do better, however, to take a few lessons in the art, or let a regular canine beauty shop operator do the job. If you wish to take care of the coat yourself, you can purchase trimming charts containing excellent directions for each breed at your department or pet supply store. You can also buy the right tools for doing the job properly.

With Poodles, especially, the amateur may have a difficult time making his dog look right. There are various kinds of hair-dos for this breed—the English Saddle, the Continental, the Dutch Clip, etc.,—each one finishing the dog off with a radically different outline. It is a big job to be sure; the Poodle has a wealth of coat which must be taken off in some places, left on in others, and shaped according to the particular pattern preferred. Better have this done at the beauty shop, and then later perhaps take a few lessons from a professional in the accepted manner of doing the work yourself.

Care of the Eyes

The dog's eyes are his most attractive feature. They are the "tie that binds" him to mankind. Let him look at us just once with that expression of entire trust, and he lifts himself up and away from all his kind and becomes our best friend among the beasts.

Sight is not one of the dog's strong points. It need not be, since his hearing and power of scent are so phenomenal. He cannot see colors very well; on the other hand, he can differentiate degrees of brightness better than we can. He sees motion in a flash because, as an animal of the chase, he had to get his food on the run. Although he has an eye very much like ours, the eye-white surrounding the iris or color portion does not show as much. Lids cover the white except perhaps for a tiny speck at the inner corners.

The expression of the normal dog is bright, intelligent, knowing; his eyes in health are clear and clean. The moment the eyes appear at all different, we suspect that something is wrong. A staring, dazed expression, with whites showing, may mean over-excitement and the possibility of a fit. Watery, weeping, squinting or heavy-lidded eyes alert us to watch for distemper or some other infection.

Departure from the normal is not always serious. Weeping and pus discharge may be caused by a cold (see page 137), by a blow on the eyeball, or by weed seeds caught beneath the lids. Serious or slight, however, eye troubles require prompt attention to prevent the sight being endangered.

A dull heavy expression may be caused by an enlarged haw, the triangular stretch of reddened membrane across the eye's inner corner. This enlargement is sometimes so small that it escapes attention; at other times it may be raised halfway across the eye and highly inflamed. The swelling can be treated with cotton pads dipped in warmed tea or boric acid solution; but since it will probably occur again, minor surgery may be required.

Weeping eyes should be cared for without waiting for them to cure themselves. Bathe the eyes very gently with cotton swabs dipped in boric acid or sodium bicarbonate solution to remove any dirt or pus. Then use a simple eye ointment like mercuric oxide, and as you finish roll the lashes up and off the eyeball. Castor oil and cod liver oil are old-fashioned eye soothers. Place a drop of one or the other in each eye before taking the dog out for a run in woods and fields. They help insure against the scratching and discomfort caused by dust, pollen and weed seeds. Commercial eye preparations for humans are excellent for dogs. There are also modern eye ointments which your veterinarian can get for you.

Inverted eyelids and in-growing eyelashes sometimes occur. They cause continual weeping and pawing of the eye. Don't wait. Let your veterinarian prescribe before the eye is scratched.

Blue Eye

Another quite usual condition known as "blue eye" may set in with distemper, a lack of riboflavin, continual weeping or injury. The cornea changes from its natural color to an opaque blue. While the dog will not be able to see, he is only temporarily blind in the affected eye. After several days the blue gradually fades from the edges inward until only a tiny spot remains. Several months may pass before this scar disappears; possibly it will never disappear. Modern ointments are excellent in preventing infection of the cornea, so see your veterinarian before the sight is permanently damaged.

When his eyes hurt, the dog crawls under the bed or seeks someplace where the light is dim. Take this as a tip to provide a semi-dark shelter throughout the course of all eye illnesses. Keep his bed out of the sun, or throw a blanket over it to shadow the light. Also, since the dog will rub the painful eye with the foot on the injured side, tape the nail as described under "nail taping" (page 129).

Care of the Ears

The dog's sense of hearing is better than ours; actually he hears twice as well as man. And though he has an ear very much like our own, its flap or leather is quite different from the ear-shell of man. Made to catch the sound, it also moves to find the direction from which sound comes.

Selective breeding has resulted in a wide variety of ear flaps. In certain breeds the flap stands erect or pricked, in others it rises half-way and then tips over. In still others it is "buttoned" or turned down though slightly raised at the base, while in many breeds it falls flat to the head when it is said to be dropped. The kind of flap seems to have no bearing upon the dog's hearing but it does influence the amount of care required. The drop ear or turned down flap interferes with ventilation, and must be watched more closely.

When the puppy is born, the ears lie flat to the head. In breeds whose ears stand up at maturity, ear cartilage strength changes so much during the process of growth that the exact age when the ears should come up cannot be stated. They may begin to stand quite early in life and then, while the teeth are changing, drop again or flare around uncertainly for weeks or months, after which they finally stand strong and straight.

During play the puppy may injure an ear tendon. The upright ear may then drop and never recover. Some people have helped weak or injured ears to stand by winding them with a quarter-inch wide strip of adhesive or Scotch tape into a cone-shape. Do not wind too tightly or you will interfere with circulation. Leave the strip attached only for a week or less at a time. As far as possible avoid sticking the hairy portion of the flap with the tape since this makes it more difficult to remove. Use benzine when you take off the tape and then apply an antiseptic.

Ear flaps that stand when they should drop are taped down lightly for short periods. But do not attempt to shape the ears in any manner without first looking up the breed section (pages 163-232). Make sure you know exactly how your dog's ears should be carried when he is fully grown.

Scratched or Fly-bitten Ears

Diseased ear conditions if not treated may cause deafness. Trouble should be suspected if the dog shakes his head or carries it sidewise, or if he rubs an ear against the floor or attempts to massage it with his paw. Cuts, scratches and fly bites can injure the flap so that it becomes scabby and perhaps infected. A gentle soap-and-water cleansing will remove the crusts, after which a light dusting with antiseptic powder will soothe the irritation.

For fly-bitten ear-tips, you might try bathing the flaps with the following: Oil of clove, 3 parts; bay oil, 5 parts; tincture of eucalyptus, 5 parts; alcohol, 15 parts; water, 200 parts. Your druggist can make this up for you.

Ear Canker

Canker of the ears is often serious. Caused by mites, wax accumulations, dirt, eczema and even by a generally weakened condition, it can be suspected when your dog constantly scratches at his ears, shakes his head or rubs it on the floor. Look for inflammation inside the cup or base and leading down into the canal where pus of brownish color can be seen. This pus can be cleaned out with a cotton swab. But never probe deeply into the ear! You may injure the delicate interior or push down material which should be brought up. Removal of pus and dirt is followed by antiseptic powder dusting. Dogs with drop or hairy ears which prevent air reaching the ear canal need special attention. Air is important in all cases of ear treatment. Severe canker is a task for the veterinarian and should be attended to promptly. Ear mites so tiny that they cannot be seen by the naked eye can cause deafness if not removed before the inner ear becomes involved. These ear mites are the most frequent cause of a dog shaking his head and scratching at his ears.

The Nose

So keen is the dog's sense of smell that his world is full of scents, some soothing, others exciting, each with a definite message to influence his behavior. Take your dog out to walk and watch him closely—to him, half the fun is sniffing places where other dogs, other animals, have passed.

Scenting ability differs in certain kinds of dogs. It seems to be sharpest in those with a long nose, long ear and hanging lips, such as the hounds and sporting breeds. Shape and color of the nostrils also may be important. The keenest noses are usually those whose nostrils are large, black and wide open. Exceptions to the color rule are the brown-nosed hunting dogs. A temporary fading of the nostrils from black to brown is usually caused by some "off" condition; it happens frequently to females in season.

The dog around the house, be his nose long or short, can recognize smells to an amazing degree. He feels safe and at home on his blankets because they carry *his* scent. He likes your old sweater or coat to lie on because it carries *your* scent. When he rides in the car, head out the window, he knows you've turned homeward because he recognizes *neighborhood* scents. It is almost unbelievable, but true. A dog can smell formic acid, for instance, in a solution containing only one part of the acid in ten million parts of water; and he can recognize your scent on an object you have held in your hand for a mere two seconds.

Since the nose is also the organ of breathing, it does its best work when the nostrils are cool, clean and mucus-free. The cold nose, by the way, as a sign of the healthy dog has been over-rated. A snooze under blankets or a huddle beside a radiator can warm the nose of an animal in the best of health. Dryness, however, usually indicates fever rather than warmth. When in any doubt, take the temperature. (See page 127.)

Watery or mucus discharge is more serious. It suggests distemper or bronchial ailment, but may also result from a simple cold. Clean off the nose with a soft cloth, remove the mucus within the nostrils with a swab and then grease them with vaseline or olive oil to keep them soft. This is important in illness since mucus makes breathing difficult, and prevents smelling and tasting food.

Care of the Feet

Normal exercise should wear the toenails down to comfortable length. Proper length helps the dog grip the ground. Nails which are too long may cause his foot to slip and his arch to weaken.

Trim the nails with clippers sized to the breed (ordinary scissors will not do), then file them smooth. Don't cut into the quick which is very sensitive and may cause bleeding and fright. Nip off only a little at a time since you cannot see the line of the quick in dark-colored nails. Pay special attention to the upper inside nails or dewclaws. Since these do not touch the ground they continue to grow, sometimes curling around to pierce the flesh and cause infection. In such a case, cut off the nail point and soak the foot in warm sodium bicarbonate and water. (The dewclaws may be removed by your veterinarian; see page 10).

Thorns in or between the pads, shown usually by limping, should be taken out with tweezers. Cuts and abrasions will need thorough washing in soap and water. Then put on a good healing ointment. Until healed, protect the foot with a bandage or boot to prevent infection. Also watch out for possible fungus infection of the toes which dogs occasionally pick up from the ground. This is a case for the veterinarian, not the amateur. Whatever ointment you use, however, remember that the dog will lick it if he can, so be sure it is not poisonous.

CHAPTER 9

HOUSEBREAKING

Housebreaking is not a pleasant chore, but it is not nearly as difficult as it sounds. And once done, it is done for life. The dog rarely forgets this lesson. He is by nature a very clean animal, but he cannot stay clean without our help. In taking him into the home we make him live our kind of life. He must depend on us to take him out at the right time. Housebreaking is not teaching the dog to be clean; it is, instead, giving him a chance to stay clean.

The age at which housebreaking can be started varies among sizes and kinds of dogs. Intelligence has a bearing also, although not as much as people think. The problem is this: the earlier you try housebreaking, the more careful and alert you must be. In other words, the younger pupil needs relief more often; so the teacher must always be ready to take him out.

If housebreaking is started too early, progress will be so slow that you may think the pupil is stubborn or stupid. When the teacher gives enough time to the lessons, when he allows for the pupil's age and needs, progress may be surprisingly swift and sure.

When to Begin

Breeders and individual owners often disagree: one tells you that he started house-training his dog at three months, while another insists that seven months is the earliest age at which to expect a dog to be house trained. Each can be right, each can be wrong. A great deal depends upon the teacher.

To housebreak a dog quickly, arrange to teach him full time. If you train a dog in the morning and not in the afternoon, or train him for a few days and then go off and leave him alone for a day, you will have a confused and very slow learner. Keep at it hour after hour, day after day, and your dog, whatever his age, will become a model of cleanliness.

Be patient. The slightest sign of temper will cause fear and slow learning. No matter how exasperated you feel, don't let it show. Be quiet, relaxed, gentle but firm and, above all, cheerful. Your manner is going to have a great deal to do with the way your puppy acts. He has much to learn. It is harder for him than it is for you since he has to understand your language. You are not half as good at understanding his!

With these things in mind you *decide* at what age you are going to start the housebreaking—at three, four, five or six months. But make it easy for yourself as well as for the dog. Don't begin it until you can see it through.

How to Begin

If you have watched your puppy closely, you will know about what his needs are. At four or five months of age he still urinates and defecates often. Cold, excitement and confusion add to the usual number of paper or outdoor visits, while feeding almost always promotes the urge. In other words, you will have to take him outside at least every two hours, and always the first thing in the morning and the very last thing before going to bed.

This seems like an awful lot of trouble. You are tempted to put off the housebreaking until, with growth, the puppy's needs are less frequent! Bear in mind, however, that regular outdoor visits teach cleanliness and control as well. So, the earlier you start housebreaking, the sooner regular habits will be formed.

Also watch the puppy's manner just before he relieves himself. When about to urinate he hurries along usually sniffing the floor or ground; when about to defecate he goes round and round as if to select a particular spot. These habits are helpful since they tell you of his need.

To start the lessons, shut the puppy in his crate, room or pen, at night after he has had his regular outing or visit to his paper. Leave the usual pillow or blanket and a square of newspaper. He is going to need the paper during the night for a while. However, the paper should cover just a small section of the sleeping quarters. As he grows, his instinct for cleanliness increases. He becomes more and more unwilling to soil the floor close by. Do not leave him room to get far from his filth since he is learning to dislike it. He wants to keep his bed clean even if he does not know quite how.

Go to the puppy the very first thing in the morning and take him out. Beter carry him out to be safe—he is likely to do his business the minute he is set down—and carry also the newspaper from his bed if it is wet. Set the paper on the ground, set the pup down, and when he has performed properly, praise him, pet him and bring him in again. The soiled paper tells the puppy what to do and is a very sound idea. There is also a commercial preparation which you can sprinkle on the spot you wish the puppy to use, whether indoors or out. The odor is like dog's urine. Do not hurry the youngster back inside since he may have a bowel movement to make. If so, so much the better.

After his breakfast, take him out again. Either lead or carry him out the same door so he may learn which door means *go out*. And as you walk toward the door, say "Want to go out? Go out?" This will help in teaching the pup to go to the door when he feels the need to go out.

Be a clock watcher. At least every two hours, say *"go out,"* and stay out until something has been done. Also, watch the puppy in case your timing is not quite right. The moment you see him sniffing or hurrying, or trotting round and round, get him out.

Mistakes and Corrections

At first there will be mistakes, perhaps many of them, until he learns control. To correct him properly you must be right there *at the time,* not five minutes or even two minutes later. Stoop down, look him in the eye and scold "Shame!" "Shame!" Take him out at once even though this particular visit may not have results. If, however, he continues to make puddles where he should not, in addition to the scolding, slap the floor smartly with a newspaper paddle.

Do not spank the puppy for mistakes. Do not mishandle him in any manner whatsoever except perhaps to grasp him by the back of the neck to hold him still as you look him in the eye. Spanking will frighten the puppy and he may hide his filth next time in a dark corner or beneath a chair. To terrify him by spanking makes him think his filth is wrong, or at least that would seem to be the way he figures it out. Puppies spanked while being house trained will continue this unpleasant behavior.

Remember that the young puppy does not have full control over his bladder. Petting or an unexpected motion on your part may cause instant dribbling. This is an accident, a nervous reaction. Never scold him at a time like this. As it usually occurs in the rather shy pup, ignore it completely. He will outgrow it.

Clean away all mistakes, using soap and water and strong-smelling disinfectant until the spot cannot be recognized for what it was. A little ammonia or vinegar in water can be used on rugs. Careless cleaning is a strike against the pupil, since he will always want to visit a spot that has been visited before, either his own or that of another dog.

Vary the Procedure

Once the dog is fairly well housebroken, use a different door to get to the yard. Also, change the place the dog is expected to use. If a particular spot becomes too firmly fixed in his mind, he may refuse to go anywhere else.

Attach his leash and walk him around to another section of the yard or along the street. Lead him over grass, gravel, dirt, pavement, anywhere at all so long as the footing differs. Variety of terrain is very important. Dogs broken only in grassy yards have to be taught to use the highway; and city dogs, knowing only pavements and streets, have refused to use natural ground until trained to it.

Some dogs become so dependent on their owners that they will not listen to anyone else. When taken out by a person other than his owner, such a dog may make himself sick rather than relieve himself. Once the dog is house trained, let a neighbor or have a responsible child walk him occasionally. This will teach the dog that *going out* is more important than *who takes him out*.

Curb Training

Curb training is done in the public interest to keep the sidewalks clean. *"Curb Your Dog"* signs are found in many towns and cities and owners who do not do so are fined. Whether or not your town goes this far, remember that at some time or another your dog may have to be walked in a city where such laws are enforced.

Watch the dog closely as you lead him along and, just as he makes ready to squat, pull him gently but firmly toward the curb and down into the street. It is not difficult; most dogs take to the idea quite readily. The same trick can be used when crossing the gravelled paths of parks, and other public places. Those who try to keep all such areas free from fouling can do much to further the cause of dog-owning everywhere.

Housebreaking a Grown Dog

More difficult to housebreak is the dog who grows up without regular lessons in cleanliness or whose training has been slipshod. Cases of this kind are often the fault of owners who have left the dog shut up alone for long periods of time.

Here the closed crate night and day is useful. Or, the dog may be leashed to a radiator or any firm support and taken out only when relief is needed. Since the dog dislikes to soil his own quarters he will be more likely to control himself when penned or tied up short than when allowed to roam the house freely. Take him out at regular, stated times; the very first thing in the morning, the last thing at night, and a few times during the day. When he does what is expected of him outside, be liberal with your praise. You may offer a reward of some relished tidbit. As for mistakes, clean them thoroughly with soap and water and a strong smelling disinfectant. And scold but do not spank.

Let one person do the training, if possible the one who feeds him. Let that person be on hand all day and every day as long as needed. And let the teacher give the dog a great deal of affection. Many of these difficult-to-housebreak dogs have had no one to love, no one to please. Every dog wants to please his master; if given a master he will want to please him as soon as he understands how.

When housebreaking is delayed beyond one year of age, the dog may be very stubborn; on the other hand, he may catch on very quickly. In either case, it can be done, and it is well worth doing. Many a so-called "dirty dog" has been sold for a song simply because it was claimed he could not be made clean around the house. But it does take time since bad habits must be broken as new ones are learned.

The dog sold as "guaranteed housebroken" may be a problem for a while. Strange voices, a new bed and an unfamiliar house or back yard can make a very homesick animal. Give this one time to get acquainted. The dog rarely forgets his house manners but he is understandably confused when moved to a new home. Don't rush the training now; your first job is to gain the dog's confidence.

The Reason for Mistakes

Even the perfectly house-trained dog will misbehave upon occasion, such mistakes being caused by illness or the call of scent. Illnesses when the dog is not to blame for mistakes include cold, the beginning of "season," and intestinal upsets. In such cases neither scolding nor punishment will help; instead, they add to the dog's trouble by making him nervous. The house-trained dog has a sense of shame for mistakes. To punish him for an act he already knows is wrong is to worry and confuse him unnecessarily. When the dog is ill, take him out more often, or give him an indoor spread of newspapers.

The age-old call of scent is powerful and may cause mistakes. Food and urine are the two smells to which the dog reacts most quickly. Whenever and wherever he finds the scent of urine, whether on trees or posts along his line of march or previously soiled spots within the home, it is natural for him to leave his own mark.

This is what may happen. The neighbor and his dog come to see you. The visiting dog leaves his calling card. Immediately your perfectly housebroken dog forgets he ever was housebroken; maybe for two or three days he has to be tied up. This was not his fault. It could have been prevented. In fairness to _your_ dog it should be solved. Speak plainly to the visitor. Ask him to hold his dog on his lap, or leashed. When the visitor leaves, watch your dog carefully; when he sniffs around, speak sharply to him and hustle him outside. Even a single mistake at such a time may encourage a return of habits you have tried hard to break.

Eternal watchfulness is the price you must pay when your dog entertains another dog in your living room. Lifting the leg is the characteristic greeting of dog with dog, a form of greeting he will never out-grow. Be on the alert with a sharp _"Stop that!"_ or a quick slap at the offender.

Another annoyance is the dog that decorates your porch in early morning, sprinkles your milk bottles and bakery bag, and your choice evergreens too. If your female is in season, the males for miles around will know it. The male dogs are not to blame, of course, since this is their natural method of announcing their willingness to call. Confine the female inside your home or in a securely fenced yard (see page 47).

Keeping the Yard Clean

Cleaning the yard is one of the niceties of dog-keeping. In its way it is just as important as cleanliness inside the house. Yard cleanliness means: disposing of the droppings, and watching for over-acidity of the soil which is caused by too much urination in one small area.

If droppings are left in the yard flies collect instantly and then leave to spread germs far and wide. The flies from a neighbor's dog yard enter *your* home just as those in your yard visit theirs! Therefore, droppings should be picked up daily and put in a covered container or, better still, buried. This helps stop the spread of disease and prevents reinfection of a dog that has been wormed.

To keep the lawn clean, dog owners frequently use the one-spot method of housebreaking. That is, they teach the dog to go to one corner of the yard. The advantages of this method are obvious, but the small section of ground becomes sour, moldy and evil-smelling from urine. Grass is quickly burned out and the soil is hard-packed.

If you do limit the dog's toilet to a small section of fenced yard, the soil will have to be refreshed from time to time. Cover the surface with lime and spade it in thoroughly. Dig down around all fence posts and paint them with carbolic whitewash. Rake the dirt over fine and level, leave it alone for a while, then sow it to grass or clover. Meantime assign the dog to a different section of the yard. Where lack of space makes this impractical, floor the dog's yard with gravel or sand. Concrete yards are good, too, for they can be hosed out frequently; however, they must be properly graded to throw off the water, or equipped with drains or screened cesspools.

CHAPTER 10

TRAVELING WITH YOUR DOG

Today's dog is quite a traveler. In former years he was boarded out or given to a neighbor when the family went away. Today he goes right along in the car, often touring great distances to vacation spots. Whether he is to be a comfortable companion or something of a nuisance depends largely upon his training for the open road.

Lessons in Riding in the Car

Start with short drives to get the puppy used to the motion of the car. Do not feed or water for at least two hours before riding. A few short rides will probably be enough to get him used to the motion of the moving car. Hold him on your lap at first, or sit him on the seat beside you. Keep your arm around him for confidence and support as well as to guard him against being thrown to the floor in case of a sudden stop.

If he is large and you want him on the floor, order *Sit* and see that he remains there. Most dogs prefer to lean out the window to enjoy passing scents. Constant rush of wind, however, may cause cold in eyes and ears, although keeping the head up does seem to discourage car sickness.

Car Sickness

While it is not unusual for dogs to become car sick when riding, it is less likely among those trained to ride while young. The car vomiter can sometimes be helped by driving with him for short periods each day; when this fails, speak to your veterinarian. He may prescribe Dramamine or Bonamine to overcome car sickness. It is a good idea to be ready for car sickness on a long journey. A sedative such as sodium bromide (3-5 grains) given before starting and perlodically during the trip may help to control drooling and vomiting. The dog that is always nervous and sick in a car can often be "cured" by sitting with him in a standing car and petting him there for short periods each day. In some cases, the nervousness disappears after the dog has been fed a meal or two inside the motionless car. Letting him see out helps, too.

Trunk Carriers

If the dog is not too large, or if you have a station wagon, take along a cage or crate in which your pet can ride in comfort. The dog does not sleep as long at any time as we do; he takes many short naps. The crate lets him snooze for an hour or so along the way. But let him out often for relief.

The large dog is more of a problem—perhaps there is not enough space for him inside the car. But beware of carrying him in an open-backed crate fitted beneath the lifted lid of the trunk compartment. The rush of wind around the back of the car makes this a cold and drafty place for the dog to ride. Also, dogs are easily poisoned by carbon monoxide gas sucked into the trunk from the exhaust pipe.

If you must carry your dog in the trunk compartment be sure to guard against gas poisoning. One way to make sure the dog gets enough fresh air is to make a fairly large opening in the deck between the back of the rear seat and the rear window. Cover the opening with wire mesh. This will allow air from the car's opened windows to flow back into the trunk. It is also important to extend the exhaust pipe with a length of hose; run it upward (never downward) against the car's body so that the exhaust gases are carried off at the top of the car well above the dog's nose. Rubber suction clamps will hold the extension pipe in place, and it can be attached and removed at will. A commercial trunk ventilator can be purchased at little cost. Trunk-carrying is only for cool weather. In hot weather, no matter how well ventilated, the hot metal of the lid makes an inferno of the trunk.

Planning the Trip

The trip will be more enjoyable for you and the dog both if planned ahead. Take along your pet's own food and water pans. Take a few cartons of his favorite food since you may not be able to buy it in out-of-the-way places. Also take a thermos or gallon jug of water for drinking. Dogs are affected by water change, and may develop an upset stomach or diarrhea as a result. Have his collar attached, complete with license and identification tags. Take a good stout chain, as well as an extra leash for you will need this for exercising along the way. No matter how warm it is when you start, pack a sweater, too, if your dog is used to wearing one in cool weather.

Take a few bath towels and also some clean rags for wiping up in case of accidents. If the pet is small enough to be kept in a carrying case, take one with you. If you are stalled along the way, it may prove invaluable. Also it can serve as a comfortable bed in hotels and rooming houses. You might even pack a bottle of triple bromides or whatever pills your veterinarian recommends.

Before starting out make sure you have in the glove compartment of your car a copy of the "Touring With Towser" booklet put out by the Gaines Dog Research Center, 250 Park Avenue, New York 17, N.Y. There is a charge of 25 cents for it, but you will find it very helpful, since it lists hotels and motels throughout the U.S. that accept travelers with dogs.

The Health Certificate

Look into the laws about dogs of the various states you plan to visit or cross over. Most states require a health certificate which you can get from your veterinarian. Some states also require a certificate of the dog's vaccination against rabies. If you are shipping a dog by rail or air this certificate is absolutely necessary. When traveling by auto you and your dog may never be stopped, then again you may be. Dog regulations differ from time to time, so before you go you might check with the Health Departments at the capitals of the states you plan to visit.

Be very careful in national parks since they may have special laws. There are usually areas where dogs are allowed if they are on leash or under control of the owner. You can send for a pamphlet from the National Park Service, Department of the Interior, Washington, D.C., or ask, when you arrive at the Park, exactly what the rules are.

Dogs in Parked Cars

There will probably be times when you will leave your dog in the car while you eat, go shopping or sight-seeing. Park the car in the shade of course, but more than that, be sure the sun cannot get to it before your return. Sun on glass makes a furnace of the car and the dog may easily suffocate.

Be sure to allow for enough air. Lower a window a few inches on either side and also open both side wings—provided the dog is too large to squeeze through and get out. And always place a pan of water on the car floor if you will be gone any length of time. Do not leash the dog—he might hang himself. Besides, only when he is free inside the car can he protect it against theft.

Traveling in Hot Weather

Owners rightly fear for the safety of their pets when crossing the desert by car. Dogs probably suffer from the heat even more than human beings. This is where your bath towel will come in handy. Place a wet towel on the car floor for the dog to lie on; then over him place another wet towel. These help to keep him as cool as possible.

A folded sheet of wet cardboard may also be used to prevent overheating. Your thermos of cold water, too, may be a life saver; offer the dog a drink often, and feed lightly.

Conduct in Public Places

Not all hotels and motels accept dogs. The number of those that do, however, is increasing because dog owners are learning the importance of making their dogs behave.

Exercise the pet where you are told he may be exercised, and nowhere else. Guard the bushes and greenery against damage by your dog; keep the paths clean by curbing him. (See page 96.) Insist that he be clean indoors also, and spread newspapers thickly on the floor in case you are not positive of his house-training. Do not bathe the dog in the hotel bathtub, and do not use the management's towels to freshen him up. Such things as this have made enemies of friendly hotel-keepers.

You may have to leave the dog alone in the room at times. This is where trouble often starts. Tie the animal securely, with leash, or better, a stout chain, else he may escape and try to find you when the maid enters the room. Watch the windows, too. Never leave a window open from the bottom, since this is where the dog may try to get out—even through a screen. Leave the room as clean as when you found it, and you and your dog will be welcomed again. If furniture or bedding is damaged, pay willingly for the damage. Do not try to hide it, or the next fellow and his dog may be turned away.

Foreign Travel

Traveling with your dog abroad, of course, is more complicated; be sure that you get up-to-date information well in advance about the laws of the countries you will visit.

England, Sweden, Denmark, Finland and Hawaii have a definite quarantine period during which a dog must be held before entering the country. At this writing there is no quarantine in other countries. Many, however, do require a health certificate stating that the dog has been inoculated against rabies during the previous six months. These places include Canada, France, Germany, Italy, Switzerland, Nassau, Virgin Islands, Mexico, South America and Cuba.

Some but not all steamships offer kennels for about $50 per dog. Be sure to ask, before booking passage, which boats carry dogs and which do not. All the major airlines carry dogs to Europe at a cost of about $1.17 per pound of the dog's weight. Here, also, it is best to get in touch with the company about special regulations. Or, you can obtain the services of a kennel or agent which specializes in the boarding and shipping of pets to and from most anywhere in the world. They will arrange travel reservations, necessary documents, etc., and provide special traveling crates.

If your dog has been out of the United States, when he re-enters, you must have a certificate from a veterinarian stating that he has been vaccinated against rabies within the last six months.

CHAPTER 11

A FEW SIMPLE TRICKS

Training Can Be Fun

Tricks can be a lot of fun for the dog and for the family. More than this, they give the dog something to do. The trained dog is a busy dog and is less likely to be mischievous and destructive. And the more you train, the more you *can* train since ability to learn usually grows as it is used.

Trainers say that two years is a favorite age at which to begin. If your dog is older, however, don't despair! You *can* teach an old dog new tricks! Some puppies, too, can learn simple tricks at fairly early age, but do not expect too much of the very young.

Rewards get results because the dog understands them. When he obeys and gets a tidbit as a reward, he is happy because he has pleased you and he'll want to do it again. Show him that doing the right thing and a pleasant reward go together. Repeat this lesson often enough and he will learn!

Be cheerful, happy, sociable in all your teaching, and your dog will just about fall all over himself to do what you want. If you can arrange it, teach before meal-time, when he is hungry. Use a dog biscuit or other food as the tidbit. When the lesson has been learned, you can skip the "eats" but never forget that pat on the head or the spoken "good dog."

Short, regular lessons which will not over-tire the pupil are best. Two or possibly three daily lessons of ten minutes will be enough. Work on one trick at a time, and do not go on to a second trick until the first has been mastered. When beginning on a new trick, review the tricks he already knows; this gives the puppy confidence in himself. Do not smoke while teaching, for the fumes bother the puppy's nose and eyes. And do not keep your dog repeating a trick—or obeying a command—until he is weary and bored.

Shake Hands!

Even a six month old puppy can learn to "shake hands" because it takes no special strength or skill. It is natural for any dog to lift a paw in greeting or to attract attention. The point is to make him put out one paw when you tell him to do so.

We will now realize the importance of the *Sit* and the *Sit-Stay* exercises. (See pages 51-52 and 59.) If your puppy has not learned these, teach them first. You will have to use them constantly. In the *Sit* of course the dog sits beside you facing straight ahead, while in the *Sit-Stay* he sits and remains seated as you walk away from him.

Order the leashed pup to *Sit-Stay*, as you stand facing him. Now stand quite close and a little to one side. Lean toward him. This will make him draw back and raise one foot. If he does not raise his foot tap it lightly. Whichever paw he raises as you lean over him, take that paw in your hand and shake it gently as you say *"Shake hands!"*

There seem to be right-handed and left-handed dogs, so at the start you never know which "hand" you are going to shake. Take the one offered, then later you can teach the pup to shake first with one and the other. After you shake the first, say "Now the other one!" If he keeps offering the same paw, just nudge the other one and he will give it to you. Remember the praise, "Good Buster" as you give him a tidbit. As this trick is mastered—it won't take long—stand away from the dog rather than close to him, and finally do it without the leash.

Speak!

In some ways the *Speak* is like *Shake Hands* because you are telling the dog to do something he does anyway. See when the pupil barks readily; perhaps when the doorbell rings, when a stranger comes in, or when you are preparing his dinner.

Make him bark. If yours is one of those very quiet dogs you may have to "bark" yourself to start him off. At any rate, be ready. When he barks order *"Speak!"* Do not shout; don't be nasty about it. Use an encouraging tone of voice—you and the dog both are having a good time. When the bark answers your command, pet him and feed the tidbit.

The *Speak*, however, should be one or two yips and no more. If barking continues, pick the dog up and fondle him or, if he has learned the meaning of *No!* or *Quiet!* use one of these to stop him.

Beg!

Most beloved of all tricks is sitting up. However, since we use the word *Sit* for another exercise, we had better use the word *Beg* so that the puppy will not be confused. In all orders we must avoid words which sound the same.

Use a corner of the room where a rug or carpet will keep him from slipping. Have the dog *Sit-Stay*, his back close to the corner. Hold a tidbit in one hand and give him a chance to smell it. He will follow it with his eyes and straighten up as you slowly raise this hand above his eye-level. At the same instant, with your other hand raise his forelegs off the ground as you order *"Beg!"*

Holding his head up to sniff the tidbit will help him stiffen his back and keep the unnatural, upright position. The moment he stiffens his back, hold your hand under his chin instead of under his legs. The first few times, he may stay upright for a second or two. This is enough. Praise him and give him a nibble of the tidbit.

This trick is not hard for the dog to learn, but it is very hard for him to master before 4 or 5 months of age. A younger puppy's weak back muscles and poor sense of balance make "sitting up" practically impossible. The wall close behind him of course helps to support his back. After a few lessons he may not need it, and then the lessons can be given anywhere at all so long as the footing is good. If he rears on his hind feet as you lift his fore-legs, take your hands away, order *"Sit!"* then start over. Some breeds and shapes of dogs find it easier than others. If your dog cannot sit up, do not try to make him do it, but choose some trick for which he is better suited.

Steady!

Steady is an interesting outgrowth of *Beg*. When the pup has learned to sit up and beg without wobbling around, try to make him hold a piece of the tidbit on his nose while sitting up.

When he is in the *Beg* position, put the tidbit on his nose as you point a finger at him and say *"Steady!"* You will have to speak firmly now since all he wants to do is to eat the tidbit. He must hold it on his nose and remain still until you say *"All right!"* or *"You can have it!"* which means he may flip the tidbit off and swallow it.

This may take a little time, but sooner or later he will learn that he may eat the tidbit only when you tell him to. Until then he must keep absolutely still. If he moves his nose and drops the piece on the floor, do not give it to him. Start over. Dogs like this trick because they know that in the end they always get the prize. They will learn to hold the pose for several moments.

Dance!

When the dog's back is strong enough for him to learn begging, he is ready to learn dancing. Put him on leash and work up a little excitement by letting him sniff the tidbit in your hand. Hold the hand fairly high above his head but not too close or you will throw him off balance.

As he rears up on his hind legs, slowly move your hand in a circle so that he can follow its direction. As you do this order "Dance!"

At first, he may need the taut leash to keep him on his hind legs as he twirls around. As soon as he learns to balance himself upright, skip the leash. Do not give him the tidbit if he jumps to get it. In this case, order "Sit!" and start over.

Catch!

The game of Catch! is the delight of dogs big and little since it also means something to eat. You will throw a piece of biscuit or other food to the dog who must catch in his mouth without fumbling. This may be difficult because you must aim the biscuit correctly. In fact, the timing and direction of the teacher's cast are as important as the pupil's ability to catch the object. Use a smaller tidbit than usual.

Stand well away from the dog. With a slow, underhand movement throw the tidbit in the direction of the dog but slightly higher. The dog can then follow it with his eyes and try to catch it as it comes down toward him. If he misses it, remove it; let him eat it only when he makes a clean catch.

This trick leads to ball playing. Take care to use a ball large enough to be grasped but not swallowed, and soft enough to avoid injury to the teeth.

Lie Down!

Have the dog on leash and order him to Sit-Stay. He is facing you, sitting about three feet away. With the leash in your left hand, crouch or kneel, and as you say *"Lie down!"* or *"Down!"* pull down on the leash. If he goes down flat, with forelegs stretched out before him, praise him for a job well done.

The chances are he will not drop at first. Try again. Repeat the order, pulling down on the leash. At the very same instant run your right hand under his forelegs and with one quick motion slide both forelegs out from under him. Both legs must be pulled at once; if you pull one at a time, he will pull back, using the other leg for support.

Once he is in the down position, forelegs outstretched, praise and reward him. With practice he will stay down until you tell him to rise by saying *"All right!"* But while he stays down, you too must kneel. If you stand, he will also, at least until the trick is thoroughly mastered.

Roll Over!

When the dog has learned the *Down,* you may go on to *Roll Over.* Order *"Down"* first. Then with your hand push him over on his side as you say *"Roll over!"* If he resists as he may at first, hold a bit of food in front of his nose to signal the direction his body should take. Crouch closely over him so he will not get up. How fast he learns will depend upon whether or not he is at ease in the down position.

Retrieving

You may not have a retriever which you use for duck hunting but if you want your dog to fetch and carry, whether a ball in play or your newspaper from the front lawn, the same steps in training are used.

First, you teach him to accept or take, an object. Use a favorite toy that he enjoys carrying around—a burlap roll, or an ordinary small dumbbell.

Stoop low or get down on the floor and waggle the dumbbell to attract the dog's atention. If he picks it up, say *"Hold it!"* If he doesn't, stand over him; with your left hand hold the muzzle from above, and press your thumb and middle finger into the corner of the mouth between the lips and teeth. This makes him open up.

Slip the dumbbell between the teeth just far enough back for him to hold it. He may resist. There is no telling how he will react at first. When he holds it for even a few seconds, praise and reward him. If he drops it, correct with *"No!"* and start over.

When he gets the idea of holding for a moment or two, tell him to release it. Kneel down before him, gently take the toy out of his mouth and say *"Out!"* or *"Drop it!"* If he won't let go, force the mouth open as described above. He must learn to let go of the object only when you tell him to.

Carrying an object comes next. But make sure the pupil knows *Hold it* first. Put on the leash. With the toy in his mouth lead the dog around the room or out in the yard. Since holding a hard object is a strain on teeth and jaws, you may use a newspaper or an old shoe or anything soft. The dog usually enjoys this; he'll walk as far as you like. But do not overdo it. Every so often say *"Sit"* and *"Out."* Remove the object and wait a while before you give it back.

The next step after holding and carrying is to teach the dog to get an object, pick it up, bring it back, sit and drop it. This may be difficult since the pupil will want to run and play with the object instead of bringing it back. Therefore, it is best not to try this trick until the dog had learned to come when called. (See page 60.)

With the dog on a fairly long leash, take the object in your hand and waggle it before him to attract his attention. Throw the object a short distance away. Then run with him to it and order *"Hold it!"* Wait until you are sure he has it firmly in his teeth—he may mouth it and play with it, so you must insist on the hold before giving the next command.

Now say *"Fetch!"* as you crouch down and slap your knee exactly as you did when teaching the *Come.* When he gets fairly close to you, order *"Sit"* and then *"Out."* You may skip the *Sit,* but it may be helpful in teaching control.

Hold, Carry and *Fetch* should be taught in just that order, but use the same command so as to simplify things for the dog. Each should be thoroughly mastered before the next is attempted. Actually, they are one trick, taught in three stages to avoid confusion. You will use the *Fetch* around the house as well as out in the yard as the dog learns to bring your slippers, his leash, his bone, a ball, or the newspaper.

Climb Up!

If yours is a tiny dog or one so short-legged he cannot jump into your lap, teach him to climb up. This seems to give little dogs a great deal of pleasure and it can be learned in about one minute. As he rests his forepaws on your knee, asking to be picked up, place the palm of your hand against the back of his head and say *"Climb up!"* Stiffen your hand as he braces his head against it and he will walk right up into your lap.

No Jumping

Jumping is a favorite pastime. It is a rather showy trick at which some dogs are very good and others no good at all. But don't let your dog jump unless he is full grown, strong and sturdy. By nature the dog is a broad jumper rather than high jumper. He can go across a ditch more easily than he can go over a fence. If allowed to jump too young or too hard he may seriously injure the tendons of his legs and feet.

A word of caution. The dog who learns to jump very high may be able to scale the very fence you built to keep him safely at home. However, if your dog is sturdy and enjoys doing tricks you can teach him to jump over a stick or broom handle. First, hold the stick close to the ground; have an assistant help the dog over the stick as you say *"Jump!"* Holding a tidbit on the other side of the stick also helps in teaching this trick. The stick can be raised gradually, but do not try very high jumps.

The Forbidden Chair

To the tricks taught for pure amusement, you might add one aimed at better conduct around the house. In some homes there are sad little dogs tied up all the time because they refuse to stay away from the best furniture. Maybe they nap on your bed when they are not supposed to; maybe they prefer the best living room chair! You have tried to discourage Rover from sitting in this chair but he cannot understand because he has been allowed to sit in other chairs.

A dog can usually learn to stay off all or certain chairs, if he is told *"No!"* every time he starts to get up on them or is found there. If this doesn't work put a pie plate or other tin dish on the arm of the forbidden chair. Place it so that it will fall off with a great clatter when he jumps up. The loud noise should frighten him away. Or the snapping of a set mousetrap placed on the chair, although not for small dogs it might catch. He soon learns which chairs, couches and beds mean unpleasant sounds, and he will be sure to stay away.

How to Talk to the Dog

The average house pet understands more words than most people realize, and, by talking to him in the right way, an amazing increase in his understanding is possible.

In the first place, use a friendly, conversational tone, not too loud and not too soft. The sharp, quick manner of speaking is for correction, whereas the softer, slower, manner of speaking is for teaching. Talk clearly, using as few words as possible. Short sentences are the rule. Use the same words each time for the same idea. For instance, do not send him to *Bed* one time, and to *Box* the next. Decide on one word and stick to it.

Talk to the dog as you would to the child whose understanding of words is limited. When you say to the child *box* and then show him a box, he learns to connect the sound with the object. The dog will also. Say *shoe* every time you show him a shoe or give him a shoe; he'll soon learn what the sound means.

If you keep this up with many objects, he will become so smart you may have to spell out certain words when you don't want him to catch on. In time, you may even have to spell backwards!

☆ CHAPTER 12 ☆

DOGS AS A HOBBY

Whatever kind of dog you have chosen, you are going to be proud of him. You take him with you wherever you go, and put him through his paces for visitors to see how smart he is. Sooner or later somebody says: "Why don't you put him in a show? I'll bet he could win!" At once your curiosity is aroused. What about this place where dogs are shown?

Dog shows are competitions for purebred dogs involving prizes, ribbons, trophies and championships. There are hundreds of such shows held yearly throughout the country, some in big buildings like armories, amphitheaters and Madison Square Garden, others under canvas on outdoor grounds. There may be 2,000 or more dogs competing at a time; there may be a hundred or two.

If you want to enter your dog in a competition, you should first register him.

How to Register

When you get your puppy, if it is a purebred, you should have received a partially filled in printed form. This is an application for registration. Of the several agencies which register dogs, the American Kennel Club is the largest. Their records list most of the purebred dogs in this country.

Let's consider, then, that you have been given an AKC form with your puppy. You sign it, and send it with the re-required fee, to the American Kennel Club, 221 Park Ave., South, New York, N.Y. If the form is correct, you will receive a certificate of registration. This contains your dog's official number which must be used, with his name, when he is entered in a show.

How to Enter in Dog Shows

There are many local dog clubs, both all-breed and specialty clubs for one breed, throughout the country. Many of these hold informal sanction "match" shows which are excellent training for the puppy and novice exhibitor. No advance entry is required, and fees are low. Local newspapers sometimes carry announcements of matches, or you can write to the AKC, 221 Park Ave. South, New York, N.Y., for the names of any clubs near you. This organization will also send a list of coming dog shows throughout the country, upon request.

It is a good idea to go to a match, or attend a show without your dog, so you will know what is going on. Watch particularly how your breed is groomed and shown in the ring, then practice at home. If he has learned the simple obedience lessons of heeling on leash, standing when told to, you will have little trouble.

Choose a nearby show, then write to the listed superintendent or secretary for the "premium list." This booklet gives advance information about the show and contains an entry form which you fill out and return with the fee as directed. In order to compete, your dog must be over six months of age, he must be registered (or listed) and, if a female, not spayed.

The entry form will tell you to choose the class in which your dog is to be shown. Classes include puppy, novice, American-bred, open, etc. Since this is your first experience, you had best enter one of the easier classes, that is, the puppy class if your puppy is between six months and one year of age, or the novice class if he is more than a year of age.

The dog show is a series of competitions, each more difficult than the last. The dogs of each sex first compete in their classes. Then the first prize winners of each class compete for *winners, dogs* (males) and *winners, bitches* (females). These two compete for *best of winners*, and then finally with certain champion dogs for *best of breed*. All bests of breeds next compete according to their group—Sporting Dogs, Hounds, Working Dogs, Terriers, Toys and Non-sporting Dogs. The six group winners then compete for the grand prize, *Best in Show*.

Now this may seem complicated. Don't be discouraged. You do not have to understand it all straight off. In fact, if your dog wins first in his class, or even second, third or fourth you have every right to be happy about it. You can take the ribbon home and proudly show it to your friends. When a dog is awarded *winners,* he earns points toward his championship, but you do not have to keep on showing him if you do not want to. Just one show alone will be an interesting experience. Later you can exhibit again if you wish and learn step by step as you go along.

Competing in Dog Shows

When you take your dog to a show for the first time, this is what you do. At the entrance gate, show your ticket, which admits you and your dog. The number on your ticket is his bench number, if the show is benched. If not, you do not have to stay after your judging is through, and you can keep your dog with you. If the show is benched, take your dog to his stall as soon as you have let him to into the exercise ring to relieve himself. He must stay in his stall except when he is being groomed and judged.

Your next job is to have the dog examined by the veterinarian, and it is up to you to see that this is done. The veterinarian may be at the entrance gate or in quarters of his own somewhere else. Find him. He will look your dog over to see whether he is in good health, then stamp his ticket. This insures that only healthy dogs are admitted.

Be alert to take your dog into the ring at the right time. You received a timetable in the mail with your ticket, and it gives the starting time for judging of your breed. Be prepared in plenty of time, but let your dog relax in his bench until just before his class, so he will be clean and fresh. You will receive a numbered armband at the ring entrance, and then you are in the ring.

Your dog will be expected to stand still for examination, and then to trot up and down for inspection of his gait. Do exactly as the judge directs and you will get along all right.

In each class there are four ribbons awarded for quality. You may get one of the four, you may get nothing. It depends upon how your dog measures up with others in the class. If you win nothing, never mind; there will be other days, other shows where you and your dog can try again.

In addition to all-breed shows there are "specialty" shows where only one breed is featured. If there is a dog club in your neighborhood, get in touch with the secretary who will tell you something about the meetings of his group. You will be welcome to attend and can learn a lot about dogs, shows, and dog breeding.

Educational Phases of Dogs

All such meetings can be quite educational, because like you, everyone is interested in purebred dogs or they would not be there! You will be excited by other people's enthusiasms, sympathize with their troubles, and you will learn a great deal by getting to know folks who admire the same kind of dog that you do.

The subject of purebred dogs is fascinating. Once interested, you will want to learn more and more. Visit your nearest public library. You will find many volumes telling the histories of the dogs of all nations, from pole to pole.

Veterinary Care Available

There are 20,000 veterinarians in the United States. Most of them handle dogs as part of their general practice. There are about 4,000 small animal hospitals for the treatment of dog ailments.

Canine blood banks and X-ray, medical care and surgery on a par with that for humans, are all available to dogs today. Many of the new drugs developed for man, the serums, vaccines, hormones and antibiotics, also serve dogs.

The veterinarian of today has long and intensive preparation for his profession. He must have had at least two years of college before he can enter a veterinary school. Then he has four years to study at one of the twenty veterinary colleges or universities in the United States and Canada. This is usually followed by a year or more as an assistant in a small animal hospital. He must pass school examination to get his degree in veterinary medicine and then pass State Board examinations to get his license to practice.

Much research for dogs is done in college laboratories, as well as in private laboratories of pharmaceutical companies and dog food manufacturers. The result is that dogs live longer and healthier lives today than ever before. Thousands of dogs that would have died 20 years ago now recover from serious illnesses.

Schools and Training Centers

There are even schools and "colleges" where dogs are prepared for AKC degrees of "Companion Dog," "Companion Dog Excellent," "Utility Dog" and "Tracking Dog." These degrees are awarded at obedience trials which are held along with regular dog shows or independently. While developing dogs mentally, obedience instruction also teaches good canine citizenship. There are several hundred training organizations for dogs and their owners in states across the nation. So if you are not getting good results in training your dog at home, you might join one of these classes. For a free list of such classes in your locality, write to the Gaines Dog Research Center, 250 Park Avenue, New York 17, N.Y.

Breeding Your Dog

You do not have to become a regular dog breeder, but you may consider mating your female just for the fun of watching the puppies grow and develop. It is quite an experience that will teach you a good deal about the ways and wonders of nature.

First, be sure the female is normal, average-sized for her breed, and in top physical condition. You might have her examined by the veterinarian. Ask him whether he considers her fit for mating. The chances are that she is, but it is wise to get an expert's opinion. If the veterinarian gives her a clean bill of health, then go ahead.

The age of the first mating is important. With time, the bones become more set and rigid, hence the female bred for the first time at four or five years of age might have difficulty in delivering the pups. If you plan to breed your female, do it while she is young. Not too young, though. It is unwise to breed a female at her first "season." Most females are not mature enough to handle a litter at this age and it becomes a strain on them both physically and mentally. With small dogs it is far better to wait for the second season, and with very large breeds perhaps even the third. Plan ahead for the breeding.

Selecting the Stud Dog

Well in advance decide on the male to which your female is to be mated. If possible, select a dog offered at stud by a regular breeder rather than some unknown, untried dog in the neighborhood. For this service you will be asked to pay a fee, but it is well worth it. Occasionally a stud owner will mate his dog without fee, instead having first choice of a puppy or two in the litter. If such an arrangement is agreeable to both parties, then go ahead, but get some sort of contract in writing to show exactly what the arrangement is.

If you cannot find a stud of your breed write to the AKC for a list from which you can select one near your home.

Go and see this breeder's dog or dogs and select the one you like or, better, chose the one recommended. Some pedigrees combine better than others, so take your female's pedigree along and be guided by the breeder's advice.

Having decided on the dog you will use, make a reservation for his services then and there. You will know the approximate date when the female is due in season. She will probably be ready for mating on the twelfth day after the first sign of color discharge. If it is the right day, you can take her to the male, have her bred, and bring her home again the same day, although more than one breeding may be advisable.

Care of the Bred Female

When you bring her home, be sure to *guard her carefully* until she has gone completely out of season and has returned to normal. Then let her live her life as usual, exercising her every day without fail. Feed her as before. As she gets bigger, she will need more food. But give her an extra feeding each day rather than overload her stomach with more at one time.

Guard her against jumping and rough-housing, for as the size of the carried litter increases, she may injure herself or her puppies. If you must pick her up, be very careful. Support her hindquarters and set her down gently. Don't let her squeeze through swing doors. Watch her bowels; she may need an occasional dose of a mild laxative like milk of magnesia. If in any doubt about her condition, let the veterinarian look her over.

Dogs usually deliver sixty-three days after the mating; often, however, it is a day or two more or less. Keep a record of the date of mating. Figure the probable delivery or whelping date and be ready for it.

The Whelping Bed

Choose a room where the temperature can be held at about 60 to 70 degrees. Prepare a box and let the female sleep in it for two weeks or so before the whelping date. If she objects to new sleeping quarters give her one of your old sweaters or coats to lie on. The box of oblong shape is best. It should be as deep as the female is long, and about twice as long. You might attach upright posts in the corners so you can throw a blanket over the box, in case the room grows chilly. The best flooring is a removable, canvas-covered slide. Make two, so one can be washed and sunned while the other is in use.

If you do not care to go to all this trouble, and your female is a little one, you can use ordinary cardboard cartons. Get several since, once damp, they are useless. The hardy female of larger size, used to living outdoors, can use a stall set up in the cellar or garage; but it must be arranged to keep the puppies in a limited space. Young puppies need warmth and protection from drafts—do not forget that when preparing the whelping bed. Finally, place in the box a piece of rug or quilt which the female can dig into and pull on during labor.

The Whelping

As the due date draws near, the nipples swell, the carried litter sags. As long as the patient eats she is probably all right; if she refuses food, then she will probably whelp very soon. Also, her temperature will drop about two degrees, to below 99 degrees, about 12 hours before whelping. She will pace back and forth and, perhaps, crawl under tables and chairs where she will lie panting. Now and then she scratches vigorously, tearing papers or anything she can dig her claws into. Do not leave her alone; she may want you nearby.

Watch carefully for the first sign of labor pains. There will be regular straining, with panting and a stretching of the entire body. Look at the clock and note the time. More than two hours of straining without the birth of a puppy will mean that your female needs a veterinarian.

When the whelping is normal, you may see a lump between anus and vulva. With a few more painful strains a dark fluid-filled bag or sac begins to come out. It may be expelled without assistance; if not, use a rough-textured washcloth to grip on its slippery surface. Hold the sac to prevent its going back and with each succeeding labor pain, pull gently but firmly down.

Each puppy should come in its own enclosing sac—the afterbirth or placenta attached to the umbilical cord should come right along with the puppy. Should the connecting cord break, never mind for the moment—it will probably come out later. However, keep track because if any placentas are retained, they may cause an infection. A hormone shot must be given by the veterinarian if any placentas are retained, or if he thinks there may be another puppy left.

Ordinarily the mother takes care of the whelping without help. Don't be too eager and, in any case, there should never be too many people around. She will usually tear open the sac with her teeth, but sometimes she just sits and waits. In this case, you must work fast to get the puppy's head out or it will smother. Tear the sac down and around the head, and off the body. If the umbilical cord is still attached, saw it off with scissors leaving at least a two-inch length from the pup. If it bleeds tie it with silk thread.

Give the puppy to the female to wash. If she is the old-fashioned sort, she will lick the little one and tumble it about roughly to start the infant breathing. If she is an ultra-modern, "just sit and watch" kind, do this for her. With a dry towel rub the baby all over. Wipe any mucus from the mouth with your index finger. Don't be too gentle; really rub and rub. When you hear a tiny squeal you will know the puppy is breathing; otherwise keep rubbing or shake it, head down, until it shows some sign of life; then place it on the matron's breast.

If the after-birth does not follow the puppy, it will probably come out with the next puppy. There is one for each pup and each must be accounted for. Let the matron eat one or two. They contain healthful substances and it is natural for the mother to clean the nest by eating them, but too many will make her nauseous and lose her appetite when she needs to eat food.

The puppies will continue to arrive—perhaps ten minutes apart, perhaps a full hour or more. The same digging, scratching, straining will go on for each one or she may hardly know when she has them. While straining for the next birth, the mother may injure an earlier puppy; in any case it will get cold and wet if kept with her. You may remove the little ones to a basket nearby (be sure they are warm) until the whelping is completed. Then give the puppies back to the mother to nurse.

Feeding the Puppies and Matron

If the mother doesn't have enough milk, or if there is too large a litter for her to take care of, then you must give extra bottle feedings.

A commercial product may be used or you can make your own formula with two teaspoonsful of Karo syrup, two cupsful whole milk, and two yolks of egg. Or use two parts of evaporated milk to one of water, adding a small amount of Karo syrup, and a yolk of an egg. Mix thoroughly and keep the formula in the refrigerator, warming whatever amount is used at each feeding. An ordinary doll or baby nursing bottle can be used for hand feeding. A baby lamb nipple or the anti-colic nipple used for premature babies are the best types for puppies. Make sure that the hole allows the formula to pass through readily but not too fast. For puppies raised solely by hand the feedings should be given every 4-5 hours around the clock.

For hand-fed puppies it is important after each nursing to take a swab of cotton, dip it in olive oil and massage the puppy between its hind legs until it has had a bowel movement and urinated. This takes the place of the mother's washing which keeps the pup clean and bowels open.

For the first day or two, following the whelping, feed the mother only meat, milk, egg and other solid foods. She will refuse bulkier food which would make her have to leave the puppies more often. Soon dog meal will be added. She needs even more food now than when she was in whelp. Ask your veterinarian about any extra vitamins or minerals that may be needed. As time goes on the matron will need more food; she is feeding her growing litter as well as herself, and she must be well-nourished if she is to make enough milk for her brood. Feed her three times daily plus a bedtime snack if she wants it.

The Matron's Job

The matron takes entire care of her puppies throughout the nursing period, feeding, washing, warming and otherwise making them comfortable. She should not, however, be expected to lie with her brood constantly. Gradually she will leave them for longer and longer periods to stretch her legs and perhaps lie in the sun. Arrange the box so the dam (but not the puppies!) can come and go as she likes.

By the third week the mother will be getting good and tired of the brood. Their toenails will scratch her breasts, so nip off just the tips with manicure scissors. Then, every day, offer the puppies baby cereal and milk to lap; the commercially prepared milks for orphan puppies are excellent. Pups learn to eat finely ground beef almost immediately. Shortly they will also lap cow's milk or slightly thinned evaporated milk with only a little cereal, and then soaked dog meal added. But stick to one type of milk. And see that each pup gets his share.

Gradually begin to add dog meal as thickening for the milk. Or give beef broth and meal occasionally. At about the fifth week you may notice that the matron vomits her partially-digested meal for the puppies to eat. It won't hurt them—in the wild state it was the natural way for the mother to feed her pups—but on the other hand, the mother herself needs the nourishment, so take this as a sign that the puppies need more food.

Weaning Schedules

The following program is one weaning method. You need not follow it exactly since there are other methods just as satisfactory. Remember that new foods are introduced gradually to avoid upsetting the puppy's digestion.

3-4 Weeks

Twice daily: milk and baby cereal or meal lapped from a dish.
Once daily: beef.
Nursing as usual.

4-6 Weeks

Three times daily: milk with dog meal—very moist.
Twice daily: beef broth and dog meal.
Nursing twice daily, then only at night.

6-8 Weeks

Three times daily: milk thickened with dog meal.
Twice daily: dog meal, moistened with beef broth, perhaps adding scraped raw or cooked beef.
Nursing only during the night through the 6th week but no longer except perhaps for a backward puppy.

The following program is recommended as the most modern method of weaning puppies and the best for weaning to self-feeding.

3 Weeks

Make a mixture of dry dog meal or burger-type food and milk to the consistency of a malted milk shake and put this before the puppies for a three-hour period while the mother is away from the litter.
Nursing as usual after the feeding period.

4 Weeks

Feed a thickened version of the above mixture for a six-hour period while the mother is away.
Nursing as usual after the feeding period.

5 Weeks

Feed a thick gruel of meal or burger-type food and water over a 12-hour period while the mother is away. Feed two batches a day to eliminate spoilage and contamination.

Nursing as usual after the feeding period.

6 Weeks

Feed the same mixture on a self-feeding basis. The pups are now totally weaned. Make the mixture as dry and crumbly as possible, deciding on the proper moisture based on the size of the puppies and the ease they have in eating.

Until you are feeding the foods dry, prepare several batches of the mixture a day to eliminate spoilage and contamination.

7-8 Weeks and on

Use the self-feeding method and gradually eliminate the liquid until the food is served dry. Be sure to keep drinking water available at all times.

Gradually cut down on the amount of food given the mother dog in order to reduce her milk supply. When she is removed entirely from the puppies, daub her breasts with camphorated oil to hasten the drying-up of her milk. A jacket bandage (see pages 128-29) may also be helpful. And keep her away from the puppies until all traces of her milk have disappeared. For weaning to the self-feeding method, see pages 8-9.

CHAPTER 13

NURSING AND SPECIAL CARE

You don't have to be an expert to know when the pup is sick. All you have to know is how he should look and act when he is well. The healthy dog is responsive and willing, runs and plays, is happy and reasonably fearless. His tail wags with enthusiastic messages. His face is expressive, his eyes bright and clear, his nostrils clean. His nose does not have to be cool but it usually is. There is a certain springiness about him that shows pleasure in all he does. He eats eagerly, drinks rather sparingly.

Signs of Illness

When the puppy is too good, when suddenly he stops his mischievous ways, we begin to suspect that something is wrong. Maybe he acts dumpish, droops his tail and doesn't care about cleaning up his dish. Or perhaps he eats as if he were starved, or drinks so much water that he vomits it right up again. His stomach may be bloated.

The stools should be medium brown in color and well formed. The puppy may defecate 4-5 times a day, the grown dog once; don't worry so long as color and consistency are right. If the stools are black, watery or blood-streaked, and there are more movements than usual, then something should be done.

In a puppy, the eyes and nose are often first to show on-coming illness. The eyes may weep, possibly with pus collecting at the inner corners; the nose may discharge either clear water or mucus. He may pant continuously, his breathing may be difficult, his expression strained.

Not all of the symptoms will be noticed, of course, when the puppy is getting sick; certain symptoms point to one ailment, others to another. However, they are signs that should be watched for. Any one of them is enough to tell the owner that something is wrong. Don't wait to see whether the condition will correct itself. The chances are that it won't. Don't experiment with remedies suggested by well-meaning neighbors. Get the advice of an expert—your veterinarian. Quick action at the first sign of illness is the best short-cut to its cure.

The Sick Room

When the dog is ill he needs a room or corner of his own. Protect him from noise and confusion, and from the well-meant attentions of children and unthinking adults. He will be comforted by the quiet presence of his owner, but don't talk too much. You'll tire him out.

He needs first of all, peace and quiet. The dog recovering from a serious disease like distemper, may be thrown into fits by nothing more than the slam of a door or the shrieks of children playing. Or a frenzy of fear may be caused by the raising of a window shade and the entrance of sudden, stabbing light. Use dark shades, and keep the light fairly dim. Over one side of his bed throw a blanket to further shield the light which will pain him if his eyes are affected.

Remove rugs and carpets so the floor can be easily cleaned, and cover the floor with newspapers. Arrange for enough air without draft, and moderate heat that will remain even. Hang up a thermometer so that you can watch room temperature. Have some water bottles handy in case the patient needs additional warmth.

A table or a chest for medicine, utensils, everything used in the course of treatment will be helpful. And do not forget a pad upon which you note each dose of medicine and the time of day it was given. Wash all utensils carefully whenever used. Wash your hands before and after tending a sick dog.

The Pet's Medicine Chest

The dog's own medicine chest will be helpful to him and to you. Put in it the things he needs or may need—no family remedies, no pills suitable for people but *not for dogs*. Just the pet's very own remedies that can be found in a jiffy when required.

Such things as sterile cotton and bandages, camphorated oil, boric acid, bicarbonate of soda, aspirin, adhesive tape, a good non-poisonous salve, a burn remedy, vaseline, antiseptic dusting powder, flea powder, and a proper cough mixture. These are some of the things you may need from time to time. You will think of others. Your veterinarian can help. Ask him what sedative is best; when to use it and the dosage. Then in case of over-excitement, fits or accidents, you will be prepared to give first aid. This may seem like a lot of unnecessary work, but the day may come when it pays off handsomely. Always remember—the dog cannot take some drugs which are helpful to people.

Keeping the Patient Clean

One of the chief problems of canine nursing is how to keep the patient clean. In mild illnesses when the dog can go out of doors for relief, the problem is less acute; when he is paralyzed or too weak to stand, his cleanliness is of real concern.

It is safe to assume that in serious illness the house-broken dog worries when he cannot perform his bodily functions outside. Also, the constant soiling of bedding causes odors in the sick-room. This may make the dog anxious and slow his recovery.

The weakened or paralyzed patient should be turned over often, not alone to ease the strain of lying in one position but to prevent bed-sores. He needs a softer under-bed than usual, and since it will be soiled often it should be of washable material. Light-weight, cotton flannel blankets, cut in yard-size squares, will do, and can be washed in the washing machine. Mattress pads are also excellent.

Make for the sick-bed a canvas-covered, removable false bottom, raised two or three inches off the floor of the box itself. Air will circulate under the bed, keeping the floor boards dry. At least two canvas slides will be needed for each bed so one can be sunned and aired after scrubbing while the other is in use.

However soft the bedding upon which the patient lies, he will also need a wrapper or diaper. Lay under him a full-sized turkish towel; bunch it up between the hind legs, across the inner thighs and around the tail. Wipe him often with a soft cloth moistened with very mild antiseptic, and then dust the skin lightly with antiseptic powder or ordinary talcum. Long-haired dogs, lying helpless for any length of time, should be clipped around the hindparts. Cut off the skirts and the hair around the tail.

If the patient is able to go outside for relief, wipe him off when he returns. Not a trace of dirt should be brought in to his bed; also, he should not lie down wet or damp. Brush his coat gently, but don't take too long since it may annoy him.

Pay special attention to the sick dog's eyes, ears, mouth. If he vomits often wipe out his mouth with a mild salt water solution. Remove discharge from eyes and ears. (See pages 87 and 88.)

The Temperature

The dog's normal temperature is 101.2 degrees. A few tenths one way or the other has little significance. It may be slightly higher under excitement or following rough play; therefore take it when the dog is quiet or has been resting. A rise of more than one degree should not be ignored. This shows that the body is fighting an infection of some sort. A subnormal temperature of 99 degrees is also cause for alarm since it may show internal bleeding, shock or collapse.

The time of day at which the temperature is taken may affect the reading. Ordinarily, the temperature rises in the afternoon and early evening, drops lower during the morning. When talking to your veterinarian, tell him the time of day the reading was made, as well as the day-to-day rise and fall.

Use a regular clinical thermometer, rectal type. Wash it carefully in tepid water, then shake down the mercury with a quick flip of the wrist. Grease the bulb and lower shaft with vaseline. Lay the patient on his side or have an assistant hold him for you. Insert the bulb at least two inches into the rectum, and hold it there for a minute or two. After use, wash the thremometer carefully with soap and tepid water, then immerse it in a jar of alcohol for one hour. Dry it, and shut it up in its case.

Phoning the Veterinarian

Many illnesses do not require daily visits by the veterinarian, yet he should be kept informed of his patient's progress. He will probably say: "I'll not be in for a few days but keep in touch with me by phone."

This means he will want *facts* about the sufferer's day-to-day condition. It is not enough to say that the dog "is about the same," or that "he seems better than he was yesterday." Give *facts*. In other words, keep a record.

Take the temperature twice daily, at ten in the morning, four in the afternoon. Watch the breathing—is it quick, strained, shallow, with pinched nostrils, or is it deep, relaxed, easy? Are there muscular spasms or jerky movements, coughing, strangling, clouded eyes, unusual bowel movements, and so on? These things can be reported accurately only when written down as you see them. So, have the record at hand when you phone the doctor. You will save him a lot of time, and you stand a better chance of saving your dog.

When the veterinarian tells you what to do, do it to the letter! When medicine is to be given every two hours, that means every two hours, and in the exact amount, no more, no less. If it is a case for twenty-four-hour medication, that is, night as well as day, see that it is done. Faithful nursing has pulled many a dog through.

Restraint

Bandage Muzzle—A bandage tape muzzle is used when a dog may be tempted to bite from fright or pain during the trimming of nails, the treatment of wounds, or when in shock or hurt from an accident, etc. The width of the bandage will depend upon the length of the dog's nose, but ordinarily the inch or one-and-a-half inch size will be correct, even if it has to be folded over for the shorter faces.

According to the size of the dog, cut a twenty-four or thirty-six inch strip. With the ends of the tape hanging down over the sides of the muzzle, place the center over the nose. Bring the tape down around the muzzle under the chin, cross the ends, tie with a fairly loose knot then bring the ends up and around to the back of the head and tie with a bowknot. Adjust the bandage tightly enough to hold the jaws closed but not so tight as to make breathing uncomfortable. Put on a muzzle of this kind once in a while just for practice; it will teach you how to do it, and the dog will learn not to mind it.

A bandage muzzle has many uses. If, for example, your dog has been struck by a car, he may be in such pain that he doesn't recognize you and so must be muzzled before you can handle him.

Jacket Bandage—The jacket bandage is used to hold throat compresses and poultices in place, in pneumonia where chest rubbing with camphorated oil may be indicated, and for drying up lactating females whose breasts have been daubed with camphorated oil or vinegar. Such coverings are helpful where fresh air is important but where draft may be deadly. They also protect furniture and bedding from being smeared with salves and oils.

Fit the jacket from belly to back. For the front legs cut two holes in a square of cloth which is brought up around the throat and ribs, then sewed or taped across the back. A few minutes and a bit of ingenuity will produce a jacket that will be comfortable and reasonably wrinkle free. The cold or pneumonia jacket is usually made of light-weight flannel while that for oil dressings is made of cotton material.

Protective Collar—The Elizabethan collar is standard equipment to keep the dog from licking wounds, tearing off bandages, and biting sores. Cut a semi-circular piece of heavy cardboard, the inner circumference fitted to the dog's neck. Make it wide enough to reach about to the muzzle tip. In the two straight sides puncture eyelets, and through the eyelets run tapes for pulling the collar together. When tied, it looks something like a lampshade worn around the neck. It is very effective and, being light in weight, rarely annoys the dog. In fact, most dogs feel "dressed up" in it and wear it proudly.

Nail Taping—We tape the nails of dogs suffering from eye disease or injury to prevent further tearing of the eye by the upper inside toenail. Even when this nail is kept trimmed, it can scratch the eye because the dog uses considerable force as he paws it.

The toenail on the same side as the injured eye is the one that does the damage. With adhesive tape, wrap this wrist completely covering the nail. Keep the tape on until some time after the eye has returned to normal. Boots can be purchased for the same purpose; here all nails are covered, which is very good in cases of eczema and skin infections that cause constant scratching.

How to Give an Enema

An enema may be needed when purgatives are too slow-acting or otherwise inadvisable. For the very little dog, a glass syringe or even a rubber syringe is sometimes used. On the whole, however, the regular quart-sized enema bag with rubber hose and shut-off valve is to be preferred.

With castile or similar mild soap make up some hot soap-and-water suds and let cool to blood heat (tepid). The amount will depend upon the size dog, but better make too much than too little. The larger amount will hold its blood-heat temperature longer in the bag. The size of the nozzle, too, is measured by the size of the dog although the baby-sized hard rubber nozzle will ordinarily be correct.

Two people are needed to give an enema. An assistant lays the dog stretched out on his side; or, if the animal fights, the assistant can hold him in standing position while steadying his hindquarters. Do not, however, place the hand beneath the stomach since this can stop the free flow of the fluid.

Hang the bag on a hook higher than the dog's body. Daub

the nozzle with vaseline, but don't clog the opening. Now, before inserting the nozzle, open the valve. This clears the nozzle and forces air from the tube. Close the clamp again, insert the nozzle well up, several inches, into the rectum, then open the clamp. The water will run slowly, and then begin to ooze out at the nozzle. Remove the nozzle gently, placing your thumb for a moment on the dog's rectum to prevent immediate release of the fluid. Wash the bag, tube and syringe nozzle carefully and hang it up to dry.

Administration of Medicines

Pills—Provided the dog is eating, the easiest way to give him a pill is to hide it in a piece of food.

In cases where the stomach is to be empty when the dose is given, the pill must be force-fed. Coat the pill with butter, honey or mineral oil to make it slippery. With the left hand beneath the dog's chin, open the mouth by pressing with thumb and middle finger against the cheeks near the back teeth. Drop the pill on the tongue, then with a fingertip guide it quickly toward the back of the throat and push it down. Close the jaws and hold them closed as you stroke the throat with a downward motion. The dog should swallow; if he does not, hold your thumb against his nostrils for an instant.

Powders—Open the jaws as described. From a piece of waxed paper creased down its center, slide the powder onto the back of the tongue, then hold the jaws closed until the dog swallows. Or, put the powder in a gelatine capsule, oil it and push it down.

Liquids—Bitter-tasting liquids should be put in capsules and given as described under *Pills*. The dog can vomit at will, and so can reject what he does not like. Mild-tasting or tasteless liquids can be poured into the mouth from a small bottle, a test tube or a spoon. Small bottles and tubes are easier to handle than spoons. If no one is helping you, back the dog into a corner so he cannot draw away. Put the left hand index finger in the right hand corner of the dog's lips, drawing out the under lip to form a pocket. Pour the liquid slowly into the pouch. Hold fast to the lip and keep the dog's head up until he swallows. When the large dog is handled without help, the attendant usually straddles the animal to control him with his knees, then he pours the dose into the left pouch.

Tasteless powders and liquids can often be concealed by serving them with the dog's regular food, or by mixing them with honey.

Hypodermic Injections—These should only be given by prescription and *all medicines for hypodermic injections should only be used upon the advice of your veterinarian.* Use the simplest type of small, all-glass syringe. Take it apart; place barrel, piston and needle in cold water, and boil for twenty minutes for sterilization. Cool and put the parts together. With the plunger draw up into the barrel the right amount of liquid, shoot out a drop or two to test the needle opening and to force out any air.

The shoulder or scruff of the neck are good places for the injection. Where time permits, clip away a spot of hair and daub with a drop of iodine or rub with alcohol. If quick action is essential, merely roll the flesh between thumb and forefinger to part the hair, then put the needle in slantwise with a quick, firm jab. Very slowly push out the contents of the barrel. Withdraw the needle carefully.

Inhalations

Vapor baths or inhalations can ease the labored breathing caused by colds, bronchitis, and pneumonia. Use tincture of benzoin, one tablespoonful to a quart of boiling water.

Small dogs may be placed in a basket or clothes hamper, raised on two chairs or other support; or they may be held in a cane-seat chair with the kettle underneath. Large dogs are best left on the floor with a bed-sheet tent over them, and the steam directed inside. Or, the animal may be shut in his crate with the steam spout turned toward the gate. If the dog fears the steam, and is small enough, he may be held in one's arms. Treatment of a few minutes several times daily will help to open up the passages and give relief. But be very careful to avoid scalding.

Nasal drops may be effective in some cases but should not be overdone. A salve such as is used for children's chest colds may be used for rubbing around the nose and throat.

Separating Fighters

If a strange dog attacks your dog on the street you are going to need help to separate the two. If someone can bring a pail of water to dash on the fighters, or better still, douse them with a water hose, that is probably the easiest way.

One dog is usually the attacker. If he can be grabbed by the tail and pulled hard, he will turn around to see what is happening and thus lose his hold. Or, if you can get assistance, have this person grab and pull on the hind legs of one dog while you do the same with your dog, thus separating them. To prevent the dog being able to turn and bite you, hold him as high off the ground as possible until he cools down.

There are any number of tricks that will surprise battling dogs into breaking apart, such as throwing pepper in their faces or holding a lighted match near the nostrils. But at any rate don't yell; the dogs probably won't hear you and if they do may think you are egging them on. If the dogs are males and you have no assistance, try to get them into a position where you can pinch the testicles. That usually takes the fight out of them for the moment.

When the fight is stopped and you grab your dog, have a helper ready to shield you. The still infuriated attacker will try to reach your dog and may strike you.

The nosy dog that bothers your dog when you go out to walk is often a cause for great annoyance. Your dog is on leash, the other dog is not so you have a difficult time snubbing him. He may not be a fighter, perhaps he merely wants to sniff your dog and follow along after the two of you. Carry a water pistol in your pocket. A squirt or two in the face will dampen his enthusiasm.

Dog Bites

If you are bitten by a dog, wash the area thoroughly with tincture of green soap and water and cover the wound with sterile gauze. The bite of a clean and healthy dog need be no more serious than any other minor cut. However, if the dog is vicious and/or unknown to you, as in the case of a stray dog, the wise course is to see your physician immediately.

CHAPTER 14

AILMENTS AND ACCIDENTS

Distemper

Although great progress has been made, distemper remains one of the most serious of all diseases. It strikes principally at young dogs, usually affecting those under one year of age. That is why vaccination to make the puppy immune to it is so common today. Once recovered the dog is almost always immune against a second attack.

Symptoms include listlessness and loss of appetite, eye and nose discharges at first watery, later thickened; coughing, vomiting, fever, thirst and diarrhea with black, evil-smelling stools. The disease with its secondary infections often lasts for six weeks. Afterward there may be chorea (muscular twitching), convulsions or paralysis.

While the death rate is high, disabling is even more frequent. Blindness in one or both eyes may result from discharges affecting the cornea. These same discharges sometimes leave the dog deaf or without the sense of smell. Permanent damage to the nervous system may cause chorea for the rest of the dog's life.

Distemper is caused by an airborne virus. It may be picked up by the dog which comes in contact with a dog sick with distemper or from the feet, hands or clothing of the person caring for such a sick dog. The bed, bedding, in fact everything used by a distemper-sick dog may spread infection.

To avoid infecting others the distemper patient should be isolated for at least three weeks following his recovery. If there is a case of distemper in your neighborhood, steer clear of the house in which the sick dog lives, and every member of his family. Do not let them visit you! They can bring the disease to your dog even though they leave their dog at home.

It is wise for every dog owner to have his dog immunized.

Temporary immunity is given by injecting the young puppy with serum, permanent immunity by vaccinating the older puppy. See your veterinarian. As in all vaccinations, for humans as well as animals, they are not 100% perfect, but failures are uncommon.

There is no drug that will cure distemper, although antibiotics and serums are helpful particularly against the secondary infections which often do the greatest damage. Good nursing is vital to bring a dog through. The patient should be kept isolated in clean, warm, dry, well-ventilated quarters. Give simple foods in small amounts three or four times daily—beef broth, coddled egg, cup custard. It is difficult to make the distemper patient eat anything and this is where liquid beef peptonoids are invaluable. Dilute this protein extract with water and spoon it into the dog like medicine several times a day.

Keep the eyes and nose free of mucus. With a piece of sterile cotton dipped in boric acid solution, wipe out the eyes, then use castor oil or yellow mercuric oxide salve to soothe the rims. Clean out the nostrils gently with a cotton swab and use vaseline to prevent cracking.

Follow your veterinarian's advice about medicines. Above all, keep the patient quiet. His nerves are on edge, so no sudden bright lights, no door slamming, no confusion, no loud talking. Dim the light in his room since his eyes are sensitive throughout the course of the disease.

Following recovery burn blankets, beds and bedding that are not too valuable to discard. Otherwise, disinfect thoroughly everything the patient has used or come in contact with. Spray his yard, including the fence posts, with a 20-per-cent solution of slaked lime. If the dog dies, do not bring another puppy into the house for at least a month and be sure to have him properly vaccinated.

Immunization

One hears so much these days about serums and vaccines—it is all quite confusing. So, just to give some idea of what they are:

Serum is the clear liquid part of blood. Taken from a highly immune animal it is sometimes injected into a healthy animal as a means of giving immediate but temporary protection against exposure to disease—for example, distemper. It is also used in treatment. To keep an animal immune by serum requires injections about every two weeks.

Vaccines are of two kinds. Live virus vaccine is weakened material of the disease itself. It creates a long-lasting immunity with a "booster" shot each year. There are also vaccines made with killed virus. These give immunity that is usually limited to a few months or a year.

Infectious Hepatitis

Infectious hepatitis in dogs is a disease of the liver caused by a virus. Like distemper, it affects young dogs most often, though it can strike dogs of any age. The mortality rate is higher in puppies. It is not the same as the infectious hepatitis or epidemic jaundice which attacks human beings. It is not air-borne but is caught by contact with saliva and the urine of infected animals. In fact, the urine of the infected animal is dangerous for some time following recovery. The disease lasts a short time, sometimes only a few days.

Symptoms include listlessness with high fever and thirst, a watery discharge from the eyes, sometimes vomiting and diarrhea. The throat, particularly the tonsils, becomes red, the glands swell.

Hepatitis works fast, so fast in fact that the puppy may die before the seriousness of his illness is realized. It may follow distemper, or may be present along with it. Consult your veterinarian immediately. Prevention is possible with a vaccine which may give life-long protection, and is usually given along with the distemper vaccine to pups.

"Hard Pad" Disease

"Hard pad" is thought to be caused by the distemper virus and has not been identified as a separate disease. It is a virus which can attack through the air or by contact, but unlike infectious hepatitis does not seem to be spread by recovered patients.

It is practically impossible, especially for the layman, to tell it from distemper until the foot-pads begin to harden. Instead of their normally rubbery texture, the pads become thickened and so hard that the feet click on certain surfaces. Vaccination against distemper is the best protection.

Leptospirosis

Leptospirosis is not a virus like distemper and canine hepatitis but is a spirochete transmitted by rats. Not only a rat bite, but even drinking water infected by rat urine, give this rapid-killing disease to a dog. Because it acts very rapidly, immunization is a must. It can be given at the same time as the other puppy shots.

Rabies

There has always been so much talk about rabies that many people believe it is much more common than is actually the case. As a matter of fact, rabies is a very rare disease in dogs. It is not limited to the summer although it seems to occur more often in warm weather. This is probably because dogs roam more during the summer months.

Rabies, or "hydrophobia," is caused by a virus. It comes from the saliva of an infected animal and in no other way. Rabid animals can infect other animals by biting them, although bitten animals do not always get the disease. This means that your dog will not get rabies *unless he is actually bitten by a rabid animal, or infected by the animal's saliva through an open wound.*

There are two forms of rabies, furious and dumb. In the former, the first symptom is a usually marked change in the dog's behavior, that is, from friendly to snappy and offish. The infected dog may become restless and wander off to hide in dark corners. His voice may undergo a change in pitch or he may howl. He grows excitable. Later his throat muscles become so paralyzed that he cannot drink. In the dumb form there is paralysis of the jaw and pronounced melancholia. There is no cure for rabies.

If your dog should show any of these symptoms, of if you know he has been bitten by a strange dog, then you must handle him with all possible care. Throw a blanket over him, gather him up, shut him in a room. The blanket will keep him from biting you if he has grown snappy. Then call your veterinarian at once. If you are bitten, wash the wound thoroughly with green soap and water; really scrub the area and cover with sterile gauze. Then be sure to see your doctor.

Many communities today are encouraging owners to vaccinate their dogs against rabies, while others have made vaccination compulsory. This cannot wipe out the disease. Vaccination can reach only some of the dogs in any community. *Responsible* owners look after their dogs, but right in the same town or city live *irresponsible* owners who let their dogs run the streets and who would disown them rather than pay license and vaccination fees.

The free-roaming dog is the chief source of infection. To help to wipe out rabies, fence your yard and exercise your pet only under control. And try to make your neighbor control his dog also. Licensing and vaccination do not entitle a dog to run free; any roaming dog can still be a neighborhood nuisance.

Pneumonia

Pheumonia may follow other diseases, or it may be an independent inflammation of the lungs. Although caused by a microbe, it may be caused by sudden changes of temperature, or by exposure to cold and dampness—particularly damp sleeping quarters.

Listlessness and loss of appetite will probably be noticed first. The temperature may rise rapidly to 104 or 105 degrees, with a husky cough and very shallow, raspy breathing. Often the nostrils are pinched and the eyes strained as breathing becomes difficult.

Get your dog to the veterinarian immediately. Thanks to modern drugs, pneumonia is not the killer it used to be, but you must work fast. As in all weakening diseases, try to keep the patient eating. Give three or four small meals per day of light, easily-digested foods—beef extract, milk, egg custards, and puddings.

Colds

The dog kept in a heated house may catch head colds brought on by drafts, auto riding and sudden changes of temperature. Eyes and nose run, the dog shivers and perhaps coughs but does not show much rise in temperature. The thin mucous discharges may be cleared away, and the eyes and nose wiped with boric acid solution. Give a mild purgative like milk of magnesia, from one teaspoonful to one tablespoonful according to size. If you have an ultraviolet lamp and are experienced in using it, you might try it for your dog's coughs and colds.

Worms

There are several kinds of worms which the dog can have. Some dogs go through life with little or no trouble, so do not take it for granted your dog has worms and worry about it. However, it is wise to know something about the different types of worms and how they affect general health.

Round Worms—Round worms have already been mentioned (see page 30). In addition to these there are tapeworms, whipworms, hookworms and heartworms.

Tapeworms—Spread by the flea, the tapeworm can be seen with the naked eye as flesh-colored and square-shaped when they leave the rectum. They become dry and brownish, and look like grains of rice, in the air. You may find a few sticking to the dog's bed or around his rectum. This parasite may be several feet long and continue to grow unless the head part is eliminated. It causes vomiting, restlessness, and irritation at the rectum which the dog often drags over the floor. Other symptoms include pale gums and eye-rims, loss of weight, dull hair, and diarrhea. Strong medicine is necessary to fully remove tapeworm. The usual treatment is to worm at least twice, two weeks apart. Tapeworm medicine should not be given to puppies under three months, except by the veterinarian, and never to weak or sick puppies. See your veterinarian or, if you must worm the dog yourself, get one of the commercial preparations containing Di-Phenthane-70. These are considered effective and non-toxic.

Whipworms—Usually about two inches in length, the whipworm is round and tapered. Since they live principally in the cecum (something like our appendix) they are not easily discovered and, because they are deep inside the intestines, a series of treatments is usually required. Whipworm causes loss of weight, anemia, foul-smelling diarrhea, nervousness and convulsions. It is not as common as round and hook worm but if neglected can be fatal. Treatment is sometimes by a series of injections. Surgery to remove the cecum has also been used. There is now a tablet which has proved effective and safe. Let your veterinarian decide which treatment is best.

Hookworms—Hookworms are tiny and increase very rapidly. Formerly they were found only in the South, but they are now fairly common in the North as well. They hook into the dog's intestinal walls where they suck the blood. Symptoms are pale gums and eye-rims, loss of weight and blood-streaked diarrhea. Treatment for hookworm in puppies is the same as that for round worms. Most of the leading manufacturers produce capsules for treatment of both round and hook. It is necessary for a veterinarian to treat your dog, especially in severe cases. The new injection treatment is very effective.

Heartworms—Heartworm is common in mosquito country since it comes from an infected mosquito's bite. It is also carried by fleas. Heartworm can be discovered only by microscopic examination of a blood sample from the suspected dog. The tiny organisms live in the blood stream and from there go to the heart where they mature. If present in large numbers, they clog the blood flow. The first symptom, therefore, may be exhaustion following exercise when the dog gasps for breath and perhaps collapses. Ordinary worm medicines have no effect. Diagnosis and treatment cannot be done by the amateur.

Treatment for Worms

There are special medicines for each kind of worm, but the particular parasite must be known before the right drug can be given. Worm medicine is powerful stuff, irritating to stomach and intestines, weakening to the patient, and often dangerous unless given in an amount, carefully measured by the age, size, strength and condition of the individual dog.

It is safer to let your veterinarian worm your dog for you. But if you prefer to do it yourself, have the veterinarian make the examination and tell you the correct dose. Take a sample of your dog's stool to the veterinarian. By examining it under the microscope, he can tell if your dog has worms and what kind. Follow his directions carefully. Many of the patent worm medicines are excellent but it is vitally important to follow directions. When they state that the dog should not eat for a number of hours before giving the medicine, make sure he is put on a fast with no "tidbits" or even milk to "tide him over." Be sure that you give the right dosage and never the amount for adult dogs to puppies.

Coccidiosis is another disease which causes the same symptoms as worms, particularly loose and bloody stools. It is treated like tapeworm with Di-Phenthane 70 and with supplementary use of antibiotics and sulpha drugs.

Skin Troubles

When in normally good condition, the dog's skin is elastic. When you grasp it over the back, then let it go, it springs right back to its tight fit. In most breeds it is a light pink color; in a few it is blue, dark or spotted. Part the hair and look at the skin just to make sure it is healthy. Skin troubles travel fast, so when anything is wrong take steps to correct it before a large area becomes affected.

Dandruff—Not at all unusual in a dry scaliness like dandruff in man. Brushing will raise many dusty little scales. This may be caused by too much washing which dries out the coat's natural oil; it may also be caused by not enough rinsing after the bath. The remaining soap dries and irritates the skin. A little cocoanut oil, olive oil or castor oil massaged into the skin usually helps. The larger dog may be rubbed all over with linseed oil or with a dressing made especially for dogs.

Distemper Pustules—Often during the course of distemper little pustules appear on the abdomen. They will disappear when the disease has run its course. Meantime, keep them soft with vaseline.

Eczema—Eczema is one of the more serious skin troubles. Remove the cause, whatever it may be—external parasites (see page 83), dirty bedding, overheating, too strong soaps, and use a healing ointment. The skin should return to normal in a week or two.

So-called dry eczema is the most common form. The skin looks scaly and hair may fall out in patches. Constant biting and scratching makes the condition spread. A mixture of seven ounces of alcohol, an ounce of balsam of Peru and a teaspoonful of Creolin may help relieve the itching. Sometimes the dryness is caused by a lack of fat in the diet. A few tablespoonsful of a vegetable oil, bacon drippings, or lard in the dog's food will help. Medicinal soaps or strong mange "cures," however, may only set up further irritation. There are patent soothing lotions that ease the itching and irritation. But, don't expect miracles. If there is no improvement within a couple of weeks, get professional advice. It often takes quite a while to diagnose and treat any skin condition successfully.

A moist condition of the skin, with red, flushed appearance, suggests improper diet and constipation. Give simple purgative such as milk of magnesia (from one teaspoonful to one tablespoonful according to size). Also, you might dust with soothing antiseptic powder. It is important to prevent scratching or biting and here the Elizabethan collar (see page 129) can be very useful.

It is always well to check skin troubles with your veterinarian. If the rash is caused by nutritional deficiencies, he may suggest vitamins to help overcome it. This type of skin trouble is more common in summer so watch out for it from the onset of warm weather. Don't let it get ahead of you and spread!

Mange—Mange is caused by a particular and pernicious parasite. The veterinarian identifies it by examining skin scrapings under a microscope. *Sarcoptic mange* sets up an intolerable itching, causing the dog to bite and scratch. It spreads rapidly and strips the skin of hair. *Follicular mange* is less itchy, but more serious. Just when it seems cured it may break out again. The hair falls out and pustules dot the skin. It may start with bare spots around the eyes, inflammation, and scaliness similar to dandruff. Go to your veterinarian immediately and do exactly as he says. For years a home remedy was flowers of sulphur powder mixed to a paste with crude oil. Today there are other more effective treatments. Mange is catching from dog to dog, from utensils and grooming tools, bedding, etc. It is not impossible to cure if steps are taken quickly and if strict sanitary practice is observed. Watch for new spots, too, until the complete cure is certain. Good nutrition and vitamins help build resistance.

Ringworm—Ringworm is caused by a fungus which, like mange, can be identified only under the microscope. At first it may appear as a round, rough and scaly patch raised above the normal level of the skin. The spots may be dry or moist, may even discharge pus, and should not be handled except with gloves. Iodine two or three times a day is a commonly-used treatment. Take your dog to the veterinarian as soon as any condition like ringworm appears.

If you see a bald spot or irritation on your dog's skin, do not get upset about it since it may be unimportant. On the other hand, do not pass it by entirely. The naked eye cannot diagnose it properly; the veterinarian and his microscope can. So to relieve your mind and to cut short the disease, let your veterinarian take care of it.

Skin troubles similar to hives in humans may be due to allergies to certain plants or weeds, in injected serums, or, in rare cases, even to certain foods. Suspected allergies should be handled by your veterinarian. Often these cases respond well to antihistamine drugs.

Poison Ivy

Ordinarily, dogs suffer no ill effects from contact with poison ivy although they can carry the poison to people. When they walk through it, or roll in it as they often do, the oil from the leaves rubs off on their coats. A person who pets or strokes the dog may then be affected. When you know your dog has been in contact with poison ivy, put on a pair of rubber gloves and give him a good bath with brown laundry soap and water.

Vomiting

Vomiting occurs often in dogs of all ages because the dog can vomit at will. Dose him with an evil-tasting medicine and he'll throw it up because he does not like the flavor. Feed him a peppermint candy, and possibly he will throw this up too. The same thing may occur with cinnamon, ginger, cloves and nutmeg. Therefore, vomiting may merely show dislike. It is often caused by grass which the dog eats when his stomach feels uncomfortable.

Frequent vomiting is caused by many diseases and upsets. It is cured by eliminating the cause. Overloading the stomach is a common cause; the cure, less food fed at more frequent intervals. Worms can be responsible; getting rid of them solves the difficulty. Over-excitement, fatigue, and boisterous play can be avoided. Then there are what may be called mechanical causes, among them poisons. (See pages 144-45.)

Persistent vomiting of just a little food may mean a change in the menu is needed. Mix the food with less water. For the time being, limit water and offer a lump of ice to lick. Withhold solid food if the condition is serious and substitute a preparation like liquid beef peptonoids, (see page 134), from one teaspoonful to three tablespoonfuls every two hours throughout the day, according to the size of the dog. This allows the stomach to rest, easing whatever irritation must be causing the upset.

Pepsin and bismuth powders, five grains of each, given three times daily may help. Afterward, feed little and often, slowly and carefully. However, do not experiment with a persistent vomiter too long. Better see your veterinarian.

Flatulence

Indigestion is often suspetced when a dog passes foul-smelling gases, but this is sometimes the result of a diet consisting largely of meat or many eggs. It can usually be corrected by feeding a meal-type or a biscuit-type dog food. Adding small amounts of charcoal helps correct flatulence. One Neocholan tablet twice a day for a dog the size of a Boston Terrier will often remove the cause of the trouble.

Diarrhea

Diarrhea is often caused by bad feeding. If it happens only once or twice it may be nothing more than a slight intestinal upset. A sudden change in food can bring it on, so a change from one brand of food to another is best done by easy stages. Often it results from nervousness or fright brought on by unaccustomed journeys or excitement. Spoiled food, too, will cause it.

Diarrhea accompanies the intestinal form of distemper in which case the stools emit an especially foul odor. Intestinal worms are also a major cause. Serious diarrhea, involving several daily evacuations, evil-smelling or blood-streaked, should be treated immediately by the veterinarian. Mild or occasional cases may be relieved by milk of bismuth given twice daily in doses of from one-half to one teaspoonful according to size.

Constipation

Constipation, which is more common than supposed, can be dealt with easily, but its cause should be eliminated or it will happen again. Eating bones, or a diet composed largely of meat, are frequent causes. When evacuation is difficult, a single dose of mineral oil may be enough. Where the system has become poisoned by long-standing constipation, a purgative dose of milk of magnesia—for small dogs a teasponful, for medium size dogs, one or two tablespoonfuls; for large dogs, two or three tablespoonfuls—will help clear the intestines. For quicker action use a tepid soap-and-water enema (see pages 129-30).

Except in the case of very old dogs, persistent constipation can usually be avoided by balanced feeding and additional exercise. Be sure to consult your veterinarian if the condition continues as there may be an impaction.

Fits or Convulsions

Puppy fits may be caused by teething or by worms. They sometimes result, too, from the fright of sudden noise, from too much sun, from lack of water, and from faulty feeding. In several diseases such as distemper, fits are almost always present.

The attack may last for only a few moments as the dog barks excitedly, stiffens and stares glassy-eyed, champs his jaws and froths at the mouth. Or he may stagger and fall unconscious as his legs continue to push and pump. Remove the sufferer to a quiet, semi-dark room or place him in a crate where he won't injure himself. When he is conscious and able to swallow, give a simple sedative; triple bromides or whatever your veterinarian had advised for just such a happening. Whether the fit is mild or severe, it should be followed by a complete physical checkup. The fit is not a disease in itself; it is a sign that something is wrong somewhere in the dog's body. Dogs do have epilepsy, but rarely.

Frothing at the Mouth

Frothing at the mouth causes fear among folks unfamiliar with dogs and their ways. However, simply frothing needs cause no alarm. An occasional puppy may froth during teething. Following pungent or bitter medicines, the dog drools, bubbles and froths. He may do the same thing when sampling carrion or anything evil-tasting. Frothing ordinarily precedes a fit. The champing of the jaws cut the tongue and perhaps flecks the foam with blood.

Lameness

Lameness, limping and a stiff gait, may be due to a variety of causes. Rheumatism is brought on by lying on cold ground, concrete, or damp bedding. Internal treatment as well as a dry play yard and a warm bed are suggested; while sprains and stifle injuries, which cause the dog to coast on three legs, require the skilled assistance of the veterinarian.

Long-neglected constipation is a source of stiff and stilted gait. Lameness is usually associated with footpad injuries, and this, of course, can account for uncertain and faulty gait. Inspect the feet for thorns, cuts, splinters, corns, etc. (See pages 91-92.) If there is no abnormal foot condition, have your veterinarian look for possible bone dislocation.

Burns

In mild burns, when the affected area is small, trim away the hair, then apply tannic acid jelly, or strong, freshly-made tea. When using tea, first cover the burn lightly with sterile cotton and pour the liquid into it. Bandage well, but not tightly. Ordinary burn ointments or a sodium bicarbonate solution may also be used.

Cough

Whether or not breathing is difficult, a cough is serious. It suggests distemper, bronchitis, pneumonia or pleurisy. The cough may be no more than a barely audible hack, or it may be severe enough to choke the animal temporarily. Something may have stuck in the throat; more probably, however, the cough may be accompanied by fever and labored breathing.

Penicillin has become standard for lung troubles, but this should not be used unless prescribed by the veterinarian. However, you will not go wrong by dosing with honey and lemon. Into the juice of a lemon mix enough honey to make a thick syrup, and give this to the dog several times daily to ease the irritation.

Poison

We usually think of poison as a dose planted by a fiend to kill the dog next door. Such cases are rare. More often someone's ignorance or carelessness causes the dog to poison himself. Perhaps he swallows lead by chewing on painted objects or by licking paint cans. Maybe he sniffs some cockroach destroyer and gets himself a dose of phosphorus. Or he picks up a tasty piece of rat bait with Paris green inside. When playing outdoors he nips the leaves from bushes that have been sprayed, or licks his feet after running over areas sprayed with arsenic poisoning.

The garbage can, too, so attractive to all dogs, must bear its share of blame for such tragedies. It is here that the dog often finds old pills and powders. Occasionally, a dog comes to grief when, with the best of intentions, he is doctored with remedies from the family medicine chest. Tonics containing an amount of strychnine beneficial to human beings can be extremely dangerous since the dog is highly sensitive to this drug.

Poisoning can floor a dog suddenly when large doses are swallowed, or it can sicken him gradually if taken in small amounts. Signs are ordinarily quite definite, and include trembling, jerking and twitching, shallow breathing, vomiting and convulsions, blue gums, severe stomach pain and blood-streaked diarrhea. One or more of these, depending on the poison, may be seen.

Emetics

When poison is suspected an emetic is given—like any liquid medicine (see page 131)—to make the dog vomit. Among the usual emetics are hydrogen peroxide mixed with an equal amount of water; common table salt, two teaspoonsful to the cup of tepid water; mustard, one tablespoonful to the cup of tepid water. Vomiting should follow in a few moments.

The veterinarian within easy reach is a godsend, for there is no time to be lost. Act with all speed if your dog is to be saved. If you know the particular kind of poison your dog has eaten, take along the package. This will help the veterinarian choose the right antidote. Packages containing poisonous material state clearly on the label the correct antidote. This has saved many a victim since different antidotes are used for the various poisons.

Snake Bite

Snake bite, another rush job, is not uncommon among dogs given free run in country where poisonous snakes abound. Tie the leg above the bite, that is, between the bite and the heart; use your handkerchief, necktie, stocking or anything of the kind handy. With knife or razor blade, slash an X across the bite to start bleeding. Squeeze out the blood. If you have brought along a snake-bite suction cup, keep sucking the wound with this; if not, suck it with your mouth (provided your mouth is not cut or injured) and spit out the blood. Wash the wound with full-strength hydrogen peroxide, and get the dog to the veterinarian as quickly as you can. Carry him; do not let him walk even if he can.

Hunters who take their dogs into snake country carry anti-venom serum for use in the emergency. If you live or are summering in a snake-infested area, ask your veterinarian about this. Do not, however, depend entirely upon the serum. Removing the poison by squeezing or sucking the blood from the wound as soon as possible is most helpful.

Encounter with a Skunk

If your dog has had an argument with a skunk, you will want to do something about getting rid of the odor, for your own sake as well as the dog's. Wash the dog as thoroughly as possible with soap and water. Follow with a 5-10 percent ammonia rinse. Good results are obtained in getting rid of the odor by bathing the victim in tomato juice! Skunk odor will, however, wear off. When a skunk sprays the dog's eyes it is painful. You will see the dog dig at his eyes in misery. In such cases bathing the eyes with boric acid solution is helpful.

Porcupine Quills

The dog that tangles with a porcupine is going to be stuck with a lot of quills particularly around the head and face. These quills are barbed and will work in more deeply if not removed promptly by a veterinarian or yourself. Since it is painful for the dog, give him a sedative first. If you have nothing better a couple of aspirins will do. Work slowly, and with small pincers or tweezers pull out each quill carefully with a slow steady pull—do not jerk—cleaning each wound with antiseptic.

Bee Sting

Stings by bees, wasps and hornets are common. Those on the body are not so serious since the coat serves as a protection, but those on the head, where the hair is usually shorter, can cause pain and swelling.

Extract the stinger with tweezers if you can. Apply a paste

made of bicarbonate of soda and water, or boric acid powder and water. Ice-cold compresses will help to reduce the swelling which may not go down for twenty-four hours. If the dog is frightened or excited give him a simple sedative.

Insect stings are not considered dangerous unless the eye or the nearby flesh is involved. Here the pain is so intense that the dog scratches and frequently tears the eye with his nails. A local anesthetic can be injected by the veterinarian to relieve the pain.

Cuts, Scratches and Bites

Cuts and scratches of the type the dog gets from slithering through fences, or from thorns in heavy wood cover, are sometimes so slight that they need no treatment other than the dog's own licking. However, all abrasions should be washed with antiseptic soap and water to stop infection.

The dog's saliva is helpful in keeping the wound clean, but licking, if overdone, can delay healing. In such a case use a healing ointment and bandage the wound. Since the bandage may be torn off, be sure to use a non-poisonous ointment. If the dog does tear off the bandage, put on a protective collar. (See page 129.)

If your dog is bitten by another dog, clip away the hair around the puncture, wash the area thoroughly with strong soap and water. Get the name and address of the attacking dog's owner and make sure of that dog's health. It is always wise to have your veterinarian inspect all animal bites.

Swallowing Foreign Objects

It is not unusual for the puppy to swallow things he shouldn't—a tiny rubber toy, for instance, a piece of a glove, or a shoe, some bolts and washers. If you can get to the veterinarian immediately, so much the better; with his fluoroscope he can look inside and see exactly what has been swallowed and where it is lodged. If help is not available, feed soft food like bread and milk, then give an emetic or common salt—two teaspoonfuls in a cup of tepid water. The chances are that the puppy will vomit the food and give up the object at the same time.

Drowning and Artificial Respiration

Dogs have been known to drown in pools that they cannot clamber out of. Remove the collar and hold the animal up by the hind legs to drain the water from the lungs. Then place him on his side, forelegs stretched out front, hind legs stretched out behind, and give artifical respiration.

Place your two hands over his chest. With your weight press down and release, regularly timed at the rate the patient would breathe. To keep the rhythm reasonably correct, as you work slowly, say "out goes the bad air" (press down); "in comes the good air" (release). Keep at it, keep at it, keep at it. Do not give up.

The moment breathing starts, let the dog inhale just a little aromatic spirits of ammonia. When he is fully conscious and can swallow, give a few drops at a time of well-diluted whiskey and water. Wrap him in a warm blanket and get him to the veterinarian.

Automobile Accidents

No matter how careful you are to protect your dog from street traffic there may come a time when he is hit by a car or truck. Always approach a hurt dog cautiously, reassuring him with your voice. His fear and pain may make him bite. For easier handling use a bandage muzzle of a strip of cloth, or even a necktie if nothing else is available. (See page 128.) Slide him carefully on a plank, a blanket, or your coat and carry him to a quiet spot, or into your car. If a leg seems to be broken, keep it as straight as possible. If the bone has broken through the skin attach a stick as a splint by tying it above and below the break. This will prevent the sharp point or edge from cutting a blood vessel when the dog moves or struggles.

Where there is a gash or cut, put a wad of cloth over the wound and hold it in place with a bandage. In a leg injury always start at the foot and work upwards. Apply the bandage firmly but not tightly as this would stop the blood. If the head has to be bandaged take two turns around the neck, again loosely, then carry it between the ears over the head, down by the side of the face, under the jaw, up over the other side of the face, across the head between the ears to the neck, repeating until several layers have been applied. The bandage should be tucked here and there to keep it in place.

If the blood from a wound is spurting you can be fairly sure an artery is cut and in that case, haste is essential. Apply a tourniquet (a twist of cloth on whatever is available to cut off circulation) between the cut and the heart. For example, in a leg injury, put the tourniquet above the wound on the leg. A tourniquet must be loosened every ten or fifteen minutes or the blood will be stopped entirely, causing gangrene.

After an accident a dog will suffer from shock. This is shown by pale and grayish lips and gums. This may also mean internal bleeding. First aid in shock is to wrap him in a coat to keep him warm and let him rest quietly.

Even if a dog seems unhurt, he should always be examined by a veterinarian as soon as possible after an accident as there may be internal injuries that you cannot see.

Hunting Accidents

Accidents that happen to dogs in the home and on the street plus a few more, can also occur on hunting and camping trips where you may be miles from the nearest veterinarian, or even your car. Broken glass and opened tin cans hidden in rock piles or brush where the dog is hunting may cut a pad or leg. Sometimes a poorly-directed shot or another hunter mistaking your moving dog for the quarry causes a gunshot wound. Burns with gun powder should be treated as any burn. A dog that is more severely wounded may go into shock, falling down, breathing shallowly with eyes staring and glazed. Heat hysteria, prostration or running fits often occur when dogs are being hunted in warm weather after a long lay-off. In all such cases of shock keep your dog as quiet as possible, cover him with your jacket, place him in a shady, comfortable place and let him alone. When he regains consciousness give him a bit of diluted whiskey or black coffee. Treat wounds as needed, applying a tourniquet if necessary (see above) making sure to loosen it every ten or fifteen minutes. Afterwards keep him quiet for several days, feeding lightly with broths and milk.

Cuts from barbed wire should be treated to prevent infection. In camp close all discarded empty tin cans. This not only prevents the chances of a cut foot but also food poisoning for the dog may lick the putrified food still inside. Food poisoning can also come from eating spoiled food., so all garbage should be burned or buried and the spot covered with a heavy stone.

A dog's tail sometimes becomes injured. Put packs of boric acid solution to the bruised part. If the skin is broken use an antiseptic, followed by boric acid ointment or petroleum jelly. A broken tail should be properly set by your veterinarian.

First Aid Kit

A first aid kit for your dog needn't be too bulky. It need only contain a pair of large-sized tweezers for removing porcupine quills or fish hooks; a small bottle of hydrogen peroxide for use as an antiseptic and also as an emetic in case your dog eats poisoned vermin bait or garbage (see pages 144-45); a bottle of metaphen for cuts (this doesn't burn and is easier to put on a dog than iodine); a small bottle of boric acid solution which has many uses including the important one of eye wash for weed seeds, etc., that gather in the eyes; a tube of one percent yellow mercuric oxide is handy for inflammation or abrasions of the eyes; and, finally, a roll of three-inch bandage and a roll of absorbent cotton should be included.

In snake country carry snake serum. It may mean the difference between life and death for your dog. Also carry a sealed packet of razor blades as they are more efficient than a pocket knife for opening snake bites.

Your dog may get a foot caught in an animal trap. First apply an emergency muzzle (see page 128). If you have nothing with which to make a muzzle, wrap your coat around his head to prevent his biting. Place the trap flat on the ground and step on the spring so the jaws open and you can pull out the dog's foot. Treat cuts and if the foot is broken get to a veterinarian as soon as possible.

Suppose your dog is hurt so badly that he can't walk and must be carried for a long distance. If you have a companion make a stretcher, if possible, or use your coat as a sling. If you are alone lean down and place your dog over your shoulders like a sack of meal, holding his head and front legs over one shoulder, his hind feet over the other.

CHAPTER 15

THE SELECTION OF A DOG

The selection of a dog is more of a problem than it used to be because there are now so many available from which to choose. There are more than 100 kinds or purebreds alone, to say nothing of the crossbreeds and mongrels. Our dog population is more than twenty-five million, one-third of which are purebred. Nineteen million families, or about forty percent of all American homes, shelter one or more dogs. So, if you own a dog, in more ways than one you are not alone.

Purebred, Crossbred, Mongrel

The purebred is a dog of only one breed, that is, both its parents are of the same kind of dog. For instance, the puppies of a purebred Pointer male and a purebred Pointer female are purebred Pointers. If different kinds of dogs are mated (for example, a Pointer with a German Shepherd), the pups of this crossing are called crossbreds. The mongrel is a mixing of many breeds. In fact, the mongrel is such a mixture that no one breed can be recognized as such. Is there any difference between the three kinds as far as companionship is concerned?

Basically, all normal dogs are much alike—big-hearted, faithful, kind. However, the fact that the crossbred or mongrel is usually "given away" whereas the purebred often costs quite a sum, suggests certain differences. Cost does not always mean value, but it is a guide. What one gets for nothing is often worth nothing, or else it comes with strings attached. There must be a reason, then, why we can get a crossbred or a mongrel for little or nothing, and why we must pay for a purebred.

The crossbred and the mongrel are usually given away because someone wants to get rid of them. Often bred by accident or neglect, they are an unnamed product, with no market value. The purebred, on the other hand, has always been bred from selected parents and raised under the best conditions for health and good development. Each pure breed has its own standard of perfection, that is, a detailed list of characteristics which together make the "model" or perfect Boxer, Poodle, etc. Therefore, when you buy a purebred, you know more nearly what you are getting. You may be sure that the purebred puppy has a good chance of looking like his parents; that his size when he is full grown, his coat, ears, tail, and so on, will be fairly close to those of his father and mother.

When you get a dog other than purebred, you are getting uncertain quality and quantity; you never know exactly what he will look like nor how big he will be when matured. But his heart is in the right place, and he will give just as much devotion to you. Far better a mongrel than no dog at all! And many a home has been blessed with handsome, hearty and happy mongrels.

Origin of the Breeds

We mentioned a while back that there are more than 100 kinds of purebreds, that is, more than 100 different breeds of dogs from which to choose. What do we mean by a breed? Insofar as dogs are concerned, a breed is a group of similar dogs kept alike by selective breeding. Man selects the dogs which have the qualities he admires or considers best for his purpose, and by breeding them over a period of time gets pups which look alike and which, when grown and mated, will produce pups like themselves. That is why this type of breeding is known as selective breeding—man selects the dog and the bitch he thinks, mated together, will produce the kind of puppies he wants.

Now, man did not start this idea. He borrowed it from nature who used just such a method in the wild for producing animals fitted to live under widely different natural conditions. When nature does the selecting we call the method natural selection. Man took up the work of perfecting the breeds where nature left off, for way back in the dim past evolution had begun to produce different kinds of dogs.

Fifteen million years ago there lived a dog-like animal called *Tomarctus*. Small in size, he looked somewhat like the civet-cat which may be seen in zoos. Long before the time of Christ, down from *Tomarctus* came four main lines: the herd dogs, the northern dogs and spitz-type toys, the hounds and the terriers, and the guard dogs. From these have come our modern kinds of dog.

Much as we would like to classify them for the sake of easy understanding, we cannot be too exact about it because we can only guess what happened ages ago. Over the years, nature, it would seem, divided and subdivided dogs to fit them for different climates, terrains and occupations. Nevertheless, in tracing the paths of evolution, we find much overlapping, and so our groupings of type and breed can never be absolutely correct.

The herd dogs were the shepherds on Old World hillsides. Practically all countries had their sheepdogs: the Shepherd Dogs of Germany, for instance, the Collies of Scotland, the Komondorok of Hungary, the Briards of France. These were the natural type animals produced by nature rather than by man's selective breeding. Most of them were rectangular in body, had weather-resisting coats and great endurance.

The northern dogs were the cold-country types of the Arctic Circle: the Samoyed, Siberian Husky, Chow Chow, etc., all had the wedge-shaped head, ears which stood straight up, heavy coat, and an upcurled tail that screened the nose from subzero air while they slept. Here, too, developed the tiny dogs, the toys, some like Pomeranian closely related to Arctic types, other more or less removed from them as, for instance, the Maltese, the Pekingese, Pug, and Japanese Spaniel.

The hounds are either sight hunters like Greyhounds and Deerhounds, or scent hunters like Bloodhounds and Beagles. The sight hounds were tall and reachy-necked, streamlined for speed; they watched their prey as they chased it. The scent hounds ran nose-to-earth, and they had longer ear flaps which waved over the ground to stir up the scent.

Then there were the spaniels, that large group which includes pointers, setters and retrievers. Hunting with head high to catch airborne scent, these were the soft-mouthed finders and retrievers that brought in their birds without a toothmark. The terriers were so-called from the Latin *terra* or earth. These were the ground diggers, with strong forelegs, and with powerful jaws for ratting and trapping vermin. They were made so hard-mouthed they could literally snap their quarry to death.

The guard dogs are descended from the lion fighter of ancient Greece. Down from them came Mastiff, Bulldog, Boxer and Great Dane. Here were the stout-hearts of the dog family, with size, weight and courage to spare.

These at long last developed into the hundred-odd breeds we know today. For thousands of years of course they were not thought of as breeds but as different types of workers, Only within the last 100 years or so, have we known enough to breed dogs according to definite patterns, hence to call them breeds.

For judging in the show ring, we have tried to group dogs along somewhat the same lines as those early natural groupings. Instead of the four original groups, however, modern fanciers have six groups—sporting dogs, hounds, working dogs, terriers, toys and none-sporting dogs. Here, again, we cannot group them strictly—we can only decide the division to which they seem best to belong.

Which Is the Best Breed?

There are so many breeds. How are we to know which is the best? Which breed is smartest, which the most affectionate, which cleanest in the house, the least likely to run away? To all such questions, we must give the same answer: there is no best breed. All are brothers and sisters under the skin, all very much alike, all very much what their owners make them.

The average person can be forgiven for thinking that one breed is smartest, one cleanest, one most affectionate, because for a long time owners and breeders have given their favorites just such labels. In their enthusiasm they have put mistaken ideas into the minds of buyers. Many expect to find special personalities in the dogs they select, and then perhaps are disappointed. Let us not blame these enthusiastic owners; let's try to understand them. In their loyalty to a favorite dog, they give him all the good qualities in the book! In time you will do that very same thing!

Just remember this: No puppy comes with a special personality ready made. It is strictly up to you, the owner, to develop by teaching such qualities as you want your pet to have.

A dog of any breed will run away as fast and as far as another if he is not *taught* to stay at home. A dog of one breed will be as clean as another in the house if he is *taught* to be clean. There are differences of course in intelligence, that is, some dogs are smarter and more trainable than others. This, however, is more a matter of the parent, it has nothing to do with breeds. There are smart dogs and dumb dogs, geniuses and morons. Even so, a dog does not have to be a mental giant to be a lot of fun; the dumb one can still give much comfort and companionship. In short, your dog, whatever his breed, will grow up to be about the kind of pet you make him, if he had sound parents.

Which Is the Best Puppy?

This suggests the importance of the parents of the puppy you plan to buy. Try to see the mother and the father for yourself; watch them, their manner of meeting you, their friendliness, their vigor and condition. Ask all about them; were they easy to train, clean and sensible around the house? "Like father, like son" is still a fairly good rule to go by.

If you are selecting a young puppy from out of a litter, you will be understandably puzzled. They are all rollicking little balls of fur. Which is the smartest, which will love you the most? It is difficult to tell. The one that makes friends with you quickest is not necessarily the firmest friend in the end. One may be a bold little rabble rouser, another as reserved as a bashful child. Curiosity has long been considered a fairly good yardstick of intelligence, yet it is no sure guide in judging the very young.

The main thing, then, is to pick a puppy of good sound parentage, and whose health and vigor are unmistakable. The healthy puppy is sprightly but not nervous or overactive. His eyes are clear, his nose clean. His ears can hear, that is, he responds when you talk to him, when you make a noise. The cringing, dumpish pup should not be discarded as mentally backward. Such a one just doesn't feel well because, perhaps, he needs another worming or some other medication. If your heart sets on a puppy of this sort, do not take him now. Instead, ask the breeder to get him in tiptop condition, then visit him later.

There is nothing quite so discouraging as to being doctoring a puppy the moment you bring him home. It should not be necessary, and it will not be if you insist upon perfect health and nothing less in the dog you buy. Perfect health means two things: that the puppy is in good condition at the moment, and that he has not been exposed to any disease or type of infection which might develop in a few days.

Everything else depends upon taste alone. Some folks prefer a dog with a long tail, others a dog with a short tail. Some want stand-up ears, others drooping ears. Some like long coats, some short, while the larger sizes appeal to many and the medium and toy sizes to others. Color also is a matter of taste, and we have plenty of colors from which to choose. Suppose you make a list of what you want in a dog, and then read the following chapter describing the various breeds. See whether you can find one which matches up with your preferences.

After all, the pet that is going to make you happy is the

one you like. This is to be *your* dog; you'll live with him for ten or fifteen years. So get the kind of dog whose looks please you, and do not allow anyone to dissuade you. And remember that size, sex and coat will determine in some measure the kind of care you must provide.

Large vs. Small Dogs

The country place or large estate is usually recommended for the big dog since he will need more room to run than the small dog. However, a large dog can be kept just as well on a small place if you make it your business to give him enough outdoor exercise. Many a person who has to hand-run his dog on leash does a more thorough job than the one who lets his dog run free on a farm. Often the free-running dog just sits and suns himself while the hand-exercised dog must keep pegging along as far as you make him go. You cannot keep a large dog in good mental or physical condition if you shut him in the house. The little fellow can exercise running upstairs, downstairs and all around the house; but for the large dog this is not enough. Also, the large dog needs more food than the small dog, so his feeding costs will be higher.

The Child's Pet

If you want a dog for a child's pet, first consider the child. The rough little boy had better have a tough little dog, one that can take a lot of knocking around, and strong enough to keep on the go. For this youngster a terrier is the instant suggestion. For the dainty little girl, a toy dog might be best; she can cuddle it, make a baby of it. However, be skeptical about accepting this or any other such suggestions as a certain guide. As we have said before, the dog grows to be what his keepers make him. Sometimes you can make a quiet-mannered pup into a boisterous tough if you give him the idea that you want him that way; just as you can sometimes take a headstrong one, full of vigor and vim, and make him gentle as a lamb. So much depends upon the way he is handled as a young and growing puppy. The strongest trait of the domesticated dog is the desire to please his master, When he understands what the master wants, that will usually be what he will do.

On the other hand, if you want the dog to guard the child, then one of the larger breeds might be best. Even so, the dog brought up with a child, whether a large dog, a medium or a small, will in almost every case take on himself the job of protection. While he may not go so far as to bite or attack, he'll raise enough ruckus with his barking to send the intruder packing without delay.

When you go to buy a dog, beware of the seller who guarantees that *this breed* is perfectly safe with children. That is a highly questionable statement. There is hardly a breed that is any more safe with children than another. A dog, any dog, is safe with children only after he has proved himself to be so. He must learn to love the child, and he *will* learn it if he is brought up with the youngster from puppyhood. When he has attached himself to the child with real affection, he will suffer any discomfort for the child's sake. Given sound parents, any puppy brought up with children learns to be loving and trustworthy. Once he is used to little people, he accepts them and follows them to the ends of the earth.

How Big Is a Dog?

In studying the description of breeds, you will find information about weight. This will tell you something about the average size of the adult and will guide you in making your selection. But, since some dogs are slender, some round, others tall and still others low to the ground—weight alone will not tell you very much. A tall dog with slender body might weigh no more than a dog of smaller but chunkier build. How, then, can we judge a dog's size? We must also measure him for height.

Now the height of a dog is reckoned as shoulder height; it has nothing to do with measurement from the top of his head to the ground. In fact, when we measure a dog we disregard the head entirely. Instead, we measure at the withers or top of the shoulder blades. The withers is the point on the shoulder blade which is the highest portion of the body proper, that is, the spot where neck and body meet.

Place the dog broadside against the wall. Balance a stick across his back, and as close to the joining of neck and body as you can get it. Then, on the wall, mark the spot which the end of the stick touches. The number of inches from this mark to the floor is the dog's "shoulder" height. These heights, which you will find in almost every case, tell you how tall the full grown dog will be. There is less size variation among puppies of the different breeds than there is among grown dogs, so when you pick a puppy, remember the height he will be. Only then will you know how much dog you have to live with when he is full-grown.

Male or Female?

Which sex do you prefer, male or female, dog or bitch? People who have always owned males are firm in the belief that the male makes a better pet, while those who have always owned females insist that the female is the only kind of dog to have around. Actually, it doesn't make much difference since the one is about as good as the other. It is a matter of taste.

It should be remembered, though, that the female will need protection twice yearly for a period of three weeks while "in season." Spaying the female will avoid this, and spaying should be considered if the female is not to be bred or exhibited at dog shows. (See pages 36-37.) The female has been called more affectionate, more of a homebody, than the male, and while this may be true, we believe it has been over-emphasized. The male, properly handled from puppyhood, may grow up to be as sweet and loving as the female. If not trained to stay in his own yard he may run away at the first opportunity; but so will the female if she feels so inclined. We can think of no breed that is less likely to run away than any other. If fact, the answer to the run-away problem is training in obedience, plus a good tight fence.

Breeding Is Not Necessary

One common mistake about dogs should be exploded right here: the female *does not have to be bred*. She does not have to have a litter of puppies in order to remain healthy.

Sentimentalists have said that no female can be perfectly happy unless she has suckled a litter. Nonsense! You are her world; with you she will be completely happy even if she never sees another dog. She doesn't know she is a dog, she thinks she is a part of your family, as indeed she is. The carrying and whelping of a litter means a certain amount of danger. Do not subject your pet to it just because you have been told it is good for her.

The same goes for the male dog. It is not necessary to mate him. Mating the male pet in our opinion is a big mistake since even the cleanest dog may forget his manners. If there is one thing above all others that makes male pets run away, it is occasional mating. Where before, such a dog was a quiet, contented pet satisfied with the joys of human companionship, he now becomes filled with the big ideas about his place in the scheme of things. Every female dog he sees is fair game, and every time he scents one in season, off he goes!

There's that man up the street—he owns a female. He says bring your dog over, let's breed them, it will be good for them both and we'll divide the pups! You take your pet along. You all sit in the cellar for hours as the two pets fuss and fuss, accomplishing nothing, except that the female grows weary and the male all but exhausted. You see, when a male is raised by the breeder for stud work, he is expertly trained. Your dog may bungle things, even injure himself because no one knew how to assist both dog and bitch throughout the mating. Then the male comes home, a wiser but not by any means a better dog. In fact, he is not the same; he's not quite as much yours as he was before.

The Kind of Coat

When choosing a dog the type of coat is important because you will have to learn to care for it yourself or pay someone to do it for you. The short-haired, smooth-haired kinds of dogs need no trimming; brushing and an occasional bath will keep the coat in good shape. The long, heavy-coated breeds like the Collie and the Pekingese, will need more brushing-time to keep the hair in good order, but you will be able to manage it yourself.

When we consider a dog like the Poodle, with his wealth of coat usually trimmed to pattern, you will have to spend considerable time learning how to do it or pay an expert beauty-shop operator to do it for you. It has to be done fairly regularly to keep the dog looking presentable. The wire-haired terriers are something of a problem also since their hard coats must be trimmed twice yearly if they are not to grow soft and fuzzy, and the dog shapeless because of the extra hair growth. The Kerry Blue is an exception to this rule —his coat is naturally soft—while the Cairn and the Norwich are among those on which little trimming is needed. On the whole, however, terriers need frequent plucking.

Ears and Tails

Some people object to the cropping of ears and the docking of tails. If you should favor a breed where this is usually done, remember that you do not have to do it. If the tail is to be docked, it is done at a very early age, in fact, long before the puppy goes to the new owner. As for ears, in certain breeds trimming is done very early, in others, Bostons for instance, not for several months.

It is quite usual for a buyer to take a puppy in the nest, that is, he chooses it while it is still nursing, pays a deposit on it for future delivery. In such case, you can say, if you so desire, that your puppy is not to be docked or cropped. There is no law against docking tails, but there are laws in several states which prohibit the cropping of ears.

The Black Mouth Theory

Also mistaken is the notion that roof of the dog's mouth must be black or at least dark-colored if he is a purebred. This is not true, so do not use it as a yardstick when selecting a puppy. Of all the purebred dogs at the present time, the Chow Chow is the only one whose tongue and inner mouth membranes are always black or huckleberry color. If any other dog has a dark mouth, it is mere chance. It means nothing.

The "Police" Dog

While studying the section on breeds, do not be disappointed when you fail to find one called the police dog. There is no such breed. The expression *police dog* means only a dog used for police work.

Police dogs are used in factories and department stores as night guards against thieves, on farms to protect stock and poultry, in warehouses to protect equipment, and on war fronts to find the wounded and to carry messages.

Dogs of many breeds have been trained to do this work— German Shepherd Dogs, Doberman Pinschers, Boxers, Airedales, Irish Terriers, and various others.

The Dog's Background

Perhaps, too, when you read the chapters on breeds, you will be disappointed because not one is just called a pet. I don't want a hunting dog, you say to yourself; I don't want a herder of sheep, or a dog that fights bulls and badgers. I want merely a pet, a friendly dog to play with, walk with. Do not worry. No matter what kind of dog you select, you will get a pet if you bring him up to be a pet. His past is so far behind him he will forget all about it.

The dog of ancient times worked hard for his living. Man worked hard also, and the dog was the only animal that worked with him, the only animal that turned from his own kind to be the friend of man. Down through the ages the dog has stood by man's side as hunter, guard and protector, helping him to find food and clothing, to track the snows and the jungles, to make life possible oftentimes where it might not have been possible without his aid.

And so these brief breed histories will show you that the dog you take into your home has a long and honorable history of service as selfless and as untiring as he will give to you. The very qualities of devotion that was his in ancient times are his today. Count on him for faithfulness and love of man the master. Take the dog, then, and teach him to be the well behaved friend you want him to be.

CHAPTER 16

THE STORY OF THE BREEDS

AFFENPINSCHER

The Affenpinscher is a pert little fellow often called the monkey dog because of his big, bright eyes, bushy eyebrows, prominent chin and hair tufts about the face. His coat is shaggy but hard and wiry, his tail is docked and carried straight up. Ears stand erect when cropped. The breed has been known in Europe for three centuries.

WEIGHT: 7-8 pounds. HEIGHT: under 10 inches. COLOR: black, black and tan, red or gray.

AFGHAN HOUND

The Afghan Hound is thought to have originated in Afghanistan about 3000 B.C. A lithe, slender, but very powerful hound, he was swift enough to hunt the leopard, gazelle and hare of his native land. He has a distinctive look, with a heavy, silky coat, upcurved tail and long feathered ears.

WEIGHT: 50-60 pounds. HEIGHT: 24-28 inches. ANY COLOR, usually cream and black, black and rust, blue-gray.

AIREDALE TERRIER

The Airedale originated about a century ago in England's Valley of the Aire. Produced by crossing the now extinct Old English Terrier with the Otterhound, he was used for hunting otter, fox, badger and rats. He is upstanding, squarely built, with long head and powerful jaw, a hard, wiry coat, and high-carried docked tail.

WEIGHT: 40-50 pounds. HEIGHT: 22-23 inches. COLOR: rich tan with black or grizzle markings.

ALASKAN MALAMUTE

The Alaskan Malamute is an old breed of Arctic sled dog named after the Malamute tribe in Alaska. In recent years they have been used for racing and in polar expeditions. They are big and sturdy, with a thick, fairly short coat, erect triangular-shaped ears, slant eyes and unusual face markings consisting of cap and mask. The tail is carried over the back.

WEIGHT: 50-85 pounds. HEIGHT: 20-25 inches. COLOR: wolf gray or black and white.

AUSTRALIAN TERRIER

A sturdy, sprightly terrier of small size, with a heritage as a hunter, farm dog and companion in his native Australia. Introduced into the U.S. in the first quarter of the century, admitted to AKC registry, 1960, and increasingly popular. Requiring no trimming, the slight or gradual shedding of his harsh coat, is a point in his favor as a house pet.

WEIGHT: 12-14 pounds. HEIGHT: About 10 inches. COLOR: blue-black or silver-black, tan markings head and legs.

BASENJI

Tracing to the time of the Pharaohs, the Basenji was used in his native Africa on various types of game. He was especially valuable as a hunting dog for he did not bark—even today he is known as the "barkless" dog. He is smooth-coated, short-bodied, clean-limbed and lithe. His rather large ears stand up straight, and his expression is puzzled due to the wrinkles over his forehead. His tail is set high on the rump and carried in a full curl slightly to one side.

WEIGHT: 22-24 pounds. HEIGHT: 16-17 inches. COLOR: black, tan and white or chestnut with white feet and tail tip.

BASSET HOUND

The Basset is a smooth-coated, slow-moving hound descended from the ancient St. Hubert hound and raised in France and Belgium to trail deer and other game. A tireless hunter, he is noted for scenting ability. He stands low to the ground on heavily boned, crooked legs. His body is long; his tail is long and carried gaily. He's a sad-faced dog with large, pendant ears and flews or hanging lips.

WEIGHT: 25-45 pounds. HEIGHT: 11-15 inches. COLOR: white, tan and black, or any combination of two.

BEAGLE

A very old breed, the Beagle is descended from the scent hounds known in the days of King Arthur. The earliest settlers to America brought their hounds with them; these they gradually refined and later mated with dogs from England to produce the merry little hunter of rabbits we know today. He's clean-limbed, with tight-fitting short coat that feels quite hard, and a voice melodious and bugle-like. He has large, soft eyes, long drooping ears and a moderately long, always-wagging tail.

WEIGHT: 18-30 pounds. HEIGHT: there are two sizes; under 13 inches, and from 13-15 inches. COLOR: usually white, tan and black.

BEDLINGTON TERRIER

The Bedlington is named for a mining region in England, where he was bred a century ago for hunting rats and drawing badgers. The inch-long coat is thick and soft, with a topknot which when trimmed gives a Roman-nosed appearance to the head. The long, tapering ears hang flat. The tail is fairly long, tapered and carried gracefully curved.

WEIGHT: 22-24 pounds. HEIGHT: 15-16 inches. COLOR: combinations of blue, liver, tan and sandy.

BELGIAN SHEEPDOG

There are several different varieties of Belgian Sheepdog. The Groenendael, most often seen, is descended from the oldest known strains of Central European sheepherders. Wide use abroad as a police and war dog led to his importation to America. A big, upstanding animal, the coat is thick, heavy.

WEIGHT: 55-60 pounds. HEIGHT: about 23 inches. COLOR: black.

BELGIAN TERVUREN

Formerly a variety, but given separate breed distinction in 1959, he is the same as the Belgian Sheepdog except for color: rich fawn to russet with black overlay.

BERNESE MOUNTAIN DOG

The Bernese Mountain Dog was brought into Switzerland 2000 years ago by invading Roman soldiers, and later used to draw wagons for the basket weavers of Berne. He is still quite rare in this country. A hardy dog, the Bernese has a long, silky coat, and a fairly long, white-tipped tail carried low. He is short-backed and quite compact; his head is strong, ears v-shaped.

WEIGHT: 50-75 pounds. HEIGHT: 21-27½ inches. COLOR: jet black with tan markings and white feet.

BLOODHOUND

Probably the world's first "police dog," the history of the Bloodhound goes back to the St. Hubert Hounds of 6th Century Gaul. From that day to this, he has put his incomparable scenting ability to good use in trailing murderers, kidnapers and lost children. Very mild-mannered, he never attacks the person trailed but merely finds and holds him. His ears are long and drooping, his face sad and wrinkled.

WEIGHT: 80-110 pounds. HEIGHT: 23-27 inches. COLOR: black and tan, or red and tan.

BORDER TERRIER

The rare Border Terrier, one of Great Britain's oldest breeds, was raised in the Scottish borderland to kill its hill foxes. The Border has a rather narrow but square-shaped body and an otter-like head. The v-shaped ears are wideset, dropping forward close to the cheeks; the tail is thick, tapering and carried high, the coat hard and wiry.

WEIGHT: 11½-15½ pounds. HEIGHT: 12-13 inches. COLOR: red, grizzle, blue and tan, or wheaten.

BORZOI

Borzois or Russian Wolfhounds were used centuries ago in Russia for chasing wolves across the steppes. Extremely tall, they hunt by sight. The body is narrow and graceful, the head long and inclined to be Roman-nosed; the drop ears are small, the eyes slant. The coat is fairly long and silky with a heavy neck frill, while the long tail is carried in a graceful curve.

WEIGHT: 60-105 pounds. HEIGHT: 26-31 inches. COLOR: white, with lemon, tan, brindle or black markings.

BOSTON TERRIER

The Boston Terrier is the outgrowth of a mating made about 1870 of a cross-bred Bull Terrier or white English Terrier, named Hooper's Judge, with a Bulldog-like female named Gyp. The breed actually started in Boston, Massachusetts. Square-headed, short-nosed and square-bodied, the dog has erect ears, large, round eyes, and a short, satiny coat marked with white. The tail is naturally very short, fine and tapering.

WEIGHT: from about 12-25 pounds. HEIGHT: about 16 inches. COLOR: brindle or black, with white markings.

BOUVIER DES FLANDRES

First a cattle driver in Belgium, the Bouvier des Flandres gained fame later as police and army dog in his native land. He is a powerful dog, upstanding, short in back, medium long in head, with moustache, beard and bushy eyebrows. The ears are erect when cropped. The tousled body coat is rough and hard, the tail docked.

WEIGHT: about 70 pounds. HEIGHT: 23-27 inches. COLOR: black, fawn, gray or brindle.

BOXER

The Boxer, descended from the ancient Tibetan Mastiff and the Bulldog, was developed in Germany about a century ago. His name probably comes from the way he uses his forepaws when fighting or playing. Clean-limbed but muscular and rather stocky, he is square-headed and short-backed, with smooth, short coat. His black-masked muzzle is broad, his ears erect when cropped, his tail docked.

WEIGHT: 62-75 pounds. HEIGHT: 21-24 inches. COLOR: fawn or brindle, usually marked with white.

BRIARD

Named for the Province of Brie, the Briard goes back to the 12th century when he worked as sheep tender in France. He has been in America since the Revolution. Square and powerful, the back is short, the head rather large and long, with heavy hair falling over the ears, eyes and muzzle. The ears are carried semi-erect, while the tail is long, low and well-feathered. The coat is long, slightly wavy and stiff in texture. The hind legs have double dewclaws. WEIGHT: 70-80 pounds. HEIGHT: 22-27 inches. COLOR: dark colors preferred: mainly black, gray or tawny.

BULLDOG

The Bulldog is England's own breed, used for bull baiting until 1835 when the sport was abolished by law. His low-slung body protected him from the thrusts of the bull, just as his short nose and long, heavy under-jaw made possible the famous lock grip. He is smooth-coated, massively made dog, deep-chested, round-ribbed. His head is broad, his face wrinkled, his ears small, thick, and folding in and backward. The tail may be straight or screwed.

WEIGHT: 40-50 pounds. HEIGHT: about 15 inches. COLOR: brindle, white, red, fawn or piebald.

BULLMASTIFF

A combination of Bulldog and Mastiff, the Bullmastiff was developed about a century ago by English game-keepers for use against poachers. He was called night dog because he could see well in the dark. Because they were less easily seen, the darker brindles were preferred to the more usual fawn colored Mastiff. He is a short-backed, compact dog with large, square head, and a fair amount of wrinkle on the black-masked face. Ears are v-shaped and carried down close to the cheeks. The tail is long and low, the coat short.

WEIGHT: 100-115 pounds. HEIGHT: 24-27 inches. COLOR: any shade of fawn or brindle.

BULL TERRIER (WHITE)

The Bull Terrier resulted from a cross made about the year 1835 between the Bulldog and the now extinct white English Terrier. All-white in color, he was named the White Cavalier because he was the most fashionable fighting dog of England. Today he is a most friendly fellow unless provoked. His head is long, with unbroken profile—that is, without any step down from skull to muzzle—while his ears are erect, his eyes small and slanting. His body is short, strong, muscular, with big-boned, straight legs. His thick, short coat fits like a glove, and his tail is straight, rather short and carried off from the body but not above back level.

WEIGHT: 25-60 pounds. HEIGHT: 19-22 inches. COLOR: white.

BULL TERRIER (COLORED)

The Colored Bull Terrier is exactly like the White Bull Terrier, except that the color may be anything other than white. The color commonly seen is a rich, dark brindle, often with white markings.

CAIRN TERRIER

The Cairn is an ancient working terrier from the Isle of Skye and named for the cairns or stone heaps where he helped destroy vermin. The head is unusual since it is more cat-like than dog-like; it is broad and strong, its muzzle neither as long nor as heavy as most terriers. Ears are small, pointed and carried erect. The coat is hard and weather resistant, with a dense, furry undercoat, while the tail is moderately long, heavily-haired and carried gaily, usually at back level.

WEIGHT: 13-14 pounds. HEIGHT: 9-10 inches. COLOR: usually wheaten, tan or grizzle, but not white.

CHIHUAHUA

This tiny dog gets his name from the Mexican state from which he came a century ago. He was larger then and he had both long-coated and short-coated varieties just as he does today. He is still all dog, alert and active. His head is unique in its soft spot on the skull. His ears are large, usually erect and flaring slightly outward; his eyes are full, dark and shining. The back is short, the bones rather fine, the tail fairly long and carried away from the body.

WEIGHT: 1-6 pounds. HEIGHT: about 5 inches. COLOR: any color; solid, marked or splashed.

CHOW CHOW

The only breed with a true blue-black or huckleberry tongue, the Chow Chow is a northern Chinese dog dating back more than 2000 years. Aloof and scowling, he is a massive, compact dog with short back and well-rounded ribs. His head is large with short muzzle, eyes deep-set and almond-shaped, ears small and carried stiffly erect. He is heavily furred with off-standing coat and ruff around his neck, while his tail is held closely up over his back.

WEIGHT: 50-60 pounds. HEIGHT: 19-20 inches. COLOR: black, red, fawn or blue.

COLLIE (ROUGH)

The Collie, named possibly from the "colley" or black-faced sheep he guarded in the Scottish Highlands, is one of the oldest of the shepherd types and undoubtedly appears more often in literature than any other breed. With his long, heavy coat, mane and frill, his proud carriage and lithe gait, he is the perfect picture of grace. His head is long and slender, his eyes almond-shaped and slanting. His ears half-raised and turning over to the front. His body is just a trifle longer than it is high, and his legs are straight and strong. His very long tail is carried low with a slight upward twist or swirl.

WEIGHT: 50-75 pounds. HEIGHT: 22-26 inches. COLOR: sable and white, tri-color, blue merle and white.

COLLIE (SMOOTH)

The Smooth Collie, which is quite rare, is exactly like the rough variety except for his coat which is short, smooth and thick.

COONHOUND (BLACK AND TAN)

Coonhounds have been popular for many years in certain sections of the country where they have been bred from Bloodhound and Foxhound stock. They are used for trailing and treeing the raccoon. However, they also trail almost any kind of four-footed game. Alert and quick, these dogs cover ground easily, tirelessly. The body is slightly longer than it is high, the back is level and strong, chest deep and ribs well sprung. The head is cleanly modeled, the flews or upper-lips hang in true hound style, while the long ears drop in graceful folds. The coat is short and thick, the tail long and carried high when on the trail.

WEIGHT: 50-60 pounds. HEIGHT: 23-27 inches. COLOR: black with rich tan markings.

DACHSHUND

The Dachshund is Germany's badgerhound, known since the fifteenth century. Brought to this country almost a century ago, the breed has long been popular here. It comes in three varieties—smooth or short-coated, longhaired and wirehaired. Exceptionally short-legged, long-bodied and deep in

Smooth Dachshund

chest, the Dachshund is sturdy, quick and determined. His head is tapered, his ears broad, long and drooping. Forelegs are not quite straight with feet turned just slightly out. The tail is fairly long and carried off from the body but not high. The miniature Dachshund is smaller in size but otherwise exactly like the standard.

WEIGHT: 5-20 pounds. HEIGHT: 5-9 inches. COLOR: red, shades of tan, black and tan, chocolate, dappled, tiger or gray.

Longhaired Dachshund

Wirehaired Dachshund

DALMATIAN

The spotted Dalmatian, named for the former Austrian province of Dalmatia, may have descended from an Italian Pointer some 300 years ago. Although originally a hunting dog, his love of running under carriages as guard and companion nicknamed him "Coach Dog." He is known as a firehouse dog also, and will run with or ride on the engines. He is clean-limbed, with head of fair length. His eyes are rimmed with black or liver. His ears are rather wide and tapering, falling close to the head, while his tail, which is only moderately long, is carried with a slight upward curve. His short coat is thick, fine and glossy.

WEIGHT: 35-50 pounds. HEIGHT: 19-23 inches. COLOR: a ground of pure white marked with fairly small, well defined spots of black or liver.

DANDIE DINMONT TERRIER

The Dandie Dinmont was bred from the rough-haired terriers of the Scottish Border country where he was known for his gameness on badger, fox, otter, rats and weasels. The breed gained popularity and a name, from a leading character in Sir Walter Scott's novel, *Guy Mannering*, published in 1814. The Dandie is a long-bodied dog with an arch over the loin, a well-developed chest and very short legs. His rounded head is covered with soft, silky hair like a broad topknot, while his long ears hang close to the cheeks. Eyes are large and expressive. The tail, thick at the root, is just moderately long and carried in a curve. The body coat is a mixture of hard and soft hair about two inches in length.

WEIGHT: 14-24 pounds. HEIGHT: 8-11 inches. COLOR: pepper, from dark bluish black to silvery gray; or mustard, from reddish brown to pale fawn.

DEERHOUND (SCOTTISH)

The Scottish Deerhound has been called a rough Greyhound, and he does belong to the Greyhound family of long ago. He was the sight hunter of Scotland in the seventeenth century, so valued that a lord condemned to death could purchase his reprieve with a leash of three. One of our largest dogs, he has a very deep chest and black line arched over the loin. His head is long, skull rather flat, muzzle pointed and covered with a soft mustache and beard. The ears are small, set high and folded back, sometimes being raised semi-erect in excitement. The tail, which reaches almost to the ground, is carried dropped or curved, and the coat, harsh and wiry, is three or four inches in length.

WEIGHT: 75-110 pounds. HEIGHT: 28-32 inches. COLOR: dark blue gray, brindle, yellow, sandy or reddish fawn.

DOBERMAN PINSCHER

The Doberman Pinscher takes his name from Louis Dobermann, a German who founded the breed in 1890 by crossing Shepherd, Rottweiler and black and tan Old English Terrier stock. Pinscher is the term used for European terriers. Known far and wide as an outstanding police and war dog, he is very clean of line throughout. His head is long and rather wedge-shaped, his ears small and carried erect when cropped. His eyes are almond-shaped rather than round, and his lips are tight. The back is short and the tail docked, while the smooth, hard coat fits close to the skin.

WEIGHT: 60-75 pounds. HEIGHT: 24-28 inches. COLOR: black, brown, or blue with rust-red markings.

ENGLISH TOY SPANIELS

The English Toy Spaniels, probably native to China or Japan, have been known for four centuries in England where they were pets and favorites of royalty. The four varieties are similar in type but different in color. They are compact and short-bodied, rather broad in chest. The unusual skull is almost round, with eyes widely set, large and full. The stop, or indentation between the eyes, is unusually deep, while the short nose is slightly tipped up as is the underjaw. Long ears hang flat to the cheeks, and the legs and feet are feathered.

WEIGHT: 9-12 pounds. HEIGHT: about 10 inches. COLOR: King Charles—black and tan. Prince Charles—white, black and tan. Blenheim—red and white. Ruby—red.

American Foxhound

English Foxhound

FOXHOUNDS

Bred from English and French Foxhounds imported by early settlers, the American Foxhound has been used here since 1650 in fox hunting. Another breed, known as the English Foxhound, similar to the American but sturdier in build, was brought to this country in 1738. The Foxhound head is fairly long with straight, square-cut muzzle. The drop ears are set low, their tips being rounded. Eyes are of good size and very soft in expression. The body is long.

strong and muscular, with legs as straight as a post, and gaily-carried tail. Coat is smooth, close and hard.
WEIGHT: 60-70 pounds. HEIGHT: 21-25 inches. COLOR: any hound color allowed, but usually black, tan and white.

Smooth Fox Terrier

Wirehaired Fox Terrier

FOX TERRIERS

The Fox Terrier, a centuries-old English breed, gets his name back in the days when he was brought in to dig the fox out of his hiding place. He's a very stylish dog, short-backed, straight of leg, strong, muscular and active. His head is long and lean, his small eyes sparkling bright. His small, v-shaped ears drop forward toward the cheeks, and the docked tail stands upright. The Smooth Fox Terrier differs from the Wire only in coat. The Smooth coat is quite thick but short and hard, while the Wire coat is longer, broken and wiry.
WEIGHT: 15-19 pounds. HEIGHT: 14½-15½ inches. COLOR: white predominating, with markings of black or black and tan.

FRENCH BULLDOG

The French Bulldog comes from the toy Bulldogs of England sent into France. He is a rather heavily built little dog, with short, well-rounded body broader at the front than at the back. His head is large and square with slightly rounded forehead, short, broad muzzle and well developed cheeks. His medium-sized eyes are set wide apart. His most unusual feature, the ears, are perfect bat ears, broad at the base, long, and rounded on top. They are carried stiffly erect with the opening directly forward. The naturally short tail may be straight or screw, while the short coat is smooth and glossy. WEIGHT: 18-28 pounds. HEIGHT: about 12 inches. COLOR: brindle, fawn, white or brindle and white.

GERMAN SHEPHERD DOG

Descending from Old World sheepherding types, the German Shepherd Dog was developed as a breed in Germany late in the nineteenth century, and has been in America since the early part of the twentieth. Designed as a worker, he is a rugged animal of great intelligence. The Shepherd is gracefully rounded, his body a trifle longer than it is high; the chest is deep, the legs straight and deeply angulated. The head is clean-cut, the muzzle wedge-shaped, the jaws strong. The long, pointed ears stand erect, the eyes are almond shaped and dark, the long tail carried in a slight curve. The coat is straight, harsh and close-lying.

WEIGHT: 60-85 pounds. HEIGHT: 23-25 inches. COLOR: commonly black and tan, gray or black.

GREAT DANE

Of German origin, the Great Dane is a descendant of the ancient English Mastiff and possibly the Irish Wolfhound. Its development as a breed type began during the 19th century in Germany, where it was used as a boarhound, and slightly later in England and the United States. His head is long, narrow and finely chiseled, his muzzle deep and square. The eyes are usually dark and very bright, the ears erect when cropped, otherwise drooping forward close to the cheeks. The back is short, the legs straight, the long tail carried down except in excitement. Coat is short, thick and glossy.

WEIGHT: 120-150 pounds. HEIGHT: 28-34 inches. COLOR: brindle, fawn, blue, black or harlequin.

GREAT PYRENEES

Immense size and a majestic air mark the Great Pyrenees, named for the Pyrenees Mountains where he worked as shepherd dog and puller of carts, and guard and companion for the nobility of France. His head is large and wedge-shaped, eyes slanting, ears carried close to the head although slightly raised when alerted. His body is powerful, his tail long and low. His coat is his crowning beauty—heavy and fine underneath, with a top layer of thick, coarser hair, straight or a trifle wavy.

WEIGHT: 90-125 pounds. HEIGHT: 25-32 inches. COLOR: white with or without markings of badger, gray or tan.

GREYHOUND

Known for several thousand years before the time of Christ, the Greyhound was used by the Pharaohs of Egypt to chase the hare and gazelle. Ownership was restricted to the rulers who lavished upon the dog every care. The Greyhound still races today, but on the tracks after a mechanical rabbit. He is a typical sight hunter, streamlined for speed. Very tall and slender, his back is arched, his chest is deep, his legs straight. The head is long and narrow, ears small, thrown back and folded as if held down by the wind. Long and fine, the tail is carried in a slight curve, and the coat is short.

WEIGHT: 60-70 pounds. HEIGHT: 26-27 inches. COLOR: immaterial, usually grey or pale fawn and white.

GRIFFON (BRUSSELS)

A quaint toy, the brussels Griffon was developed fairly recently from several breeds, among them the Affenpinscher, the Pug, the Ruby Spaniel and the Belgian street dog. In his native Belgium he was an efficient ratter, but here he is usually a pet and companion. He is short-backed and chunky with an almost human expression. The domed skull bulges over large, widely set eyes, and the ears stand semi-erect. The nose is extremely short and tipped up, the muzzle broad. Bushy eyebrows, whiskers and cheek fringes complete a peculiar but appealing picture. The tail is docked and the coat may be wire or smooth.

WEIGHT: 5-12 pounds. HEIGHT: about 8 inches. COLOR: reddish brown, black or black with reddish brown markings.

GRIFFON
(WIRE-HAIRED POINTING)

The Wire-haired Pointing Griffon was first bred about 1870 by a Hollander, Edward Korthals, who popularized the breed throughout France and Germany as a rough, swamp-country sporting dog skillful at retrieving game on land and in water. He is essentially Pointer in build although somewhat more heavily cast. Strong and vigorous, he is fairly short-backed and a trifle low on the leg. His head is long and narrow, his muzzle square, eyes large and not too dark, his nose brown. His moderate-sized ears hang flat, while his tail, which is docked, is carried off from the body. The rough, rather shaggy coat is hard and stiff, with downy undercoat, bushy eyebrows and mustache.

WEIGHT: 50-60 pounds. HEIGHT: 19½-23½ inches. COLOR: steel gray or gray-white with chestnut-colored splashes, chestnut.

HARRIER

Brought into Great Britain by the Normans almost 800 years ago, the Harrier gets his name from the Norman word for hound. An excellent scent hound, the dog has been known in the United States since Colonial times and was generally used in packs to hunt hare. He looks like a smaller Foxhound, although shorter in back. He is strong and active, with deep chest, well-sprung ribs, very straight legs evenly boned, and small cat-like feet. His head is medium in size and rather long, with closely hanging drop ears, while his long tail is carried off from the body. The coat is short and hard.

WEIGHT: 40-50 pounds. HEIGHT: 19-21 inches. COLOR: hound color - combinations of black, tan and white.

IRISH TERRIER

One of the oldest of the terriers, the Irish Terrier differs from the others in being slightly hound-like in outline; in fact, he looks very much like a smaller Wolfhound. His courage and disregard for danger, particularly as a messenger dog in wartime, long ago earned him the nickname "daredevil." His body is fairly long, his back arched over the loin, legs perfectly straight, strong and muscular, his tail set high and docked. His head is rather long and narrow with especially powerful jaws and teeth. Eyes dark and full of fire, ears small, v-shaped and dropping forward close to the cheeks. The coat is thick and very wiry in texture.

WEIGHT: 25-27 pounds. HEIGHT: about 18 inches. COLOR: bright red, red wheaten or golden,

IRISH WOLFHOUND

The Irish Wolfhound was Ireland's ancient protector against wolves, and later a guard against the robber bands that rode by night. He is tallest of all dogs and possibly the most powerful. His back is long, his loins arched, legs straight and thighs very muscular. His head is long, likewise his muzzle is long and slightly tapering. Ears are small, thrown back and folded like those of the Greyhound and Whippet. His long tail is carried in a slight curve, while his coat is hard and wiry.

WEIGHT: 105-140 pounds. HEIGHT: 30-34 inches. COLOR: gray, red, brindle, black, white, fawn.

ITALIAN GREYHOUND

The ancient Italian Greyhound was one of the favorites of

Italy and later of southern France while during the reign of England's Charles I it was the special pet of the nobility. It is actually a Greyhound in miniature, slender, elegant, graceful. The skull is long and narrow, the muzzle fine; eyes rather large and very expressive. Ears are rose-shaped, soft and delicate. The body is arched over the loin, the chest is deep, the tail long, low. Legs are straight and quite fine in bone, with long feet like those of the hare. The coat is smooth, the hair quite thin and glossy.

WEIGHT: 6-10 pounds. HEIGHT: about 10 inches. COLOR: fawn, red, mouse, blue, cream or white.

JAPANESE SPANIEL

Aristocrat of the smaller orientals, the Japanese Spaniel was royalty's pet and was permitted to associate only with those of noble birth. A well-mannered little fellow, he spells quality from nose to tail. His head is large for his size, broad and rounded in forehead. His bright eyes are prominent, while his small v-shaped ears fall forward but not flat. His muzzle is broad, full and very short. Body square and compact, legs straight and finely-boned, the heavily-coated tail carried closely over the back. The long coat, which may stand off from the body, has a thick mane or ruff around the neck, as well as feathering on thighs and tail.

WEIGHT: about 7 pounds. HEIGHT: about 9 inches. COLOR: black and white or red and white.

KEESHOND

The Keeshond (plural Keeshonden), essentially an Arctic breed, was Holland's barge dog, named for Kees de Gyselaer, leader of the patriots' party during the political strife of the eighteenth century, and later made the national dog of Holland. True to Arctic type, his body is short, compact, strong-chested and straight-legged. His head is wedge-shaped with strong muzzle of medium length, and triangular ears standing erect. His dark eyes, which are slightly slanting, have unusual pencilled lines running from their corners out toward the ears. The tail is fairly long, nicely-plumed and carried up across the back, while the coat is full with long, straight hair.

WEIGHT: 35-40 pounds. HEIGHT: 17-18 inches. COLOR: gray and black, the outer layer black tipped, the under layer pale gray or cream.

KERRY BLUE TERRIER

Born in the mountains of County Kerry, and national dog of Ireland, the Kerry Blue Terrier has been known there

for more than a century as a sporting terrier used for farm work and all manner of hunting and retrieving. Most puppies are born black, but usually develop the blue color by about one year of age. The head is long, with flat cheeks and powerful jaws; small, dark eyes are very keen in expression. The v-shaped ears are carried forward close to the cheeks. The back is short, the legs fairly heavy in bone, the tail docked and upstanding. The coat is soft and wavy, unlike the customary hard wire coat of most terriers.

WEIGHT: 30-40 pounds. HEIGHT: 17-20 inches. COLOR: deep slate to light blue gray.

KOMONDOR

Imposing in size and strength, the Komondor (plural Komondorok) guarded Hungary's sheep for 1000 years or more and fought courageously against beasts sometimes larger than himself. He's a shaggy looking fellow, but that is the way he should be. His rather long body has a deep and powerful chest, wide, sloping rump and straight legs. His head is fairly broad, his blocky muzzle somewhat shorter than his skull, while his ears hang down to the sides of his head. Eyes are brown and of medium size. The thickly-coated tail is long and low. Head and body both are covered with shaggy tangled hair giving him natural protection from the bites of wild animals.

WEIGHT: about 90 pounds. HEIGHT: The bigger the better; average, 23-27 inches. COLOR: white.

KUVASZ

The ancient Kuvasz (plural Kuvaszok), another giant of the dog world, was named from the Turkish *Kwasz*, meaning "armed guard of the nobility" and used as one of Hungary's protectors from the time of King Mathias I in 1458. In addition, the dog served as a hunter. Characterized by sturdy build and light-footed gait, the body is broad in chest and back, heavy-boned and muscular. The head is fairly wide, the muzzle clean-cut and rather square, the ears small, folded back and close lying. The long tail, thickly covered with hair, hangs low, while the coat is long on neck and flanks, shorter and a trifle wavy on the body.

WEIGHT: about 70 pounds. HEIGHT: 24-27 inches. COLOR: white.

LAKELAND TERRIER

Known first as the Patterdale, the Lakeland Terrier was later named for the Lake district of England which, like so many of those northern counties, developed its own particular sporting terrier to guard against the raids of fox and otter. Probably related to the Border and the Bedlington, the Lakeland is a workmanlike dog, moderately short in body and narrow in front, with well-boned, straight legs and powerful hindquarters. Head and muzzle are rather broad and not as long as in most dogs of the kind. The v-shaped, forward-falling ears are small, the eyes medium in size. The docked tail is a trifle longer than average, and the coat is hard and wiry.

WEIGHT: 15-17 pounds. HEIGHT: about 14 inches. COLOR: blue, black, black and tan, blue and tan, red, mustard or wheaten grizzle.

LHASA APSO

The gay little Lhasa Apso, native to the Lamaseries around the sacred city of Lhasa in Tibet, was valued as watch dog of the homes of the nobles. His history dates back at least 800 years. Longer than he is high, he is covered throughout with a long, straight, heavy coat that falls down over his eyes and forms whiskers and a beard. His short legs are muscular and covered with hair right down to and including the round, cat-like feet. The head is narrow, muzzle fairly short, eyes medium in size and dark, the ears are hanging and fringed. The tail, which is feathered too, is carried up over the back, sometimes kinked at the end.

WEIGHT: about 15 pounds. HEIGHT: 10-11 inches. COLOR: golden, smoke, slate, black, white, brown or parti-color; lion-like colors preferred.

MALTESE

Named for the Isle of Malta in the Mediterranean Sea, the Maltese was the favored lap dog of highborn ladies of Greece and Rome; a toy so small that he was called a squirrel dog and carried about in milady's sleeves. He is a sprightly little dog, hidden under a straight, silky coat which, parted down the back from nose to tail, hangs down long on either side. He has no undercoat. The head is fairly long, the muzzle fine, the feathered ears dropped. Eyes are dark and preferably black-rimmed. The body is short and the tail carried over the back.

WEIGHT: 2-7 pounds. HEIGHT: about 5 inches. COLOR: white.

MANCHESTER TERRIER

The Manchester Terrier comes from the old Black and Tan Terrier of England's Manchester district where rat catching and rabbit chasing were the principal sports. A very fast and alert dog, he is sleek, streamlined with narrow chest, short back and arched loin. His head too is narrow, wedge-shaped and tapering to the very tight-lipped jaws. Eyes are small, sparkling; thin ears erect when cropped, while the short, fine coat fits tightly to the skin. The tail is fairly long and tapering to a fine point.

WEIGHT: 12-22 pounds. HEIGHT: about 16 inches. COLOR: black and tan.

MASTIFF

Probably of Asiatic origin, the Mastiff comes down from the fighting dogs of 2000 years or more ago. He fought beside his masters when Caesar invaded Britain in 55 B.C., and in Rome when dogs were pitted against bulls, bears and lions. So useful was he as a guard against wild animals that Anglo-Saxon law required him on large estates. He is a massive, powerful dog, slightly arched over the loin, his forelegs straight and hind legs muscular. His head is short and broad, the muzzle blunt, forehead a trifle wrinkled, eyes set far apart, and v-shaped ears falling close to the cheeks. His face is dark colored, and his long tail hangs straight down. The coat is short, coarse and close-lying.

WEIGHT: 165-185 pounds. HEIGHT: 27½-33 inches. COLOR: apricot, silver fawn, or dark fawn brindle.

MINIATURE PINSCHER

Like the Doberman, but on a much smaller scale, the Miniature Pinscher has existed in his native Germany for several hundred years but has been developed as a breed only since 1895. He has all the characteristics of the terrier family to which he belongs—intelligence, alertness, activity. He is a compact little individual with fearless, lively manner. His flat head tapers toward the muzzle, the cheeks are lean, the lips tight. Eyes are dark and very bright, and ears erect when cropped. The short shining coat covers the body closely, while the tail is docked.

WEIGHT: 6-10 pounds. HEIGHT: 10-12½ inches. COLOR: black, with rust-red markings; brown with rust or yellow markings, red.

NEWFOUNDLAND

The Newfoundland is thought to be a descendant of Great Pyrenees dogs brought to the coast of Newfoundland by French fishermen. An exceptionally strong swimmer, he has saved many shipwrecked persons from drowning. Strength is his hallmark, together with a peculiar rolling gait. The body is powerfully built and well-proportioned, the forelegs straight, the hind legs show a paddling movement. The head is massive, the muzzle short and rather square, eyes wide and dark, and small ears set well back and lying close to the head. The long tail is carried down with a slight curve, while the coat is very heavy, coarse and oily.

WEIGHT: 110-150 pounds. HEIGHT: 26-28 inches. COLOR: black, landseer (black or bronze and white).

NORWEGIAN ELKHOUND

For several thousand years the fearless Norwegian Elkhound helped his Viking masters hunt elk, bear and other large game, in addition to serving as draft dog and herder. Built for stamina rather than speed, his body is square and compact, with great staying power; his legs straight, strong and only slightly bent at the joints. His head is broad, his muzzle medium-long and heavy, ears erect with opening to the front, and eyes dark and lively in expression. His thick-haired tail, set high, is tightly curled and his coat, which is heavy and hard, is longest on the neck, the chest, and the back of the legs and thighs.

WEIGHT: about 50 pounds. HEIGHT: 18-20½ inches. COLOR: gray with black-tipped covering hairs.

NORWICH TERRIER

To the students of Cambridge goes the credit for popularizing the Jones Terrier, later named the Norwich Terrier. The breed was first developed in England around 1880 when it became a fad with the undergraduates. This is a small but natural type of working terrier with moderately short body and level back. Legs are short but powerful, the feet round.

The head is foxy, that is, fairly wide in skull and tapering toward the muzzle. Ears are small, either erect or dropped, while the eyes are dark and very keen. The tail is docked, and the coat is very hard and wiry, with slight eyebrows and whiskers.

WEIGHT: 10-15 pounds. HEIGHT: 9-11 inches. COLOR: red, wheaten, grizzle or tan and black.

OLD ENGLISH SHEEPDOG

As breeds go, the Old English Sheepdog is not old at all, his history going back only 150 years. Whatever the length of tail when the puppy is whelped, it is docked so short as to appear tailless, hence the nickname "bobtail." The body is square and compact, the forelegs straight and thighs so long that the dog has a rolling, bear-like gait. The head is large with square, strong jaws, eyes either both or one pearl (blue), and ears flat to the head. The coat is full, hard and quite shaggy.

WEIGHT: 50-65 pounds. HEIGHT: 21-25 inches. COLOR: gray, grizzle, blue or blue-merled, with or without white markings.

OTTERHOUND

Known since the fourteenth century, the Otterhound is used for otter hunting. During the nineteenth century in England this sport became a minor vogue as the dogs were hunted in packs to keep down the otters preying upon the fish in British streams. Resembling somewhat the Bloodhound, and with a remarkable scenting ability, the Otterhound is a big, courageous dog thoroughly at home in the water. Rather ungainly in body, he has a long, gaily-carried tail and webbed feet. His head is large, ears long, thin and hanging, expression gloomy. His heavy coat is crisp and oily enough to withstand almost any amount of swimming.

WEIGHT: about 65 pounds. HEIGHT: 24-26 inches. COLOR: grizzle and sandy, black and tan clearly defined.

PAPILLON

Developed from the sixteenth-century toy, the Papillon was popularized by Madame de Pompadour and other famous ladies of the French court, whose pets were pictured with them in their portraits. The little dog's ears, flaring like the spread wings of a butterfly, gave him his name. He is a shade long-backed, with heavily-plumed tail carried up and over. The head is small, muzzle lean and moderately long, lips tight-fitting. In some specimens the ears droop flat to the head, in others they flare out; both kinds, however, have fringes. The bone is fine, the feet long and slender, while the coat is full, especially around the neck, shoulders and chest.

WEIGHT: 5-11 pounds. HEIGHT: about 11 inches. COLOR: any color, solid, tri-color or parti-color; in the last two named, marked with a white blaze.

PEKINGESE

The Pekingese was a sacred dog of the Chinese emperors as far back as the Tang Dynasty 2000 years ago; but after the British sacked the Summer Palace at Peking in 1860, one of the four dogs smuggled out was presented to Queen Victoria and a vogue began. Here is a dignified toy with courage far beyond his size. His head is broad, muzzle extremely short, the chin tipped up. Eyes are big and bold, while the heart-shaped ears hang down not altogether flat. The body is deep, compact, big-boned; much heavier in front than in back. The forelegs are unusual in being so bowed that they are like the outline of a harp. The feathered tail rides closely over the back, and the coat is coarse, full and wind-blown.

WEIGHT: under 14 pounds; usually 6-10. HEIGHT: 6-9 inches. COLOR: red, fawn, black, sable, parti-color, etc., frequently with black face mask and spectacles.

POINTER

The Pointer has been used in England as a hunting dog since 1650, and in America since 1876. He was one of the first dogs used to point game birds, hence his name. He is a clean-limbed, natural dog with strong, slightly-sloping back and long, tapered tail carried straight out. His head is long, moderately wide and furrowed between the eyes. The thin, silky ears hang flat to the cheeks, and the eyes are usually dark. The coat is short and hard.

WEIGHT: 55-60 pounds. HEIGHT: 24-25 inches. COLOR: white with liver markings, or lemon and white, orange and white, or black and white.

POINTER
(GERMAN SHORTHAIRED)

The German Shorthaired Pointer is a rather recent development of the Old Spanish Pointer crossed with the Bloodhound to add trailing skill to pointing ability. The result was a hunter that points and retrieves. Here is a powerful, heavy dog, nicely balanced and clean-cut. His back is short and straight, his hips broad, thighs muscular. The head is moderately broad, the muzzle about as long as the skull, and deep, with full but not heavily hanging lips. Eyes are medium in size, and ears hang flat to the head. The tail is docked, the coat is short, thick and tough.

WEIGHT: 45-70 pounds. HEIGHT: 21-25 inches. COLOR: solid liver, liver and white spotted, ticked or roaned.

POINTER (GERMAN WIREHAIRED)

Formerly known as the Drahthaar, a distinct breed in Germany since 1870, and one of its most popular hunting dogs, used on game birds and waterfowl. First brought to America about 1920 and best known in the Midwest. His rough, wiry coat protects him in rugged cover and weather.

WEIGHT: about 50 pounds. HEIGHT: 22-26 inches. COLOR: same as the German Shorthaired Pointer.

POMERANIAN

A North-Country, Sledge-Dog Type, the perky little Pom came into being in Pomerania where, about a century ago, he was bred down in size from the large white Spitz of Iceland. In spite of his tiny size today, he has kept his make and shape. The body is short and compact, coat thick, legs heavily-feathered. A foxy head, small ears carried erect, and plumed tail laid flat over the back complete the picture.

WEIGHT: 3-7 pounds. HEIGHT: about 7 inches. COLOR: black, brown, red, orange, cream, etc.

POODLE

An old-time hunter, herder and draft dog of Europe, the

Poodle is kin to the Irish Water Spaniel and England's rough-haired Water Dog. Originally a fine swimmer, he was trimmed to lighten the weight of his coat in the water, and thereby began the vogue of trimming him in fancy patterns. France, Germany and Russia all had their Poodles, but France really took him to her heart and made him her national dog. The breed comes in three varieties—Standard or large, Miniature or medium, and Toy or very small. Otherwise, the dogs are identical. A graceful dog, the Poodle is squarely-built, short-backed and strong, with tail docked and carried gaily. The skull is a bit full, cheeks flat, muzzle long and fine, eyes oval and dark, ears hanging close to the head. The coat is heavy, harsh and curly or frizzy.

WEIGHT: Standard, 45-55 pounds; Miniature, about 16 pounds; Toy, about 7 pounds. HEIGHT: Standard, over 15 inches; Miniature, 10-15 inches; Toy, under 10 inches. COLOR: any solid color: black, brown, white, apricot, blue and silver.

PUG

The Pug began in China centuries ago, then came to Holland, to England and to America. Everywhere he went he became for a time the most popular pet. He's a wrinkle-faced chunk of a toy, short-backed and round-ribbed, rather low on his legs. His head is massive for a dog so small, his muzzle is broad, square and very short indeed. His eyes are large and worried looking while his velvety ears hang like the down-turned petal of a rose. His tail is tightly curled over the hip, his glossy coat is short.

WEIGHT: 14-18 pounds. HEIGHT: 10-11 inches. COLOR: black, silver or apricot fawn, with black face mask and black mark running down the back to the tail.

PULI

Like most shepherd types of Hungarian origin, the Puli (plural Pulik) seems buried beneath a wealth of hair long enough to mat and cord. This was an all-round farm dog, a good water retriever and a hunter of game. Long and muscular, the body is slender, the forelegs straight, hindquarters well-developed. The head is narrow, the muzzle of medium size, and the lips tight. Eyes are deep-set, ears v-shaped, fringed.

WEIGHT: 30-35 pounds. HEIGHT: 17 inches. COLOR: black, gray or white.

RETRIEVER (CHESAPEAKE BAY)

The Chesapeake Bay Retriever is one of America's own native breeds, developed along the shores of Maryland and famous as a duck dog in the rough, icy waters of Chesapeake Bay. His one-and-a-half inch coat is crisp and oily to protect him while swimming. His short body is higher at the back than at the front, his legs are straight, his feet webbed. His head is broad, with rather short muzzle. Eyes medium and light-colored, ears hanging loosely, tail long and quite thick.

WEIGHT: 55-75 pounds. HEIGHT: 21-26 inches. COLOR: dark brown or liver to faded tan.

RETRIEVER (CURLY COATED)

Descendant of the sixteenth century English Water Spaniel, the Curly-Coated Retriever is thought to be oldest of the Retriever family. His tight curls shed the water and also protect his skin from heavy brush. His body is rather short, his chest deep, back level and moderately long, and tapered tail carried straight out. His head is long with jaws a bit lean, eyes large but not prominent, and curl-covered ears lying close to the head. In fact, as his name suggests, the dog is a mass of curls right down to the top of his tail.

WEIGHT: 60-70 pounds. HEIGHT: 22-23 inches. COLOR: black or liver.

RETRIEVER (FLAT-COATED)

Developed in England and, strange to say, of American parentage, the Flat-Coated Retriever resulted from a combination of St. John's Newfoundland and Labrador Retrievers, together with later crosses possibly involving the Setters and Golden Retrievers. Here is a powerful, active dog, short-backed, rather squarely-built and muscular, the legs straight, well-boned and feathered. The head is moderately broad, with jaws long and strong, the neck clean, the chest deep.

Eyes are brown or hazel, ears small and falling close to the head. The feathered tail is long, the coat dense, fine and flat. WEIGHT: 60-70 pounds. HEIGHT: about 23 inches. COLOR: black or liver.

RETRIEVER (GOLDEN)

Back in 1860 a troupe of trained Caucasian sheepdogs, known as Russian Trackers, while performing in a travelling circus at Brighton, England, were purchased by Lord Tweedmouth who developed them into the breed today called the Golden Retriever. Flat or wavy, dense and water-resisting, the beautiful coat popularized the Golden, although special prowess as land and water retriever has also made it many friends. The body is deep and rather short, the tail long, straight and feathered. The head is broad, muzzle powerful, eyes dark and wide apart, ears medium-sized and dropped.

WEIGHT: 55-70 pounds. HEIGHT: 20½-24 inches. COLOR: rich golden.

RETRIEVER (LABRADOR)

Imported from Newfoundland to England about 1870 by Lord Malmesbury, the Labrador was developed there from the St. John's water dog into the most popular member of the Retriever clan. In the old days he brought hooked fish to the boats, while today he is an especially good water retriever. He's a deep-chested, strong-bodied dog with almost straight back and long, thick tail rounded like that of an otter. His head is wide, clean-cut, his muzzle powerful, ears just moderately large and hanging fairly close to the head. Eyes are preferably brown or black and medium in size, while the coat is short, very thick and not at all wavy.

WEIGHT: 55-75 pounds. HEIGHT: 21½-24½ inches. COLOR: black, yellow.

RHODESIAN RIDGEBACK

The Rhodesian Ridgeback was developed in South Africa by the Boer farmers as a big game hunter and guard. It probably combines breeds brought in from other countries, two or three centuries ago, with native dogs which could withstand the temperature extremes of the South African Veldt. Since 1922 it has been a standard breed in Africa. It was imported to the USA about 1930 and a club was organized here in 1950. Unique among purebred dogs, the Ridgeback has a distinct ridge down the back where the hair grows in the opposite direction to the rest of the coat. This is a strong, muscular, hound type dog. The head is fairly long and rather broad, the medium-sized ears set rather high, dropped and carried close to the head. The muzzle is long and deep, the lips clean. The body is deep-chested and powerful, the legs straight, and the tail long and carried with a slight upward curve. The coat is short and sleek.

WEIGHT: 65-75 pounds. HEIGHT: 24-27 inches. COLOR: light to red wheaten.

ROTTWEILER

The Rottweiler gets his name from the town of Rottweil in Germany, where almost 2000 years ago the attacking Romans used him to herd cattle over the Alps. Thereafter for many a long year this capable dog drove the cattle to market and served as guard and police dog. He is a stockily-built animal, calm and quiet. His back is short, broad and level, his chest roomy, legs straight, with muscular thighs and rather heavy bone. The head is broad with muzzle about as long as the depth of the skull. The small eyes have a good humored expression while the high-set ears hang flat. The coat is short, but very dense and hard.

WEIGHT: 80-90 pounds. HEIGHT: 21¾-27 inches. COLOR: black with tan markings.

ST. BERNARD

The St. Bernard, or Alpine Dog as he was once known, gained fame in the Swiss Alps where at the Hospice of St. Bernard dogs were raised and trained to rescue travellers lost in the snow. In the three centuries they have been used at this work, they saved 2500 human lives. The St. Bernard is a large, powerful dog with broad back and well-developed leg muscles. The head is impressive with its broad forehead, wrinkles and furrow, his muzzle with flews or loose-skinned lips. The high-set ears fall quite closely to the head, and the lower eyelid fits loosely. The long tail hangs with a slight curve at the tip, and the coat is very dense, rough and tough (shorthaired), or medium length and wavy (longhaired). WEIGHT: about 170 pounds. HEIGHT: 25½-29 inches. COLOR: white with red, brown or brindle patches.

SALUKI

Sight-hunter of the gazelle in the desert, the Saluki is thought to be the world's oldest domestic animal, since his image was found engraved upon Egyptian tombs several thousand years ago. He was Egypt's royal dog, respected even by the Moslems who ordinarily considered the dog as unclean. Here is a dog built for speed; he is tall, long and slender, with deep, narrow chest, arched loin and long thighs. His head is narrow, too, his closely hanging ears long and silky. The tail which is set on low is carried in a graceful curve. The coat is fine, smooth and silky-textured, moderately feathered on the back of the legs and the tail.

WEIGHT: about 60 pounds. HEIGHT: 23-28 inches. COLOR: white, cream, fawn, golden, red, grizzle or black and tan.

SAMOYED

The Samoyed takes his name from the ancient Samoyed

people of northeastern Siberia where he served as hunter, draft dog and herder of reindeer. In more recent times he has done good work in Arctic and Antarctic expeditions as sled-dog and pack carrier. Essentially a northern type, he is rather squarely built with high-set tail, long and heavily coated and carried over the back. His head is broad in skull and wedge-shaped, muzzle tapering, eyes dark and wide apart, lips black. His well-furred ears stand erect. His heavy coat is a thing of beauty, its under layer thick and soft, its outer layer longer, harsh, shining and standing off from the body.

WEIGHT: 35-65 pounds. HEIGHT: 19-23½ inches. COLOR: white, white and biscuit, or cream.

SCHIPPERKE

The Schipperke, or Flemish "little Captain," had the job of keeping Belgian canal boats free of rats. Later he became a fashionable pet when in 1885 Leopold II's queen acquired one. For a small dog he is powerfully made, his body short, thick-set, compact. His forelegs are slightly heavier in bone than his hind legs, his rump is nicely rounded and his tail docked very short. The foxy head tapers from skull to muzzle, the oval eyes are dark and sharp, while the triangular ears stand erect. The coat, which is full and harsh, is fairly short on the body, longer around the neck and ears, and on the thighs.

WEIGHT: under 18 pounds. HEIGHT: 12-13 inches. COLOR: black.

Standard Schnauzer

Giant Schnauzer

Miniature Schnauzer

SCHNAUZERS

The three kinds of Schnauzers are almost exactly the same except for size, the Standard Schnauzer being medium, the Giant, large, and the Miniature, small. Oldest of the trio, the Standard has been a guard and watchdog in Germany since the sixteenth century, his especial work that of rat catcher around the stables. By means of out-breed crosses, the Giant was developed in Bavaria for driving cattle to market and guarding stockyards. The Miniature was reduced in size by crossing with the Affenpinscher. These are robust, rather heavily-set dogs, squarely-built. The head is long, the whiskered muzzle blunt, oval eyes dark and shadowed by bristling eyebrows. The v-shaped ears are carried close to the head or, if cropped, stand erect. The tail is docked, the coat hard and wiry.

WEIGHT: Standard, about 35 pounds; Giant, about 75 pounds; Miniature, about 15 pounds. HEIGHT: Standard, 17-20 inches; Giant, 21½-25½ inches; Miniature, 11½-13½ inches. COLOR: black, or pepper and salt.

SCOTTISH TERRIER

The Scottish Terrier is a development of the age-old terriers of Scotland, this one from the Highlands where he hunted all kinds of vermin. He's a heavy-boned small dog, with short back, wide hindquarters and very short legs. His head is long, his muzzle blunt, ears small and erect, and eyes piercingly bright. His seven-inch tail is carried up in a moderate curve. His coat, about two inches long, is thick underneath, hard and wiry on top.

WEIGHT: 18-22 pounds. HEIGHT: about 10 inches. COLOR: gray, brindled, black, sandy or wheaten.

SEALYHAM TERRIER

Named for its origin in Sealyham, Wales, the Sealyham Terrier has been bred since about 1850 for hunting badger, otter and fox. He's a rough little fellow, big-boned, moderately short in back and very low on the legs. Skull and muzzle are long, the jaws strong and punishing. Oval eyes are fairly wide apart, ears folded forward, and tail docked and carried straight up, while the coat is wire-haired.

WEIGHT: 20-21 pounds. HEIGHT: about 10½ inches. COLOR: white, or white with lemon, tan or badger markings on head and ears.

SETTER (ENGLISH)

The English Setter, probably a spaniel development crossed with pointing breeds and used in England for bird hunting at least 400 years ago, was developed principally by Edward Laverack and Purcell Llewellin, two world-famous dog breeders of the mid-nineteenth century. Here is a large dog with flat, long and beautifully feathered coat. His head is lean, muzzle long and deep with somewhat hanging lips. The silky-haired ears droop low, the eyes are dark and bright. The tail is carried straight out, its long fringes tapering to a point at the tip.

WEIGHT: 50-70 pounds. HEIGHT: 23-25 inches. COLOR: white with black, tan, blue, lemon, orange and liver belton markings, or solid white.

SETTER (GORDON)

Scotland's development of the Setter family is the Gordon or Scotch black and tan, named for the Duke of Gordon. The Gordon is a sturdy hunter, with rather short back, fairly heavy and moderately long muzzle. His eyes are bright and very wise in expression, his thin ears hang low, while his feathered tail rides out on a line with his back. The coat is soft and shining, longer on the ears, underbody and legs.

WEIGHT: 45-75 pounds. HEIGHT: 23-27 inches. COLOR: coal black with tan markings.

SETTER (IRISH)

The Irish Setter is Ireland's contribution to this respected family of bird finders. He was originally colored red and white but was developed as an all-red dog in the early nineteenth century. Needless to say, the rich chestnut sheen was widely admired. In the red setter we have a graceful, rather slender dog, deep-bodied and strong. His head is lean and long, muzzle deep and square, ears set low and hanging close. The eyes are hazel or brown. The coat is fairly short and fine, but longer on the ears, chest, underbody, legs and out-stretched tail.

WEIGHT: 50-60 pounds. HEIGHT: 23-26 inches. COLOR: red mahogany or golden chestnut.

SHETLAND SHEEPDOG

Miniature in size, like the ponies for which the rather barren Shetland Islands are known, the Shetland Sheepdog is a small edition of the Collie. Graceful, his body is fairly long and rounded, with a heavy coat including mane and frill, and feathered legs and tail. His head tapers toward the eyes, his muzzle is slender and clean-cut. The eyes are slanting, ears small and semi-erect, while the long tail is carried low with a slight upward swirl.

WEIGHT: about 16 pounds. HEIGHT: 13-16 inches. COLOR: sable, tri-color, or blue merle, with white markings.

SIBERIAN HUSKY

The Siberian Husky was used for centuries in Siberia and

later in Alaska as sled dog and general beast of burden. In fairly recent times he was used as racer in sweepstakes contests where his great energy enabled him to track a snowbound course sometimes 400 miles long. He has a powerful body, with deep chest, well-muscled shoulders and hindquarters. Of medium width, his head tapers toward the eyes, his muzzle is finely chiseled, his lips tight. The ears are erect and furred, while his keen-lighted eyes are slanting. The heavily-haired tail rides over the back in a sickle curve, and the coat is thick and furry.

WEIGHT: 35-50 pounds. HEIGHT: 20-23½ inches. COLOR: usually silver gray or tan, with cap-like mask and spectacles or other markings.

SILKY TERRIER

A toy breed from Australia, for years known as the Sydney Silky and later Australian Silky, and named for his fine, silky coat. Derived mainly from early crosses of Australian and Yorkshire Terriers but a distinct breed for over 25 years; a gay, sturdy individual with forceful personality.

WEIGHT: 8-10 pounds. HEIGHT: 9-10 inches. COLOR: blue and tan.

SKYE TERRIER

Thought to be the most ancient ancestor of Scotland's terrier family, the Skye has been bred pure, for 400 years or more, on the Isle of Skye where the long-coated, drop-eared variety was developed. His long, flowing hair protected him against the vicious small animals he hunted. His body is very long and low to the ground. His head is long and tapering. Ears may be erect or hanging. The feathered tail hangs down. The hard, straight coat veils the head and hangs heavily from the ears, the underbody and the legs.

WEIGHT: about 25 pounds. HEIGHT: 8½-9 inches. COLOR: gray or fawn, with black points.

SPANIEL (AMERICAN WATER)

Well-named, the American Water Spaniel is a true native developed especially since the early twentieth century as an all-rounder for rugged woodland hunting as well as lake and river retrieving. Sturdily-built although not too compact, he is naturally symmetrical of body with legs of medium length. His skull is rather broad and full, muzzle deep and square, eyes set wide, and long ears falling close and covered with curls. The feathered tail hangs rocker-like, while the coat is thick and closely curled.

WEIGHT: 25-45 pounds. HEIGHT: 15-18 inches. COLOR: liver or chocolate.

SPANIEL (BRITTANY)

Developed in France nearly 200 years ago, the Brittany is unique as a spaniel that points game. He is a vigorous, energetic worker, with short body and straight back, chest deep and ribs well-rounded. His skull is wedge-shaped, muzzle tapering, and deep-set eyes are protected by heavy brows. His ears fall close to the head. He may be tailless, or is otherwise short-tailed, and his coat is flat or wavy with slight feathering.

WEIGHT: 30-40 pounds. HEIGHT: 17½-20½ inches. COLOR: orange and white, or liver and white, lightly ticked.

SPANIEL (CLUMBER)

The Clumber is the heaviest of the English sporting spaniels, named for Clumber Park in Nottinghamshire, England. He is slow, very dignified, long-bodied, heavy-boned and low to ground. His head is massive, its forehead furrowed, his muzzle fairly deep and and jaws long and powerful. Gentle in expression, his large eyes are a trifle loose-lidded, while his ears, broad at the top, turn down close to the head. His tail is docked and feathered, his coat silky and straight.

WEIGHT: 35-65 pounds. HEIGHT: 18 inches. COLOR: lemon and white, or orange and white.

SPANIEL (COCKER)

Smallest of the sporting spaniels, the Cocker Spaniel is so named because, first, his forebears came from Spain and, second, he was used in his early days in England to hunt woodcock. In body he is quite square, with short back, deep chest, quarters wide and nicely rounded. His tail, which is docked, is constantly a-wag. His head is rounded, his forehead smooth, muzzle broad, deep and square. His eyes are very soft and appealing in expression, his ears long and silky. His slightly wavy coat is soft, with heavy feathering on ears, chest, underbody and legs.

WEIGHT: 22-28 pounds. HEIGHT: about 14 inches. COLOR: black, black and tan, liver, shades of red and blond, and parti-color with white.

SPANIEL (ENGLISH COCKER)

During the early nineteenth century England's Cockers appeared in mixed-sized litters, the larger specimens developing into Springers, the smaller into Cockers. Gradually the two came to be thought of as separate breeds. From these Cockers, the English Cocker Spaniel was developed as a separate breed in England and in this country. While somewhat the same in many details, the English Cocker is larger, longer in head, and less heavily feathered than his American cousin.

WEIGHT: 26-34 pounds. HEIGHT: about 15 inches. COLOR: various; solid, parti-colored or roaned or ticked.

SPANIEL (ENGLISH SPRINGER)

Named for the ancient spaniel trait of springing or flushing birds, the Springer Spaniel was recognized as a separate breed in England in 1902 and twenty years later popularized here as a gundog. He has a fairly broad head of medium length, a square muzzle with deep but not hanging lips. His rounded, feathered ears hang low; his eyes are brown or hazel. His body is fairly short, back straight and tail docked. His coat may be flat or wavy but it must be thick enough to protect him when hunting in heavy cover. It is medium in length, glossy and rather fine in texture.

WEIGHT: 42-50 pounds. HEIGHT: 17½-19 inches. COLOR: usually liver and white or black and white, also liver, black, roan.

The Field Spaniel, an old branch of the spaniel family now very rare, was bred long and low for hunting on foot; thus is is less popular now because it is so slow. The back is strong and well ribbed up, the chest deep rather than wide, and the bone fairly heavy. The skull is well developed, the muzzle long and lean with exceptional scenting power. The ears hang in graceful folds, while the eyes have a more solemn expression than is typical among dogs of the spaniel group. The tail is docked, feathered and carried low, while the coat is only slightly wiry and silky textured.

WEIGHT: 35-50 pounds. HEIGHT: about 18 inches. COLOR: black or liver.

SPANIEL (IRISH WATER)

Irish Water Spaniel history goes back to Southern Ireland when, 'tis said, the dog's first job was to retrieve arrows shot into the water. Whether or not this is true, the fact remains that here is a remarkable swimmer and retriever sometimes used for duck hunting. He is short-backed, high on the leg, rounded in rump. His forehead is high, his muzzle square and long, eyes keenly alert, and curl-covered ears hanging low. At the root his tail is thick with curls; toward the tip naked and tapered to a point. His coat is a mass of tight, crisp curls, and on his head he wears a top-knot with widow's peak between the eyes.

WEIGHT: 45-65 pounds. HEIGHT: 21-24 inches. COLOR: liver.

SPANIEL (SUSSEX)

The Sussex is another slow-moving spaniel, beautiful to look. at but no longer useful as a hunter. He was often used, however, in England years ago for upland shooting. His back is long and muscular, body low to the ground. The head is big, with heavy brows, square muzzle and hanging lips. Eyes are soft and appealing, and the fringed ears are dropped low. The tail is docked, the flat coat heavy with feathering on legs and tail.

WEIGHT: 35-45 pounds. HEIGHT: 16 inches. COLOR: rich golden liver.

SPANIEL (WELSH SPRINGER)

The Welsh Springer is an old breed from Wales where he was kept as a hunting dog. While very much like the English Springer, he is smaller, somewhat finer, and only red and white in color. His head is just moderately long, muzzle straight and square, ears hanging close to the cheeks, eyes medium in size and mild in expression. His body is deep and not long, his tail is docked and feathered, his coat flat, thick and silky.

WEIGHT: about 40 pounds. HEIGHT: about 17 inches. COLOR: red and white.

STAFFORDSHIRE TERRIER

The Staffordshire, known for some years here as the Yankee Terrier, comes from Staffordshire, England, where he was bred especially for pit-fighting. Sometimes he is also called the Pit Bull Terrier. He's a broad-chested, short-backed dog, with forelegs set wide and hind legs well-muscled. His head is broad and muzzle medium long, ears semi-erect, and eyes set wide apart. His tail is long, low and tapering, his coat short and stiff.

WEIGHT: 30-50 pounds. HEIGHT: 17-19 inches. COLOR: any color, solid, parti-colored or patched.

TOY MANCHESTER TERRIER

Known as a distinct breed for about 150 years, the Toy Manchester is another offshoot of England's Black and Tan Terrier, one of the oldest of the terrier clan. He looks remarkably like the larger Manchester Terrier. He has a long, narrow head, tapering to the nose, clean-sided cheeks and tight lips. His eyes are black and sparkling, ears naturally erect. His body is quite short, his legs straight, tail long and fine. The coat is smooth and glossy.

WEIGHT: 5-12 pounds. HEIGHT: about 7 inches. COLOR: black and tan.

VIZSLA

A pointing breed from Hungary, where he was widely used for centuries. Gentle and tractable, he is adept on upland game and waterfowl, favored by sportsmen as a keen and cautious, close working dog. Admitted to AKC registry, 1960.

WEIGHT: 40-60 pounds. HEIGHT: 21-24 inches. COLOR: light red, rusty gold.

WEIMARANER

An all-round sporting dog of German origin, the Weimaraner was developed in the 19th century at the Court of Weimar. He has been nicknamed the "gray ghost" because of his unusual gray coloring and light eyes. Clean-limbed and upstanding, he is strongly-built, with moderately short back, straight legs, long thighs. The head is fairly narrow with a long muzzle and deep lips. The ears fall to the side slightly folded, while the eyes are blue-gray or amber. The tail is docked, the coat short and smooth.

WEIGHT: 55-85 pounds. HEIGHT: 23-27 inches. COLOR: gray.

WELSH CORGI (CARDIGAN)

The Cardigan Welsh Corgi is a low-slung, Dachshund-like dog, bred pure in Cardiganshire, Wales, for centuries to run the cattle in community grazing grounds. This is a long, strong, little dog, with deep chest and small waist, short legs and long tail. The foxy head tapers toward the eyes and the muzzle. Eyes are sharp and dark, ears standing erect, rounded and rather large. The coat is short, thick and hard.

WEIGHT: 15-25 pounds. HEIGHT: about 12 inches. COLOR: red, brindle, black and tan, black and white, or blue merle.

WELSH CORGI (PEMBROKE)

Not as old a breed as the Cardigan, the Pembroke Welsh Corgi still rates as one of dogdom's ancients, its ancestors having been brought to Wales by Flemish weavers in the twelfth century and later developed in Pembrokeshire from dogs of northern type. The head is foxy, the muzzle lean, ears standing with pointed tips. The legs are longer than those of the Cardigan. The tail is naturally short or docked.

WEIGHT: 18-24 pounds. HEIGHT: 10-12 inches. COLOR: red, fawn, black and tan, blue merle, with or without white markings.

WELSH TERRIER

One of the oldest of the terrier group, the Welsh Terrier has been purebred in Wales for more than 100 years, for use on badger, otter and fox. The back is short, chest moderately wide, legs strong and thighs muscular. The head is wider than that of the average terrier, the muzzle is deep, the jaws powerful. The ears are carried forward close to the cheeks. The coat is thick, wiry and hard, the docked tail upstanding.

WEIGHT: about 20 pounds. HEIGHT: 14-15 inches. COLOR: black and tan, or black grizzle and tan.

WEST HIGHLAND
WHITE TERRIER

The West Highland was once known as the Roseneath Terrier in honor of the Duke of Argyll's Scottish estate where the breed originated. Here is a self-important little chap with a "foxy" expression. He is short and compact with wide, well-developed hindquarters and straight legs. The skull, which is fairly narrow, is as long as the muzzle, the eyes are widely set and sharp, the ears small, pointed and erect. The five or six-inch tail is carried gaily, and the two-inch-long coat is hard.

WEIGHT: 13-19 pounds. HEIGHT: 10-11 inches. COLOR: white.

WHIPPET

Probably developed by cross-breeding with the Italian Greyhound. The Whippet is a smaller Greyhound evolved in Great Britain about a century or so ago. He was first used for coursing rabbits, but later was raced on the tracks. Here is a true sporting hound with considerable speed. His body is slender, deep-chested and strong, his head lean and muzzle long and rather fine. The small ears are thrown back and folded, while the eyes are large, round and alert. The tail is long and fine, the coat short.

WEIGHT: 18-23 pounds. HEIGHT: 18-22 inches. COLOR: immaterial—usually gray or tan and white.

YORKSHIRE TERRIER

Named for the English county of Yorkshire, where it was

developed as recently as 1861 by the mill workers there, the Yorkshire Terrier is probably related to the Skye, the Manchester, the Dandie Dinmont and possibly to other terriers as well. This is a spirited even if tiny dog covered from tip to toe with a wealth of long, silky hair parted straight down the back. The body is short, compact and level-backed, the tail docked. The head is quite small and flat, the eyes dark and sparkling, the ears erect or semi-erect.

WEIGHT: about 4-8 pounds. HEIGHT: 8-9 inches. COLOR: blue and tan.

OTHER POPULAR AMERICAN BREEDS

Some breeds are not officially recognized by the American Kennel Club but are, nevertheless, well known, distinct in type and often kept pure bred. The owners of these breeds are usually persons who have no interest in registration, dog shows or other regulation competitions. However, some of these breeds—the Border Collie, for instance—have their own registry. Others are registered with the United Kennel Club, Kalamazoo, Mich.

AMERICAN TOY FOX TERRIER

The American Toy Fox Terrier is descended from old-time English terriers. Despite their small size they are game ratters as well as alert and intelligent pets. The coat is satiny and smooth and slightly heavier at the neck. The nose is black and the eyes round, dark and prominent with a soft expression. The ears are large in proportion to the head and are rounded or "bat" and usually carried erect.

WEIGHT: 5-9 pounds. HEIGHT: 7-11 inches. COLOR: usually white with black, red, or tan markings.

BLUETICK HOUND

A descendant of the English Foxhound and several other fox hounds, the Bluetick is a popular dog with coon hound field trial enthusiasts. He is fairly large, and a fast trailer. The blue ticking with tan markings is a prominent feature. WEIGHT: 60-70 pounds. HEIGHT: 23-25 inches.

BORDER COLLIE

The working Border Collie of today is a descendant of the many varieties of English and Scottish sheepdogs from which the Collie and Old English Sheepdog have also come down. They are uniform in small size and black and white or tricolor marking, but have been bred for herding ability rather than looks. In this country they are used for herding turkeys, swine and cattle as well as sheep, although they need somewhat different training for the different kinds of livestock. The Border Collie is alert and energetic and has an inherited herding instinct which is further developed by training.

WEIGHT: 30-50 pounds. HEIGHT: about 18 inches. COLOR: black and white or black and tan.

REDBONE HOUND

The Redbone is named after his coloring, and is descended from Foxhound stock, with possibly a Bloodhound cross. He is a specialist on coon hunting, but is also used on bear, cougar and other big game, and instinctively "trees" his prey.

WEIGHT: 45-60 pounds. HEIGHT: 21-26 inches. COLOR: red, with permissible small amount of white on chest and feet.

SPITZ

The Spitz, sometimes called the American Eskimo or American Spitz, is one of the most popular breeds in the U.S. and is probably known by more people than any other breed. The term "spitz" actually covers an ancient group of dogs from which were developed such breeds as the Chow Chow, the Pomeranian, the sled dogs and the Akita of Japan. All these breeds have a full coat and tails that curl up over the back. The typical American Spitz has small erect ears and dark, expressive eyes, resembling, on a small scale, the Samoyed.

WEIGHT: 16-18 pounds. HEIGHT: about 18 inches. COLOR: white.

Facts at Your Fingertips!

DO IT!
ALL BY YOURSELF!

We Deliver!
And So Do These Bestsellers.